P9-DGS-588

FAKE

FAKE MONEY · FAKE TEACHERS · FAKE ASSETS

HOW LIES ARE MAKING THE POOR AND MIDDLE CLASS POORER

ROBERT KIYOSAKI

AUTHOR OF THE INTERNATIONAL BESTSELLER *RICH DAD POOR DAD*

FAKE

FAKE MONEY · FAKE TEACHERS · FAKE ASSETS

HOW <u>LIES</u> ARE MAKING THE POOR AND MIDDLE CLASS POORER

PLATA®
PUBLISHING

If you purchase this book without a cover, or purchase a PDF, jpg, or tiff copy of this book, it is likely stolen property or a counterfeit. In that case, neither the authors, the contributors, the publisher, nor any of their employees or agents has received any payment for the copy. Furthermore, counterfeiting is a known avenue of financial support for organized crime and terrorist groups. We urge you to please not purchase any such copy and to report any instance of someone selling such copies to Plata Publishing LLC.

This publication is designed to provide competent and reliable information regarding the subject matter covered. However, it is sold with the understanding that the author and publisher are not engaged in rendering legal, financial, or other professional advice. Laws and practices often vary from state to state and country to country and if legal or other expert assistance is required, the services of a professional should be sought. The author and publisher specifically disclaim any liability that is incurred from the use or application of the contents of this book.

Copyright © 2019 by Robert T. Kiyosaki. All rights reserved. Except as permitted under the U.S. Copyright Act of 1976, no part of this publication may be reproduced, distributed, or transmitted in any form or by any means or stored in a database or retrieval system, without the prior written permission of the publisher.

Published by Plata Publishing, LLC

CASHFLOW, Rich Dad, and CASHFLOW Quadrant are registered trademarks of CASHFLOW Technologies, Inc.

 are registered trademarks of
CASHFLOW Technologies, Inc.

Plata Publishing, LLC
4330 N. Civic Center Plaza
Suite 100
Scottsdale, AZ 85251
(480) 998-6971

Visit our website: RichDad.com
Printed in the United States of America

ISBN 978-1-61268-084-2

042019

BEST-SELLING BOOKS
BY ROBERT T. KIYOSAKI

Rich Dad Poor Dad
What the Rich Teach Their Kids About Money –
That the Poor and Middle Class Do Not

The #1 Personal Finance Book of all time
A New York Times *bestseller for nearly seven years
and a book found on bestseller lists around the world*

Rich Dad's CASHFLOW Quadrant
Guide to Financial Freedom

Rich Dad's Guide to Investing
What the Rich Invest in That the Poor and Middle Class Do Not

Rich Dad's Rich Kid Smart Kid
Give Your Child a Financial Head Start

Rich Dad's Retire Young Retire Rich
How to Get Rich and Stay Rich

Rich Dad's Prophecy
Why the Biggest Stock Market Crash in History Is Still Coming...
And How You Can Prepare Yourself and Profit from It!

Rich Dad's Guide to Becoming Rich
Without Cutting Up Your Credit Cards
Turn Bad Debt into Good Debt

Rich Dad's Who Took My Money?
Why Slow Investors Lose and Fast Money Wins!

Rich Dad Poor Dad for Teens
The Secrets about Money – That You Don't Learn in School!

Rich dad often said:

"You cannot catch fish in clean water."

... referencing an ancient Chinese proverb

transparency noun

trans·par·en·cy | \tran(t)s-ˈper-en(t)-sē

plural **transparencies**

Definition of *transparency*

1. : the quality or state of being transparent

2. : something transparent

3. : the extent to which investors have ready access to required **financial** information about a company such as price levels, market depth, and audited **financial** reports

DEDICATION

TO THOSE WHO SEEK THE TRUTH

ACKNOWLEDGMENT

A **C** STUDENT THANKS AN **A** STUDENT

I failed high school twice because I could not write. I received an F In English in the 10th grade. It wasn't that I could not write. I could write—I just could not spell or punctuate well, and I was always "grammatically incorrect."

Yet, I believe the main reason for my F was that the English teacher did not agree with what I wrote. I was writing about what I thought of him. I wanted to know why he was forcing us to read books we were not interested in. And, by the way, I didn't think he was doing the job he was hired to do—when he failed over 75% of our class.

After failing the 10th grade, I nearly dropped out of school. I was crushed. Nobody likes to be called "stupid." I had learned to hate school. I wanted to learn, but not about subjects we were forced to learn about. Thank god my dad, my poor dad, talked me out of quitting... but the damage was already done. Rich dad's son also received an F in English, from that same teacher.

I got through school by sitting next to the smartest girl in my class, an A student. The school system calls asking for help... "cheating." The business world calls it "cooperation." If not for *cooperating* with an A student, I would never have made it through high school.

Today, I am known as a "best-selling author." The author of the #1 Personal Finance book of all time. I achieved that status through cooperation.

This is a long way of saying "thank you" to Mona Gambetta, an entrepreneur in the world of book publishing. Mona is my A student. She is my editor, publisher, coach, cheerleader, and friend.

We have cooperated for years, and published many books together. This book, *FAKE*, might never have been published, if Mona was not on my team... and my new A student.

FAKE should have been published over a year ago. The book was written—and then rewritten—because the world was changing so fast and we had to keep a complex subject, fake money, simple. Without complaining, condemning, or criticizing, Mona continued to cheer me on, even after starting *FAKE*... over and over again. She never gave up on me.

I dedicate this book to Mona to say, "Thank you." If not for Mona Gambetta—her encouragement and her patience and her willingness to give me feedback, even when it was difficult—I probably wouldn't be the writer, the *real* writer, that I am today.

CONTENTS

INTRODUCTION
THE FUTURE IS FAKE

This book, *Fake*, was completed in April 2018—and being edited for release in the Fall of 2018.

On May 28, 2018, I was walking past a newsstand, scanning rows and rows of magazines that were calling out, "Look at me!" "Pick me up!" "Buy me!" "Read me!"

Obviously, the magazines with pretty women and fast cars on the covers spoke to me the most loudly. Yet, it was a rather bland cover of *Time* magazine that grabbed me by the collar and said, *You must read me.* The headline on the cover shouted:

How My Generation Broke America

That magazine article—and the impact it had on me—delayed the publication of this book.

The Last Piece of the Puzzle

Have you ever worked on a giant 1,000-piece puzzle? Have you ever spent hours, sometimes days, sometimes weeks, slowly searching through the thousand pieces, until you finally find the one you're looking for, the one that makes the puzzle complete?

That article in *Time* was my last piece of my 1,000-piece puzzle. A puzzle that would create a picture of past, present, and future. *Fake* needed to include the *Time* magazine article. And that meant *Fake* had to be rewritten.

The Elites

The May 28, 2018, *Time* magazine article written by Steven Brill is about academic elites. Brill himself is an academic elite who attended Deerfield Academy, an elite private prep school in Massachusetts, then graduated from Yale University and Yale Law School.

Quoting Steven Brill from the article:

> As my generation of [Baby Boomer] achievers graduated from elite universities and moved into the professional world, their personal successes often had serous societal consequences.

Translation: The elites got greedy taking care of themselves, at the expense of others.

> They… created an economy built on deals that moved assets around instead of building new ones.

Translation: The elites focused on making themselves rich, rather than creating new businesses, new products, more jobs, and rebuilding the U.S. economy.

> They created exotic, and risky, financial instruments, including derivatives and credit default swaps, that produced sugar highs of immediate profits but separated those taking the risks from those who would bear the consequences.

Translation: The elites created fake assets that made themselves and their friends rich and ripped off everyone else. When the elites failed, they were paid bonuses. Mom, Pop, and their kids would pay for the elite's failures via higher taxes and inflation.

The First Piece of the Puzzle

Brill's article was the last piece of my puzzle. The first piece of puzzle was reading *Grunch of Giants,* published in 1983.

Grunch, which is an acronym for **Gr**oss **Un**iversal **C**ash **H**eist, was written by Dr. R. Buckminster Fuller, best known as a futurist and inventor of the geodesic dome.

The U.S. Pavilion at Expo 67

In 1967, I hitchhiked from New York City to Montreal to visit Expo 67: Man and His World, promoted (as previous ones had been) as "The World's Fair of the Future," in Canada. The U.S. Pavilion at the World's Fair was Fuller's geodesic dome.

Although I did not get to meet Fuller in Montreal, I had the good fortune to study with him several times in 1981, '82, and '83. Pictured here are Fuller and me at an event called "The Future of Business," a week-long event held in Kirkwood, California, near Lake Tahoe, in 1981. For me, each event with Fuller was transformational and life changing.

Singer John Denver called Fuller the "grandfather of the future" in his song "What One Man Can Do," which is dedicated to this great man.

Fuller passed on July 1, 1983, approximately three weeks after the last time I studied with him. I remember that I immediately got a copy of his book *Grunch of Giants* and read it. Fuller was saying many of the same things my rich dad had been teaching his son and me. *Grunch* is the story of how the ultra-rich "rip off" the world. *Grunch* was the first piece of my *new* 1,000-piece puzzle.

Between 1983 and 2018, I studied, read, and attended seminars, listening and learning from anyone who I suspected had pieces of the Grunch puzzle.

In Part Two of this book, Fake Teachers, I will list some of the real teachers I met, read, and studied—real teachers who had pieces of the puzzle.

On May 28, 2018, 35 years after reading *Grunch*, I came across that *Time* magazine with Brill's article—which was, for me, the last piece of my 1,000-piece puzzle. Brill verified most of Fuller's concerns and predictions in *Grunch*.

Fuller was a futurist. Many of his predictions and concerns in *Grunch* are coming true today, which is why Brill's article is "right on time."

Although Brill's article delayed the release of this book, I am grateful to him for disclosing his insights, insights from a world that only a few know exist—the world of America's best, brightest, and smartest academic elites.

In case you are wondering, a few of the more famous "elites" are:

1. President Bill Clinton
2. Secretary of State Hillary Clinton
3. President Barack Obama
4. President George H. W. Bush
5. President George W. Bush
6. Federal Reserve Bank Chairman Ben Bernanke

7. Federal Reserve Bank Chairwoman Janet Yellen
8. Senator Mitt Romney

There are many other elites throughout the world who are running the world.

Not a Conspiracy of Bad People

I am not saying these elites are bad people (although some may be) or are part of a conspiracy. Giving them the benefit of the doubt, I trust most of these people are good people, doing what they think is "right." The problem is, because they are so smart, they often lack a self-introspection button, causing them to keep doing what they think is right, even though what they are doing is destroying the lives of billions of innocent people.

Who Is Grunch?

Grunch and the academic elites are *not* necessarily the same people. Fuller did not refer to elites as Grunch. From Fuller's lectures and books, my recollection is the elites are puppets, and the people running Grunch are the puppeteers. As you know, puppeteers are rarely seen. They prefer to remain behind the scenes, in the dark. In this book, I will do my best to bring the puppeteers into the light.

So, on to this revised version of *FAKE*...

What Is Real... and What Is Fake?

Unless you have been living under a rock, all we hear about today is "fake this," and "fake that." Almost everything we once believed in... is now fake.

President Donald Trump has popularized the term "fake news" in calling out the media—for a variety of real or perceived reporting issues. In social media, many people have fake followers. Millions of people spend billions buying fake Rolexes, fake Louis Vuitton, and fake Versace. And there are even fake pharmaceutical drugs.

On January 17, 2019, *Time* pointed to the difference between 'information' and 'disinformation' (aka: fake news) with this quote from Roger McNamee's book *Zucked*, "On Facebook, information and disinformation look the same; the only difference is that disinformation generates more revenue, so it gets better treatment."

This type of disinformation loop feeds what ticks people off... and keeps them provoked, agitated, and inflamed.

Deep Fake

There is a new technology called "deep fake," which gives amateur techies the power to capture the images and voices of famous people to produce real fake videos. As expected, the most popular use of deep-fake technology is to take real movie stars and turn them into fake porn stars. A more dangerous use of deep-fake technology is to have a powerful leader declaring war on another country.

Simply said, we can no longer believe our eyes and ears.

In today's world, verification of what is real and what is fake can mean the difference between wealth or poverty, war or peace, and even life or death.

What This Book Is About

This book is about three specific *fakes*:

1. **Fake Money:** Fake money has the power to make the rich richer while at the same time make the poor and middle class poorer.

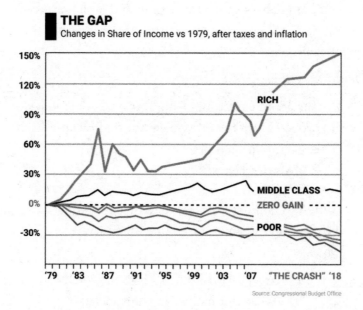

THE GAP
Changes in Share of Income vs 1979, after taxes and inflation

Source: Congressional Budget Office

2. **Fake Teachers:** What did school teach you about money? For most people, the answer is "nothing." Most teachers are great people. But, our educational system is broken, obsolete, and fails to prepare students for the real world.

Instead of guiding students into the light, our education system is leading millions of young people into financial darkness and the worst type of debt: student loan debt.

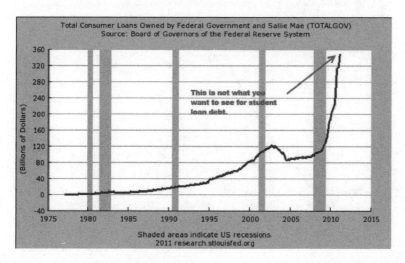

Student loan debt is over $1.2 trillion and is the number one asset of the U.S. government. In the criminal world, this is called *extortion*.

Definitions of extortion:

1. The act of extorting (using force) to take money or property, esp the offense committed by an official engaging in such practice;
2. A gross overcharge.

3. **Fake Assets:** First we need to define and understand the difference between an asset and a liability.

FINANCIAL EDUCATION LESSON
Assets put money in your pocket.
Liabilities take money out of your pocket.

My poor dad always said, "Our house is our biggest asset."

My rich dad said, "Your house is not an asset—it's a liability."

Millions of people believe their house is an asset.

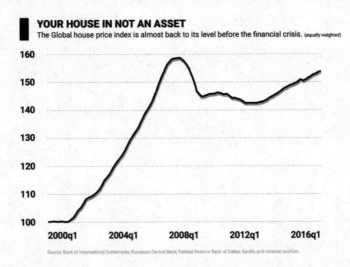

YOUR HOUSE IN NOT AN ASSET
The Global house price index is almost back to its level before the financial crisis. (equally weighted)

Source: Bank of International Settlements; European Central Bank; Federal Reserve Bank of Dallas; Savills; and national sources

In 2008, the housing market collapsed. Except for a few cities like San Francisco, New York, and Honolulu where housing prices have climbed higher, housing prices in many cities throughout the world have not yet recovered, as the above chart with data from the IMF illustrates.

Not a Real Estate Crash

The *real estate crash* was not a real estate crash. It was caused by fake assets—the same fake assets Brill describes in his article. It's worth repeating exactly what he said:

> [The elites] created an economy built on deals that moved assets around instead of building new ones. They created exotic, and risky, financial instruments, including derivatives and credit default swaps, that produced sugar highs of immediate profits but separated those taking the risks from those who would bear the consequences.

Weapons of Mass Financial Destruction

Warren Buffett calls derivatives "financial weapons of mass destruction."

He should know. One of his companies rates and insures these derivatives.

In 2008, almost $700 trillion in derivates exploded, nearly bringing down the world economy.

Many people blamed the "subprime real estate" buyer for the real estate crash.

The reality was, as Brill confirms, the elites were manufacturing fake assets called derivatives. That was the real problem.

A Picture Is Worth a Thousand Words

On the following page you'll see a chart of 125 years of the Dow Jones Industrial Average, the stock market.

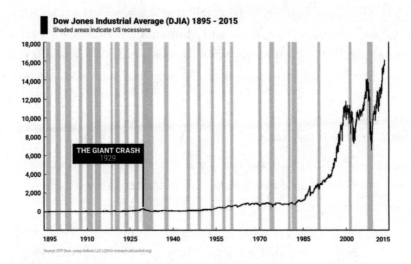

Bucky Fuller taught us to look at the big picture first, then the small picture. Unfortunately, most investors start with the small picture and then go smaller. For example, many investors wake up, check to see if their *one* favorite stock is up or down, then go to work. They may be an expert on, let's say, Amazon, but often fail to see the bigger picture. One stock among thousands of stocks in a global market does not give you much information on the future.

How to See the Future

Dr. Fuller taught his students, "If you want to see the future, you must start with the biggest picture possible."

The 125-year chart above points to the value of stepping back to see a bigger picture, a better perspective that has developed over time. Much of this book will be developed along the same lines as this 125-year chart, so you will be better able to see the future from a big picture perspective.

Money Is Invisible

Another thing you will learn, in this book, is that money is invisible. Charts and graphs offer you the ability to see "invisible money" moving in and out of various markets. In *Rich Dad Poor*

Dad, I wrote about the importance of cash flow, and that's why my wife, Kim, and I created the *CASHFLOW*® board game in 1996. Rich dad often said, "The rich have more cash flowing in, and the poor and middle class have more money flowing out."

And Fuller has taught that, "You can't get out of the way of something you can't see moving toward you." That's why *seeing* the future is so important.

I used the notion of KISS—*Keep It Super Simple*—as I was writing this book. That is why I will use more visuals like charts and graphs, rather tiny facts and figures, which are boring to most people.

The Giant Crash

On the Dow chart, the Giant Crash of 1929 is highlighted for a reason. If you step back, and look at the 1929 crash, and then compare that crash to the "dot.com crash" of 2000, and the "subprime crash" of 2008, you get a better perspective on why Fuller wrote *Grunch of Giants*, why I wrote *Rich Dad Poor Dad*, and why Steven Brill wrote "How My Generation Broke America."

I'm repeating Brill's statement, yet again, because it is important:

> *[The elites] created exotic, and risky, financial instruments, including derivatives and credit default swaps, that produced sugar highs of immediate profits but separated those taking the risks from those who would bear the consequences.*

The financial booms and busts the world has been experiencing have been caused by trillions of dollars in fake money being pumped into the system by the elites.

Did the elites fix the problem? Of course not. Why fix the problem when the problem makes them rich? Why change? Why do anything differently? Life is good—for the elites.

In 2008, there were almost $700 trillion in derivatives.

In 2018, the high-end estimate on derivatives was $1.2 quadrillion

That's right. The elites made the problem bigger, almost twice as big. As I write in 2019, a quadrillion-dollar disaster is waiting to happen.

The Purpose of This Book

My purpose for writing my books and creating the *CASHFLOW* game is to give ordinary people—people like you and me, non-academic elites—the possibility of surviving, possibly thriving, maybe even getting very rich, after the coming crash. And it's expected that crash will be a *quadrillion-dollar* crash.

Running the Numbers

We're talking *lots of zeros* here…

How Much Is a Million?

Many people dream of becoming millionaires.
A million is one thousand times one thousand:
   $1,000 x 1,000 = $1,000,000

How Much Is a Billion?

A billion is one million times one thousand:
   $1,000,000 x 1,000 = $1,000,000,000

How Much Is a Trillion?

A trillion is one billion times one thousand:
   $1,000,000,000 x 1,000 = $1,000,000,000,000

How Much Is a Quadrillion?

A quadrillion is one trillion times one thousand:
   $1,000,000,000,000 x 1,000 = $1,000,000,000,000,000

This begs the question: what will happen when $1.2 quadrillion in derivatives explodes?

That is why I have written *FAKE*.

This house-of-cards economy is what happens when academic elites are in charge of our money, our teachers, and our assets.

Putting Things into Perspective

- A billion seconds ago, it was 1987.
- A billion minutes ago, Jesus walked the Earth.
- A billion hours ago, humans lived in caves.
- A billion days ago, humans did not exist.
- Every two hours, the U.S. government spends $1 billion.

In 1983, Buckminster Fuller predicted this future.

In 1996, the *CASHFLOW* game was created.

In 1997, *Rich Dad Poor Dad* was published.

In 2018, Steven Brill confirmed that the future Fuller saw coming is here today.

This is why I delayed the release of *Fake*.

I wanted you to see the completed puzzle.

PART ONE

FAKE MONEY

In 1971, President Richard Nixon took the U.S. dollar
off the gold standard.

In 1971, the U.S. dollar became "fiat money'... government money.

Rich dad called government money... "fake money."

He also said:
"Fake money makes the rich richer.
Unfortunately...
Fake money also makes the poor and middle class poorer."

That is why Lesson #1 in Rich Dad Poor Dad is:

fake
"The rich do not work for ^ money."

– RTK

Lie #1:

Saving money will make you rich.

INTRODUCTION

PART ONE

Real financial education:
Seeing with your mind what your eyes cannot see.

– RTK

Chapter One

FAKE MONEY

THE WORLD IS ABOUT TO CHANGE...

In 1972, I was a Marine Corps pilot, a lieutenant flying helicopter gunships, stationed on board an aircraft carrier off the coast of Vietnam. This was my second tour to Vietnam. My first tour was in 1966 as a midshipman, a student at Kings Point, the U.S. Merchant Marine Academy.

In 1966, I was 19 years old, on board a rusty, mass-produced "Victory ship," a cargo ship built to carry weapons and supplies to fight the Germans, Italians, and Japanese in World War II. Rather than transporting cargo for WWII, in 1966 the rusty old ship was carrying 500-, 750-, and 1,000-pound bombs… to Vietnam.

In 1972, I was a 25-year-old pilot on board another ship. This time it was an aircraft carrier.

A Letter from Rich Dad

One day aboard the aircraft carrier, I received a letter from my rich dad saying, "President Nixon took the dollar off the gold standard. Watch out, the world is about to change."

President Richard Nixon took the U.S. dollar off the gold standard on August 15, 1971. He made his announcement during the popular TV show *Bonanza*. Apparently I had missed that episode of the TV series—and the President's important announcement.

Didn't Get the Message…

In 2018, as I write, a majority of people still do not understand the importance of Nixon's 1971 message. As my rich dad said, "The world is about to change," and change it did. In taking the U.S. dollar off the gold standard, President Nixon made one of the biggest changes in world history. Unfortunately, few people comprehend—even today—how much that change affects all of our lives, all over the world.

Looking for Gold

In 1972, I had no idea why or how the world was going to change. I did not understand President Nixon's message. Yet rich dad's warning in 1972 intrigued me.

In the pilots' "ready room" onboard the carrier, I found a *Wall Street Journal* and began searching for answers. Even the *Wall Street Journal* had scant coverage about gold, except for a few comments on the price of gold rising from $35 an ounce, and fluctuating between $40 and $60 an ounce. In another publication, I found an article written by some "crackpot" predicting gold would go to $100 an ounce.

The fluctuating price of gold intrigued me. *Why is the price of gold rising?* I asked myself. *What does it mean?*

Today, as I write this book, the price of Bitcoin and other cyber currencies are rapidly rising and crashing. Once again, very few people understand how Bitcoin or blockchain technology currencies are going to affect their lives, their future, and their financial security.

The rising price of gold in 1971 and Bitcoin in 2018 are the rumblings of profound global changes, shifts in global financial tectonic plates, which will cause financial earthquakes and financial tsunamis all over the world.

Real Financial Education

Ted was a fellow pilot who was also interested in gold. During our free time, we began our own study, doing our research to better understand the relationship between gold and future global change.

The news was that President Nixon took officially ended the gold standard because the United States was importing too many Volkswagens from Germany, too many Toyotas from Japan, and too much fine wine from France. The United States had a balance of trade problem.

FINANCIAL LITERACY LESSON: Trade Deficit: A trade deficit means America was importing more than it was exporting.

The Problem: The problem was countries like France, Italy, and Switzerland did not want payment in U.S. dollars. They wanted to be paid in gold. They did not trust the U.S. dollar.

The Solution: Nixon "closed the gold window." This meant no more gold would leave America.

Real or Fake: Was this the real reason—or a fake reason—for closing the gold window?

Probably fake. The world did not call President Nixon "Tricky Dick" without reason.

Later in this book you will find out why Nixon's reason was a lie. Later in this book I will tell you what I believe to be the real reason for taking the dollar off the gold standard.

Nixon also promised to return to the gold standard once the United States got the trade deficit back in balance. He never kept his promise. And he resigned in the shadow of impeachment.

Finding a Gold Mine

Ted and I studied a map of Vietnam and soon found a gold mine. The problem was, in 1972, the United States was losing the war and the gold mine on the map was now in enemy hands.

Ted and I formed a partnership and scheduled a mission for the next day. Our plan was to fly from the carrier, cross enemy lines, locate that gold mine, and buy gold at a discount.

Early the next morning, we lifted off from the carrier and flew approximately 25 miles across the sea into Vietnam. Our anxiety increased as we flew over the burned-out, smoldering wreckage of tanks and other vehicles left behind by the retreating South Vietnamese Army. The North Vietnamese Army was heading south after the South Vietnamese. Once we crossed the line into enemy territory, Ted and I knew we would be in serious trouble if we were shot down and captured. For obvious reasons, we had not told anyone onboard the ship where we were going.

Following the map, we soon spotted a large cluster of giant bamboo surrounding the village we were looking for. The village was about 30 miles behind enemy lines. Rather than rush in, we flew low tight circles, once to the left and then right, over the village. If we had taken fire, the mission would have been over and we would have flown back to the carrier.

Not taking fire and believing we were safe, we landed in a grassy field near some rice paddies. We shut down the aircraft and headed into the village, leaving our crew chief with the aircraft.

Even today, I can still vividly recall Ted and myself, strolling down the village path of hard-packed mud behind enemy lines, waving at Vietnamese villagers as they sold vegetables, ducks, and chickens. No one waved back. Most just stared at us, apparently not believing two American pilots were stupid enough to stroll into their village in broad daylight, in the middle of their farmers market … in the middle of a war, behind enemy lines.

We smiled and raised our hands, showing the villagers we were unarmed. We had left our personal sidearms with the helicopter. Ted and I walked in without guns because we wanted the villagers to know we came as businessmen with dollars, not as Marines with guns.

We met a young boy who led us to the "gold dealer" deeper in the village. The dealer, a tiny woman whose teeth were bloodred due to chewing betel nuts, smiled and greeted us. Her office was a tiny bamboo shack, with a bamboo blind propped up, indicating she was open for business. Nixon had closed the U.S. "gold window," but her gold window was open.

Real Gold or Fake Gold?

Ted and I, both Marine pilots and officers with college degrees, soon realized we did not know anything about gold. We had no idea what real gold looked like.

The Vietnamese woman's gold pieces were tiny nuggets, held in 3-inch diameter, half-inch thick, clear, circular plastic pill cases. Holding up the plastic cases up to the light, we got our first look at real gold. Unfortunately, her gold looked like tiny dried raisins that were painted gold.

"Is this gold?" I asked Ted.

"How would I know?" snapped Ted. "I don't know what gold looks like. Don't *you* know what gold looks like?"

"I thought you did," I replied shaking my head in disbelief. "That's why you're my partner."

The pressure of doing business behind enemy lines was getting to us. Ted thought I was an idiot and I thought the same of him.

The Moment of Truth

Most entrepreneurs have many moments of truths. For Ted and me, our first moment of truth was realizing that, while we might have been great partners as pilots, when it came to gold, we were both idiots.

After we calmed down and realized we were both idiots, we began our price negotiations.

Our opening bid was $40 for an ounce. Ted and I did know that the "spot," the international price of gold, was around $55 on that day. We thought we could get a discount since we had U.S. dollars and we were behind enemy lines. The tiny woman with red teeth just smirked and was probably thinking, *The two of you are idiots. Don't you know that the spot price of gold is the same all over the world?*

Try as we might, she would not budge off her price. She knew "spot was spot." And by now she knew we were real idiots. If she had been dishonest, she could have sold us dried raisins painted gold. She could have sold us rabbit droppings painted gold and we would not have known the difference.

Panic Sets In...

Suddenly, our negotiations were interrupted by frantic shouts and terrified screams from our crew chief: "Lieutenants, lieutenants, get back now." Immediately, my co-pilot and I ceased our negotiations and ran through the villagers' farmers market and back to the aircraft. I heard a squawk and felt badly when I realized I had accidently kicked a chicken and then stepped on a duck as I sprinted back to the aircraft.

My imagination was running wild. I could see lines of Viet Cong in black pajamas and North Vietnamese Army troops in khaki uniforms crossing the rice paddies and approaching our helicopter. It was then I remembered we were unarmed and could not defend ourselves. The little woman with the red teeth was right: we were idiots.

A Sinking Feeling

Thank God there were no Viet Cong or NVA. Our crew chief was panicking because our helicopter was sinking. The grassy field I had parked it on was an old rice paddy.

Due to the weight of the engine, rockets, machine guns, and ammunition, the aircraft was settling backward and sinking slowly, the tail rotor nearly touching the mud. We had to start the engine immediately or not start at all.

Our crew chief was the smallest and lightest of the three of us, so he sat in the pilot seat to start the engine, while we, the two pilots, put our shoulders under the tail boom to prevent the tail rotor from striking the ground.

The start was flawless as the main rotor began to turn slowly. As soon as the rotor blades were up to full speed, the crew chief began to gently rock the helicopter back and forth, slowly working and lifting the skids free from the sticky mud, as Ted and I yelled and screamed, warning him if the now-spinning tail rotor dipped too close to the mud.

Everything was going according to plan until the aircraft broke free and into a hover. Immediately, stinky, gooey mud began flying everywhere, covering Ted and me in nasty crud that turned our green flight suits, faces, and hair dark brown.

I climbed into the empty pilot's seat, took control of the aircraft, and Ted climbed into the other pilot's seat, replacing the crew chief, who then climbed into the back to man one of the machine guns.

It was a long, quiet trip back to the carrier. Ted and I said nothing to each other, and the crew chief dared not ask us if we had any gold.

Landing back on board the carrier, Marines and sailors gathered around our mud-covered helicopter. After the aircraft was shut down and secured to the flight deck, Ted and I emerged from the aircraft. The sailors and Marines were now staring at Ted and me, covered with more mud than our aircraft. Crossing the flight deck, heading for the showers and our rooms, all we said to those staring at us was, "Don't ask."

Learning from Mistakes

Rich Dad Poor Dad was first published in 1997. Rich dad was a man with very little formal education. Poor dad—my real dad—was an academic genius, graduating with a bachelor's degree in just two years, doing post-graduate work at Stanford University, University of Chicago, and Northwestern University, and ultimately earning a PhD in education. While I was in school, my dad was the superintendent of education for the State of Hawaii.

I mention my two dads at this time because both dads had completely opposite philosophies when it came to how we learn.

My poor dad believed mistakes meant that a person was stupid. Memorizing "right" answers was the real measure of intelligence.

My rich dad's philosophy was that mistakes were how people learn. He often said, "You can't become a champion golfer reading a book. You've got to make a lot of mistakes before becoming a real golfer. The same is true for being a real rich person."

Since I was never an academic genius, I subscribe to my rich dad's philosophy on real learning.

Fake vs. Real

This book is about fake money, fake teachers, and fake assets. This book is also about real money, real teachers, and real assets.

Fake Money

When President Nixon took the U.S. dollar off the gold standard, the U.S. dollar became fake money.

Definition of Fake Money: Fake money makes the rich richer, but makes the poor and middle class poorer.

Fake Teachers

In school, I found out many of my teachers were fake teachers. Simply said, they did not practice what they taught.

In school, I had many fake teachers. When I got to U.S. Navy Flight School, all of my teachers were real teachers. All of my flight instructors could fly.

Fake Assets

Millions of people are investing in fake assets. As I wrote in *Rich Dad Poor Dad*, the definition of an asset is something that puts money in your pocket. For most people, their "assets" are *taking* money from their pockets. Every paycheck, money is extracted and sent to Wall Street via retirement savings programs such as 401(k)s, IRAs, or government pensions.

Millions "save for retirement" for years, hoping their money will return multiplied. Millions of people my age, Baby Boomers, will soon find out they do not have enough money to support themselves after they retire. That's because the money that was taken out of their paychecks went to fake assets, making the rich richer—and leaving them holding the bag.

Real Teacher

I have been blessed to have had many great real teachers, teachers like my rich dad. Anytime I want to learn something, my first job is to find a real teacher, someone who practices what they teach, do it every day, and are successful at what they do.

The tiny Vietnamese woman was another one of my real teachers. In just a few minutes, not only did she teach me what an idiot I was, but she also inspired me to learn more—not only about gold but about that mysterious, magical, and important subject known as *money*, a subject not taught in school.

Owning Gold Was Illegal

After Ted and I showered off the mud, we returned to the pilots' ready room for some well-deserved laughter.

Our commanding officer threatened to have us brought up on charges. The operations officer threatened to have us wash our helicopter in front of everyone. Yet it was the weapons officer who got my attention. He said, "If you had brought that gold on board ship, you would have been arrested."

"What? Why would we have been arrested?"

"Because it is illegal for Americans to own gold."

"Why is it illegal?" Ted asked.

The weapons officer did not know. And the incident was dropped. After all, there was a war to fight, and we had more important missions to fly in the morning. The meeting came to an end and we all went to dinner.

But I had a new question in my mind: Why was it illegal for Americans to own gold?

That question led me to continue my ongoing financial education and seek my own answers.

Like my rich dad, I was learning from my mistakes.

In 1933, President Franklin Delano Roosevelt made it illegal for Americans to own gold. So, like most Americans, Ted and I had seen gold jewelry—but never gold coins, much less gold nuggets. The only money we knew was paper U.S. dollars and metal alloy coins, not real gold or real silver coins.

Today, most people only know fake money.

Ancient Money and Modern Money

Throughout history, "money" has been many different things. Money has taken the form of seashells, colored beads, feathers, live animals, and large stones.

Today there are three types of modern money. They are:

1. **God's money:** Gold and silver
2. **Government's money:** Dollars, Euros, pesos, etc.
3. **People's money:** Bitcoin, Ethereum, ZipCoin, etc.

The questions this book will attempt to answer are, which monies are real or fake, which teachers are real or fake, and what assets are real or fake.

YOUR QUESTIONS... ROBERT'S ANSWERS

Q: When did you first think about buying gold? And what was your plan?

Barbara E. – Canada

A: In 1972, the year I began buying gold, I was not thinking about the future. I was just curious. I was just curious about the relationship of gold to the U.S. dollar.

In 1972, I foolishly thought I could buy gold at a discounted price because I was behind enemy lines. The more I learned about gold, the U.S. dollar, and fake money, the more curious I became.

In 1983, I read Bucky Fuller's book *Grunch of Giants,* and the scale and scope of the global cash heist became clearer. In 2008, the cash heist went out of control when the central banks of the world printed trillions of dollars—in the name of saving the global economy. The central banks were saving themselves and "we the people" paid for it.

In Part Three of this book you will discover how sinister and pervasive this cash heist is today and why this out-of-control cash heist has me concerned about the future.

Q: Why is it so difficult for people to trust a start-up?

Momoh S. – Nigeria

A: Ideas are a dime a dozen. Millions of people have million-dollar ideas for a new product or business.

Without real financial education, very few people know how to take a million-dollar idea and turn it into a million dollars. That is why most people do not trust start-ups.

Q: If I hold all my wealth in fiat money will I lose it all someday?

Noah W. — USA

A: Yes, you will lose it all. If history is a guide, not one fiat currency has ever survived.

Fake money does not hold its value. Could the U.S. dollar be the first fake money in history to survive forever? Yes, but I would not bet on it.

Q: Once Nixon took the dollar off the gold standard, how were they able to determine the spot price of gold?

Tessa H. - Peru

A: In theory, the spot price of gold is determined by the international free markets. But that is in theory only. Today, the price of gold is manipulated, as are most financial assets.

In Part Three of this book I go into greater detail on how the price of gold is manipulated, why it is manipulated, and why the manipulation cannot go on much longer.

Q: Why was it illegal for Americans to own gold? What reason did they give the American people?

Gordon P. - USA

A: The Fed, Grunch, and the U.S. government wanted to take control of the money supply and the thousands of smaller banks—smaller banks that competed with the big banks and the Fed.

Not that long ago there were 20 larger banks. Today, there are only four "too big to fail" banks. Everyone is now trapped into a smaller banking system. Many suspect that having the U.S. economy controlled by a few large banks and the Fed has been the plan for a long time.

Q: How did the Vietnamese woman know the price of gold if there was no Internet?

Anthony O. - Australia

A: She was a professional gold seller. Professionals must know the price of their products. I assume she had a telephone, short-wave, radio, a newspaper, other dealers, and the owners of the mine as resources and as ways to stay in touch with global markets.

A more relevant question is: How many of your friends know what the spot price of gold is today? How many of them are interested in gold?

Chapter Two

IN GOD WE TRUST

WHO HAS EARNED YOUR TRUST?

n August 15, 1971, President Richard M. Nixon "temporarily" ended U.S. dollar convertibility to gold.

On June 17, 1972, the Democratic National Committee headquarters in the Watergate building in Washington D.C. were broken into. It was that event that led to the infamous Watergate scandal.

On October 10, 1973, Vice President Spiro Agnew pleaded no contest to charges of federal income tax evasion in exchange for having the charges of political corruption dropped. Gerald Ford, speaker of the House of Representatives, later became Nixon's new vice president.

On February 6, 1974, the U.S. House of Representatives passed House Resolution 803, giving the Judiciary Committee authority to investigate whether there were sufficient grounds to impeach President Nixon for his involvement in the Watergate scandal.

On July 27, 1974, the committee approved the first of three articles of impeachment: one for **obstruction of justice**, one for **abuse of power**, and one for **contempt of Congress**.

On August 9, 1974, Nixon resigned as president of the United States.

On September 8, 1974, President Gerald Ford **issued a full and unconditional pardon for Nixon, immunizing him from prosecution for any federal crimes he had committed or may have taken part in as president.**

And we trust these leaders... *our* leaders?

No one ever returned the U.S. dollar to the gold standard. Did they just forget? When—and why—did temporary become permanent?

Who Do You Trust?

I find it interesting that on all fake paper U.S. dollars we see the words:

In God We Trust

Why are we asked to trust in God? What happened to God's money, gold, and silver?

Gold is atomic number 79. Silver is atomic number 47.

Gold and silver were here during the formation of planet Earth.

Gold and silver will be here when the last cockroach is finally extinct.

So why then do the elites have "In God We Trust" on all our fake money?

This is not the first time in history when trusted leaders used fake money to make themselves richer and more powerful.

Paper money was first used by the Chinese during the Tang Dynasty, (AD 618–907). It was used for centuries before the practice caught on in Europe in the 17th century.

The Chinese Empire collapsed when the elites realized it was easy to print fake money to fight wars and build monuments to themselves.

The Romans used gold and silver coins. The Romans created fake money by trimming the edges of the coins.

Grooved Edges and Debasing Coins

Today, most U.S. coins have grooved edges. Grooved edges made it more difficult to shave gold and silver coins.

The Romans then created more fake money by "debasing" their gold and silver coins. Debasing meant gold and silver coins were mixed with base metals such as copper, tin, and nickel.

In 1965, the U.S. government began debasing U.S. silver coins, which is why silver coins have a copper tinge around the edge.

Gresham's Law

Gresham's Law states:

> *When bad [fake] money enters the system, good [real] money goes into hiding.*

In 1965, I began going to the local banks in Hilo, Hawaii, turning in dollar bills in exchange for rolls of dimes, quarters, and half-dollars. I would go home, unwrap the rolls of coins, pull out the real silver coins, and return the silver coins with the copper tinge on the edges to the bank.

It was not long before I had a large cloth bag filled with real silver coins.

I do not know why I began exchanging dollars for rolls of coins and then saving the real silver coins a habit. But I did. Was it Gresham's Law in action?

In 1965, I left for school in New York and never saw my bag of real silver coins again. I've always wonder if my mom spent that money, those real silver coins.

Searching the World for Gold

Between 1996 and 2012, I had a partner, a real teacher, named Frank Crerie. Frank was about the same age as my rich dad and my poor dad. Frank had taken a number of gold and silver mines public through IPOs (initial public offerings) on the Canadian and U.S. stock exchanges.

Too old to travel, Frank sent me throughout the world looking for gold and silver mines. It was an incredible and very *real* education. I remember looking at the side of a hill in the Peruvian Andes, looking at a line of holes, small gold mines, and following a gold vein in that hill. My mining geologist told me those tiny holes produced gold for the Incas, long before Francisco Pizarro arrived from Spain, killing their leaders and then stealing their gold.

I also remember traveling to Mongolia to visit another old gold mine we called "The Checker Board." It was called that because the mine was on flat ground and looked like a checker board due to the holes.

One of our best mines was an old silver mine in a remote part of southern Argentina. Our group took that mine public on the Toronto Stock Exchange when silver was less than $3 an ounce. We did very well once silver broke $7 per ounce. Today, silver bounces at around $15 an ounce. Unfortunately, we sold at $7.

Our biggest acquisition was an old mine in China. We got the Chinese mine for "nothing down." The agreement was that the Chinese government would give us the mine if we would raise money by taking the company public on the Toronto Stock

Exchange. Which we did. The good news is that we found gold, a massive deposit. Millions of ounces, "proven." For about a year, we knew we were billionaires. Our Chinese goldmine had a Spanish portmanteau: Mundoro Mining, or a world of gold.

Then one day, a government official notified us that the Chinese government was not going to renew our business license. Today, that mine is in the hands of friends of the Chinese elites, who are billionaires.

We are completely out of Mundoro. That is what I call a real education.

Lasting Impressions

The lasting impression left with me was this: isolated humans, living remotely, without any outside contact… who instinctively knew to value gold and silver.

What happened to us? What happened to our instincts for God's money? Are we too educated today?

Why do we trust people we don't even know? Why do we believe the elites just because they write the words "In God We Trust" on our fake money?

Look at this chart.

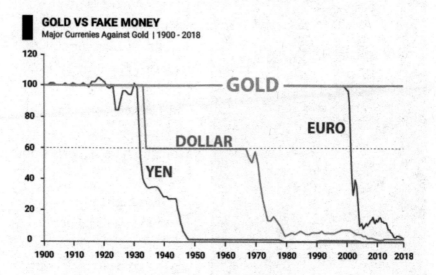

Now look at the chart of what happens to fake money, when our leaders print more fake money.

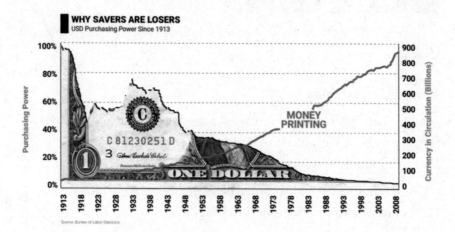

Is it history repeating itself?

This is a picture of German children in 1923 playing with money in the streets—billions in fake money. Under the Weimar Republic after WWI inflation was such that a U.S. $1 was worth 4.2 million DM.

Source: Getty Images / Corbis

The chart below shows where the kid's money came from.

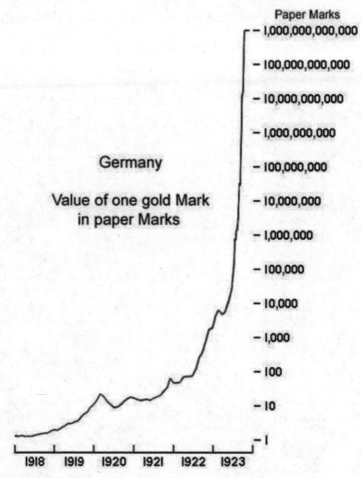

Source: Wikipedia – Delphi234

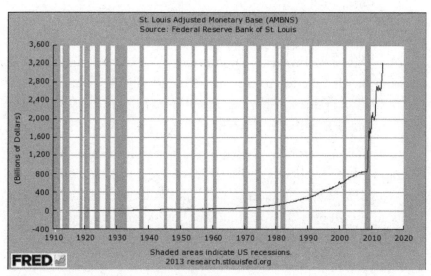

St. Louis Adjusted Monetary Base (AMBNS)
Source: Federal Reserve Bank of St. Louis

Shaded areas indicate US recessions.
2013 research.stlouisfed.org

Source: Federal Reserve Economic Data (FRED)

The FRED chart above shows the United States printing trillions in fake money after the crash of 2008.

Do you notice a similarity with the 1920s German printing of fake money, the *Reischmark*?

The bad news is, never in human history has fake money survived. Odds are that all of today's paper money will return to its true value: zero.

When it comes to your money, do you still "trust in God"?

Get the Student Back to His Studies

R. Buckminster "Bucky" Fuller wrote about "freeing the scholar to return to his studies"—in other words: getting students out of school and letting them get back to their studies.

For most of my life, I have been an average student. I was always a fake student. With the exception of flight school, I did not enjoy school. School was boring. When Fuller talked about "freeing the scholar to return to his studies," I often wondered what *my* studies were.

After reading Fuller's book *Grunch of Giants*, I knew I had found my study. I finally became a real student.

As my studies commenced, I realized I was pretty close to my studies in the fourth grade when I raised my hand and asked my teacher, "When will we learn about money?" It was asking that question that led me to meeting my rich dad, my classmate's father, and to his son and me becoming apprentices from the age of nine to well into our 30s with a real teacher.

Grunch of Giants took my study and research to a new level. I began looking for books and seminars by real teachers, anyone knowledgeable on the subject of Grunch. Frank Crerie, my partner who sent me all over the world looking for old gold and silver mines, was one of those real teachers. I will list some of those real teachers in Part Two of this book: Fake Teachers.

On May 28, 2018, while walking past a newsstand, the cover of *Time* magazine called out to me. The cover stated, "How My Generation Broke America." Steven Brill's article on elites in that magazine was another piece of the Grunch puzzle. Brill was stating the same concerns Bucky Fuller expressed 35 years earlier in *Grunch.*

In his lectures, Fuller was saying that the invisible people who control the world economy search our schools to find the best and the brightest so they can train them to run the world economy the way *they* want the world economy to be run.

Steven Brill did not say exactly that, but he did say:

> *I was one of those elite winners. In 1964, I was a bookworm growing up in Far Rockaway, a working-class section of Queens. One day I read in a biography of John F. Kennedy that he had gone to something called a prep school. None of my teachers at Junior High School 198 had a clue what that meant, but I soon figured out that prep school was like college. You go to classes and live on a campus, only you got to go four years earlier, which seemed like a fine idea. It seemed even better when I discovered that some prep schools offered financial aid. I ended up at Deerfield Academy, in Western*

Massachusetts, where the headmaster, Frank Boyden, told my worried parents, who ran a perpetually struggling liquor store, that his financial-aid policy was that they should send him a check every year for what they could afford.

Three years later, in 1967, I found myself sitting in the headmaster's office of my senior year, with a man named R. Inslee Clark Jr., the dean of admissions at Yale. ... What I didn't know then was that I was part of a revolution led by Clark, who nickname was Inky. I was about to become one of what would come to be known as Inky's boys and, later, girls. We were part of a meritocracy infusion that flourished at Yale and other elite education institutions, law firms, and investment banks in the mid-1960s and '70s.

Fuller might have said, "These very smart young people were selected and trained by those running Grunch."

Steven Brill went on to say, "As my generation of achievers graduated from elite universities and moved into the professional world, their personal successes often had serious societal consequences."

On to Prep Schools

The part of the Rich Dad story not told is that my rich classmates went on to private prep schools after Riverside School, not public middle and high schools like rich dad's son and I did. Most went to Hawaii Preparatory Academy, 80 miles away on the Big Island of Hawaii. Some went to Punahou School on the island of Oahu, where Barack Obama attended.

The future president was one of those "Inky boys and girls," like Steven Brill. Young "Barry" Obama, as he was called, went on from Punahou, eventually making it to Harvard Law, and then on to become president of the United States, a path similar to the ones of presidents Bill Clinton and George W. Bush.

When I asked my poor dad if I could go to a prep school, he said, "We are not rich, and it would not be politically correct if the superintendent of public education's son went to a private prep school."

While my rich classmates went on to prep schools, rich dad's son and I joined the students from across the street and went on to Hilo Intermediate School and Hilo High School.

The story of Rich Dad Poor Dad *begins when I was nine years old attending Riverside School, an elementary school for rich kids. The poor and middle-class kids went to school directly across the street at Hilo Union School.*

The good news was that I could surf every day. Hilo High also had one of the most powerful football teams in the state, and I loved playing football. We kicked Hawaii Prep's butt every time we played my former classmates.

Being in a school for rich kids caused me to wonder why some kids were rich and I was poor. In the fourth grade, surrounded by rich kids, I raised my hand and asked my fourth-grade teacher, "When will we learn about money?" When her reply was, "We don't teach the subject of money in school," my life-long study began. And as they say, "The rest is history."

And the best news was Mike and I became apprentices to rich dad after school and on weekends. We gained real business and financial education, all through intermediate school and high school.

It was my poor dad, the head of education for the State of Hawaii, who informed me he could only teach what the government allowed him to teach. If I wanted to learn about money, he advised me to talk to my best friend's father, who became my rich dad. And so the story of Rich Dad Poor Dad *began, a story about real financial education from a real teacher.*

Among our elementary school classmates who went on to prep school, many graduated from Stanford, Dartmouth, Yale, and other prestigious, elite universities… schools for the elite and future elite.

Serious Societal Consequences

Steven Brill went on to state of his generation of achievers, "They … created an economy built on deals that moved assets around instead of building new ones."

Translation: the elites got rich creating fake assets but did not grow the economy, i.e. they did not create high-paying jobs.

YOUR QUESTIONS... ROBERT'S ANSWERS

Q: How would we solve the financial problems of the United States? Where do we start? Do we start with putting the U.S. dollar back on the gold standard? Do we eliminate derivatives and fake assets first? How can we stop the Gross Universal Cash Heist?

Jaime M. – USA

A: These are all great questions. I had similar questions when I was younger. The more I studied Bucky Fuller and the cash heist, the more I realized there was only one answer. One of Fuller's Generalized Principles is "The Emergence through Emergency." That means there will have to be an emergency before anything changes. If you look at the word *emergency,* you notice the word *emerge* is the root word. Fuller taught our class that the next evolution of humanity would occur out of the coming *emergency*.

The great news is that many of us know this emergency is approaching and are taking action early. And I expect we'll see (or are already seeing) a new, smarter, wiser humanity emerging *ahead* of the coming emergency.

In 2004, just before the massive tsunami hit Indonesia killing hundreds of thousands of people, animals such as elephants began leaving the coastal areas as tourists headed for the beach.

The same thing is happening today. Millions of humans are evolving, choosing not to be victims, and making changes ahead of the coming financial emergency.

All of my books are written for people who know it is time to change.

Q: Is it too late to return to the gold standard?

Andrew C. – Canada

A: It depends upon who you ask. In Part Three of this book, Fake Assets, you will learn why many "academic elites" like Fed Chairman Bernanke believe gold is a barbaric relic of the past.

And then there are people such as Jim Rickards who, in his book *The New Case for Gold,* explains how the world could quite easily go back on the gold standard.

Q: What do you think the world would look like today if Nixon had not taken the dollar off the gold standard?

Joey S. – Vietnam

A: That's a very good question. I do not know. I prefer to think about what will happen in the near future and prepare for the future.

Q: Do we have fake truth?

Michael A. – Poland

A: Yes. In schools, fake truth is called "history."

If you take a closer look at the word *history,* you see it is a composite of two words: "his" and "story."

In military school, we are taught that "history belongs to the victors," not the losers.

As Joseph Goebbels said, "If you tell a lie big enough and keep repeating it, people will eventually come to believe it."

Fuller taught us to trust in "artifacts," things that you could see, touch, and feel, not a story or a lie.

For example, Columbus never set foot in America. He landed on the islands of the West Indies, so technically Columbus did not discover America. Yet there are artifacts that prove Vikings landed and lived in America long before Columbus.

So, who discovered America? An Italian or a Viking?

Q: Why the sudden change in currency over the last few years?

Kevin I. – Japan

A: If you study history, changes in currencies have been going on for thousands of years. The Chinese were the first to print paper money. The Romans "debased" their currency as the Roman Empire collapsed.

Hitler rose to power in 1933 because the Weimar government printed money to pay for losing WWI. Printed money led to WWII and the deaths of millions of people.

Many people believe 1971 was the beginning of the end of the American Empire.

Q: Bitcoin has been crashing lately. Do you still think it is real money?

Franco S. – Italy

A: Yes, but not necessarily Bitcoin. I believe blockchain technology will change the world because blockchain technology is more trustworthy than government money.

I prefer gold and silver for the same reason. Gold and silver are far more trustworthy than the people running our governments, banks, and pension funds.

Q: With so much fake (and real) news in the world today, what are some of the things you should look for to get reliable real news about the economy?

Samuel H. – Belgium

A: In this book I quote sources who worked inside the machine. They saw the cash heist firsthand. On page 288 you'll find a list of Rich Dad Radio interviews with individuals who witnessed Grunch from the inside. Listen in to the conversations and learn from real teachers the lessons on money that few people ever learn.

Q: How can this book help us survive from everything around us that is fake... and prepare for the next economic downturn or crash?

John H. - South Africa

A: Money became invisible in 1971. This book is about increasing your awareness, paying attention to signs of change—signs most people never see until it's too late.

Chapter Three

SEVEN PRACTICAL REASONS I OWN REAL GOLD AND SILVER

A CASE FOR GOD'S MONEY

Notice that I say I *own* real gold and silver. I do not say "I invest in" or "I trade" real gold and silver. There are seven reasons for the differences between *owning, investing,* and *trading*—anything.

REASON #1: Real gold and silver are not investments.

I do not own gold and silver to make money. They are insurance, a *hedge* against the stupidity of the elites… and myself.

I have insurance on my car, just in case someone hits me, or in case I hit someone else. Gold and silver serve a similar purpose.

I do not trust the elites. They believe they know everything. They believe they are always right. In their minds, they do not make mistakes. They will never admit they are wrong.

Elites are not the only ones with this affliction. All of us are afflicted with the "I am right and you are wrong" disease. We all know someone who is always right. At times, I am that person, too.

The challenge for elites is that they live in their sheltered world with other elites, out of touch with the rest of the world. They send their kids to the same elite schools with other elite kids. They believe they are doing good, working for the good of the world, yet they are out of touch with the real world. They hold massive charity events, they feel good, look good, want to see and be seen at galas, raising billions of dollars to save the world … but who saves the world from them? They were born smart, then highly educated, driven by hard work, yet—unwittingly—they have rigged the system to make themselves richer… at the expense of everyone else.

We can look to Luke 23:34 for an insight:

> *And Jesus said, "Father, forgive them, for they know not what they do." (ESV)*

Christ said this as he was being crucified. I never did well in Sunday School, yet this is one of the more important lessons I do remember: a lesson on forgiveness.

The elites may not know what they do. The problem is, the world pays for the fact that "they know not what they do."

As Steven Brill wrote in *Time*:

> *[The elites] were able to consolidate their winnings, outsmart and co-opt the forces that may have reined them in, and pull up the ladder so more could not share in their success or challenge their primacy.*
>
> *By continuing to get better at what they do, by knocking away the guardrails limiting their winnings, aggressively engineering changes in the political landscape, and by dint of the often unanticipated consequences of their innovations, they created a nation of moats that protected them from accountability and from the damage their triumphs caused in the larger community.*

Translation: The elites are above the law. They have no guardrails. They have the money to hire the best elite attorneys, often classmates from the same elite schools, to battle lower-paid government attorneys from less prestigious law schools. They have the power to do what they want without being held responsible for what they do or accountable for how many peoples' lives they damage. Their privileged education and success have turned them into despots.

Definition:
despot (n), a ruler or other person who holds absolute power, typically one who exercises it in a cruel or oppressive way.

I Do Not Know Everything

I know I do not know everything. I only know so much. I do my best, yet I make mistakes with my money. I do not trust our leaders. I do not trust our fake money. That is why I own real gold and silver, God's money.

Gold and silver are my insurance, my protection from our leaders and myself.

REASON #2: No risk.

All investments have risk. Real gold and silver have no risk. The price of gold and silver will go up and down—because the value of our fake money is going up and down.

When person invests, let's say in a stock or real estate, they expect an ROI, a *return on investment*, because they are taking a risk. When a person saves money in a bank, they expect a rate of return in the form of interest, because saving money in banks is extremely risky, especially when elites are printing money.

Look at the following chart:

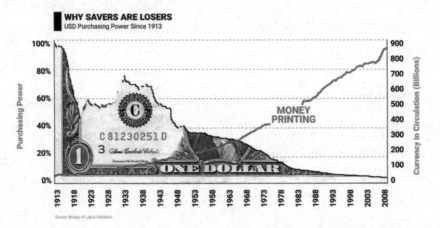

When I purchase a gold or silver coin, I do not expect an ROI, a return on investment, because I am not taking a risk. Gold and silver are God's money. Always remember, the price of gold or silver will go up or down because the value of our fake money is going up or down. Gold and silver are just gold and silver. Gold and silver will be here long after you, I, the elites, and the cockroaches are gone.

When I purchase real gold or silver, I purchase them forever. I never plan on selling. Just as Warren Buffett holds stocks forever, I will purchase gold and silver forever.

I know some of you are saying, "But I want to spend." "I need money." That is why most people are not rich. They love spending. I, too, love spending. I love nice cars, clothes, homes, and food. But even when I had no money or job, I protected those assets and never sold my gold and silver. I'll say it again: just as Warren Buffett holds stocks forever, I will own gold and silver forever.

Banks Are Not Safe

Banks are not safe. Banks are risky. I love my banker—because my banker loans me money. I use banks to store short-term cash, my operating capital. But I will not hold my long-term wealth in banks. Banks are too risky.

Reducing Risk

To reduce risk even further, my gold and silver are held in different safe-haven countries. All legally and far, far away. That way I remove all temptation and never need to worry that someone would force me to go to my local bank and get my gold and silver.

Counter-Party Risk

What is risky? That's a loaded question ...

Financial Literacy

Counter-party risk is an essential term for anyone who wants to build a real financial vocabulary and become financially educated. *Counter-party risk* is also known as *default risk*.

All investments have default risk. Simply said, a *default* occurs when someone does not live up to his or her end of the contract. For example, your friend borrows $100 from you, promising to pay you $110 in one year. The $10 return covers you taking the risk in lending your friend your $100. The $10 is for counter-party—your friend's—risk.

If your friend is unemployed and already owes you a $1,000, your interest should be higher, because the counter-party risk is higher. Better yet, just say, "No." Perhaps your friend decides to ask his banker for a loan. That is what bankers want: Bankers want to make loans. They want us to use the credit cards they issue. They do not make money from savers. Banks make money from borrowers.

Another Example of Counter-Party Risk

Here is another example of counter-party risk. Let's say you buy an insurance policy on your home. That insurance policy is only as good as the counter-party, i.e. the insurance company. If your house burns down and your insurance company goes bankrupt, your house and your insurance policy are both worthless.

THE CRASH OF 2008

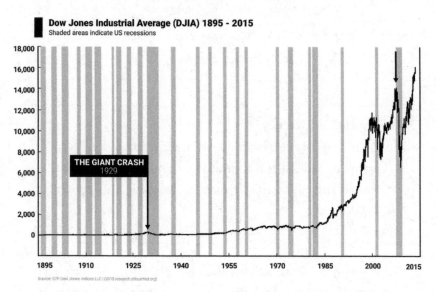

Dow Jones Industrial Average (DJIA) 1895 - 2015
Shaded areas indicate US recessions

THE GIANT CRASH
1929

Source: S7P Dow Jones Indices LLC | (2013 research.stlouisfed.org)

This is what happened in 2008:

1. Subprime borrowers, people like your friend, borrowed money to buy a house they could not afford.
2. Banks were happy to issue the subprime loan to your subprime friend.
3. The bank then sold the mortgage to an investment bank.
4. The investment bank then packaged thousands of these subprime loans, labeling them mortgage-backed securities, or MBS, a financial derivative.
5. Investment banks sold these MBS to governments, investment funds, pension plans, and other gullible people.

6. To give all parties a sense of security, these elites bought insurance policies, known as credit default swaps, CDS.

Everyone was getting rich ... because everyone was collecting "fees."

Repeating Brill's words in *Time*:

> *[The elites] created an economy built on deals that moved assets around instead of building new ones. They created exotic, and risky, financial instruments, including derivatives and credit default swaps, that produced sugar highs of immediate profits but separated those taking the risk from those who would bear the consequences.*

When the subprime borrower stopped paying, the derivates went off, exactly as Warren Buffett famously called derivatives in 2002: "financial weapons of mass destruction."

No one went to jail. Everyone who made money— from real estate brokers to mortgage brokers, bankers, investment bankers, and Wall Street—kept the money.

Millions lost their jobs, their homes, their savings, and their future. Today, the U.S. government is deep in debt, which means that taxpayers, their kids, and grandkids will be paying for those bankers' bonuses.

Credit Default Swaps

In the world of invisible money, credit default swaps are as important as insurance on your car, house, or life.

The three parties in a credit *default* swap are:

1. Bond seller
2. Bond buyer
3. Bond insurer

The **bond seller** packages debt (an IOU) and sells it, calling it a bond. The seller agrees to pay a yield, interest, an ROI over time. It is not much different from your friend asking you to borrow

$100 and paying you 10 percent interest over a year. Your friend has basically sold you a bond.

The **bond buyer** buys this bond, expecting the yield, in interest as ROI, over time.

The bond buyer is you. You loaned your friend the $100 with his promise to pay you $110 in a year.

You, the bond buyer, want to make sure your friend, the bond seller, will keep his promise. You both go to a **bond insurer**, who insures your $100 as well as the $10 in interest.

A credit default swap is the insurance policy against someone not keeping their promise.

What Is a Derivative?

A simple explanation of a derivative is to think of an orange.

When you squeeze the orange, orange juice comes out. The orange juice is a derivative of the orange. When you take the water out of the orange juice, you now have concentrated orange juice, another derivative of an orange.

When a subprime borrower bought a house he could not afford, the elites took the borrower and the house, repackaged it as a derivative called a mortgage-backed security, then the insurance companies created a credit default swap, yet another derivative. The elites made fortunes and were paid bonuses—after the house of cards collapsed.

Nothing has changed. The same people are still producing financial derivatives. Not one of the elites has gone to jail.

Brill writes:

> *[The elites'] money, their power, their lobbyists, their lawyers, their drive overwhelmed the institutions that were supposed to hold them accountable—government agencies, Congress, the courts.*

One reason why those words—*counter-party risk*—are so important is because the entire global monetary system is built on counter-party risk.

The reason I trust God's money—gold and silver—is because there is no counter-party risk.

Don't Worry...

If you do not fully understand counter-party risk, mortgage-backed securities, or credit default swaps, do not worry. Ninety-nine percent of the world does not understand the games being played *inside the world of invisible money.* If you would like to better understand this invisible world, get together with a friend or two, read what Brill and I have been writing, and then discuss what you understand. Remember, two minds are better than one—except in school, where two minds working together is called cheating.

Most important of all: always remember the entire money system of the world depends upon counter-party risk.

Is Your Money Safe... in a Bank?

The reasons banks pay you interest on your money is because there is counter-party risk.

One reason why the government insures bank deposits through the Federal Deposit Insurance Corporation (FDIC) up to $250,000 is to make savers feel safe and secure about their savings. The banks and the government do not want runs on the bank, so they offer deposit or default insurance.

Unfortunately, if the saver has $1 million in savings, and the bank goes bankrupt, the saver only gets back $250,000 of her $1 million.

When you go into your local bank to deposit money, the bank will offer you a choice between keeping your money in a *savings account* or in a *money market account.* The money market account offers the saver a slightly higher interest rate. Why? There is no deposit insurance on money market accounts. If you trust your bank with your life savings, then money market accounts will do.

Trust in Gold and Silver

Since gold and silver are real money, there is no counter-party risk. God does not default or break her promises.

By the way, I do not keep my real gold and silver in a bank safe deposit box. I do not trust banks or the government. They are only human, not God.

Private Vaults

A growing business today is private vaults with private guards. Not too long ago I was in Singapore checking out one of those private vault operations. The vault was on a private airstrip along the main airport. As I was talking to the manager of the private vault, a private jet landed at the main airport and taxied on the private runway to the private vault. The jet opened its doors and I watched two armed guards escort three locked steel boxes off the plane. The contents were locked away and papers signed, and the jet was off again, without ever shutting down its engines.

If you are not yet flying around in your private jet, you may want to keep your real gold and silver in a fireproof safe, at a location away from your home. If you tell someone where your safe and keys are, be sure your counter-party is trustworthy.

REASON #3: Gold and silver attract real wealth.
Wealth attracts wealth just as poverty attracts poverty.

I was once invited to a seminar featuring the Hindu guru Gurudeva. I was excited to attend. When it came time for questions, most questions were on enlightenment, others on spirituality, peace, or happiness. The guru was wearing a lot of gold: gold glasses, a large gold earning, gold bracelets, and a gold necklace. Since I was raised a Methodist, and Methodist ministers did not wear much (if any) gold, I raised my hand and asked, "Why do you wear so much gold?"

The kindly guru smiled and said, "Because the tears of God are made of gold." He then said, "The tears of God—gold—attract wealth." When I asked what he meant by gold attracting wealth, the guru replied, "Let's say you want to attract $1,000 a month into your life. Then you own $1,000 of real gold."

"And if I want $1 million a month, then I own $1 million in gold?"

The guru, sensing that my greed over taking my spirituality, just smiled and said, "Why don't you start with a $1,000 and see if what I say works for you. Gold does not work for everyone. There are conditions on God's generosity."

That year was 1986 and, not having much money, finding an extra $1,000 for gold was tough. But Kim and I did it. Every month, we purchased some gold and silver, and we've never stopped. For example, if we wanted to increase our income from $5,000 a month to $10,000 a month, we would acquire $10,000 in gold coins and forget about the gold. A few months later, it seemed more wealth did come in, without us really noticing the increase. If the price gold went down, we purchased more gold, and we just kept going. Today we must have private vaults in faraway, safe-haven countries. We do not need a private jet and private runways, to hide our gold... yet.

Whenever Kim and I are asked, "Will gold attract wealth for me?" we reply with the guru's reply, "Why not try it yourself, and see if gold—God's tears—works for you? God is generous, but there are conditions on God's generosity."

Spiritual Lesson on Gold

While the tears of God are made of gold, the question each of us needs to ask ourselves, are God's tears *tears of joy* or *tears of sadness?*

Much of the gold in storage is from tears of sadness.

When I was standing in the Andes looking at ancient Inca gold mines, I was reminded of my history lesson on how the Spaniards, led by Francisco Pizzaro, murdered thousands of natives, just for gold and other precious gems and metals. The Nazis did the same to the Jews. So, did most conquerors. The English did the same to the Scots, Irish, Maoris, and Aborigines. The Americans did it to the American Indians and the Hawaiians. White American slave owners did it to African slaves. The Japanese did it to the Chinese and Koreans. And, the elites are doing the same today.

This spiritual lesson applies to anything. It is not your money or your wealth that matters. It is how you *acquired* your money and wealth that matters.

REASON #4: Why real gold and silver? Why not paper gold and silver exchange traded funds (ETFs)?

I do not trust anything paper. Anything paper is a derivative, a fake, something that requires a counter-party for value.

Financial Education

Much of the global banking system runs on what is known as *fractional reserve banking.*

The world's banking system is built on fractional reserve banking, a system that has been running the world for thousands of years. The following is a simple explanation of the system.

A thousand years ago, you are a shop owner. You have 10 gold coins. You need to travel a thousand miles, through rough country with the likelihood you'll run into some bad people country, to buy goods for your store.

You go to a local "banker" who agrees to hold your 10 gold coins in his safe. The "banker" issues you a piece of paper saying that you have deposited 10 gold coins with him.

You then travel the thousand miles through rough country with only a piece of paper. Your gold coins are safe.

You then buy new merchandise for your store, give your piece of paper to the person who sold you the merchandise, and head home.

The person who sold you your merchandise goes to his "bank" and collects his gold.

After a while, both you and the person who sold you your merchandise realize that paper is much more convenient than gold coins. You both leave your gold with your bankers and use your bankers' CDs, or certificates of deposit, as paper money.

People who need money go to your banker and ask for a "loan." The banker lends out nine of your 10 gold coins. The one gold coin he holds in his vault is the "fractional reserve." In this example, the fractional reserve is one coin, or 10 percent.

This is where it gets exciting. The person who borrowed nine of your 10 gold coins goes to his bank and deposits your nine gold coins. His banker then lends out 8.1 of the nine coins to other borrowers, who do the same thing with their bank.

Your 10 (real) gold coins could easily become a 1,000 (fake) gold coins. And everything is fine—as long as no one wants real gold coins. This is the modern banking system.

The reason I want my real gold coins in my own private vault and not paper gold coins in an exchange-traded fund (ETF) vault, is because for every real gold coin, there are an estimated 100 to 500 fake paper coins.

Everything will be fine… until everyone wants real gold.

The fractional reserve banking system of banking applies to everything, not only money or gold. The entire banking system is based on counter-party trust.

After rich dad explained the fractional reserve banking system to his son and me, I laughed every time I saw "In God We Trust" on my money.

I prefer to trust God's money—real gold and silver—rather than the elites who print our money, run our government, central banks, banks, bond markets, and stock markets.

Always remember: gold and silver will be here long after you, I, the elites, and the cockroaches are gone.

REASON #5: The system is broke and broken.
The gap is growing. We are on the verge of class warfare.

Steven Brill reports:

1. Between 1929 to 1970, middle-class incomes grew faster than upper-class incomes. Income inequality was reduced.
2. In 1928, the bottom 90 percent shared 52 percent of total wealth.
3. By 1970, the bottom 90 percent's share of total wealth increased to 68 percent.
4. In 1970 the top 1 percent's share of wealth was down to 9 percent of total wealth.
5. In 1971, the trend started going the other way and accelerated.
6. By 2007, the wealth of the top 1 percent was up to 24 percent of total wealth.
7. By 2012, the bottom 90 percent share dropped to 49 percent, less than half of total wealth.

A Picture Is Worth a Thousand Words

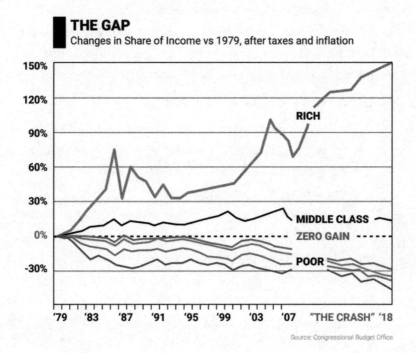

THE GAP
Changes in Share of Income vs 1979, after taxes and inflation

Source: Congressional Budget Office

Who Cares About the Poor?

In his book *Tailspin*, from which the *Time* article was adapted, Brill has this to say about the poor and middle class:

> *Politicians at least now pay lip service to the plight of the middle class, but they rarely talk about the poor, much less do enough to help them. This can only be explained by their fear that the middle class might see any attention paid to those below them as further evidence that their elected officials have abandoned them.*

Brill quotes a study done by Daniel Markovits and Ray Fisman stating, "The elites who make policy—regardless of political party—just don't care much about [economic] equality."

Translation: Who cares about the poor and middle class?

Brill notes these same elites have made great strides, championing liberal causes related to democracy such as equal rights, women's rights, LBGT rights ... but could care less about unbalanced economic power and growing income inequality between them and the poor and middle class.

I'll highlight seven facts he also notes:

1. "The celebrated American economic mobility engine is sputtering. A child's chance of earning more than his or her parents has dropped from 90 percent to 50 percent in the last 50 years."

2. "Household debt by 2017 had grown higher than the peak reached in 2007 before the crash."

3. "The world's richest country [the United States] continues to have the highest poverty rate among the 35 nations in the Organization for Economic Cooperation and Development (OECD), except for Mexico. (It is tied in second to last place with Israel, Chile, and Turkey.)"

4. "Among the same 35 OECD countries American children rank 30th in math proficiency and 19th in science."

5. "Nearly one in five of America's children live in households that their government classifies as 'food-insecure,' meaning they are without 'access to enough food for an active, healthy life.'"

6. "America's airports are an embarrassment, and a modern air traffic control system is 25 years behind schedule. The power grid, roads, and rails are crumbling, pushing the United States far down international rankings for infrastructure quality. ... On an average day in America, there are 657 water main breaks across the country."

7. "Members [of Congress] are sick and tired of spending five hours a day begging. ... [In Washington, there are] more than 20 [registered lobbyists] for every member of the House and Senate."

But who cares about the poor and middle class?

My Concerns

Studying with Fuller in the 1980s and learning how to see the future, I began to see the following storm clouds on the horizon. The storm has arrived.

1. Much of the baby boom generation has no retirement savings. This is because, prior to 1974, most workers had company pension plans. After 1974, employees were on their own, hoping personal retirement savings accounts such as a 401(k) would keep them alive after their working days were over.

2. Major employee pension funds are broke. For example, CalPers, the California pension fund for government employees, the largest government employee pension fund in America, is $1 trillion underfunded.

3. This is a chart of Social Security:

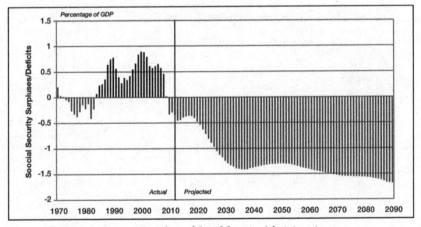

Source: The Peter G. Peterson Foundation | Social Security Administration

Medicare is an even bigger problem. The United States has been fighting a multi-year, multi-trillion-dollar war we cannot win.

But Wait… It Gets Worse

Brill notes, "[The U.S.] Congress has not passed a comprehensive budget since 1994."

The January 25, 2018, issue of *The Economist* explains the reason why American leaders cannot balance the budget and why America will go bankrupt. (Emphasis mine.)

> *The constitution gives Congress the power of the purse. Four things are odd about the way it uses it. First, annual budgets cover only the roughly one-third of federal budget spending that Congress has decided needs to be reapproval each year. Most entitlement programs, such as Medicare, health care for the elderly, are automatically funded. So, while budget-making provides for grandstanding by Congressmen about long-term fiscal problems, the process affords few chances to tackle the principal cause:* swelling entitlement spending.

Translation: The poor we have been ignoring will eventually bankrupt America. The Constitution guarantees it.

The Future?

The question is, will our elites print more money to pay for our massive entitlement programs, or will our elites put us back on the gold standard? Or will we slide into the next Great, Great Depression?

REASON #6: God's money versus government money.

A picture is worth a thousand words.

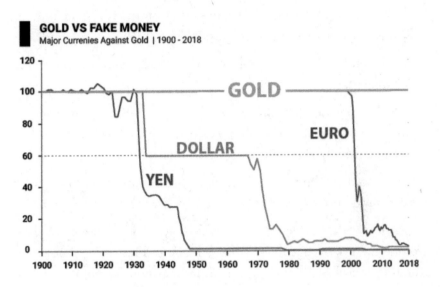

GOLD VS FAKE MONEY
Major Currenies Against Gold | 1900 - 2018

Question: How much more fake money can our governments print?

Answer: The elites can print as much as they want as long as people will work for it.

The Next Step

The next step may be for the IMF to issue special drawing rights (SDRs), a global currency… in effect, more fake money. Again, as long as people will accept it, they will print it.

Meanwhile, the elites are warehousing real gold. They know the game is over.

REASON #7: God's money is easy to acquire.

Buying gold and silver mines is hard. I know. I've bought and built two of them.

Buying gold and silver mines takes a lot of time, money, and brain power.

Acquiring real gold and real silver requires very little money, very little risk, and very little financial education.

It is much easier and less expensive to just buy real gold and silver coins from a reputable coin and silver dealer.

In 1964, I began acquiring silver coins such as dimes, quarters, and half-dollars.

Why 1965? In 1965, the U.S. Mint began *debasing* our silver coins. Debasing means the Mint was diluting the silver content of our coins, mixing the coins with base metals, like copper and tin.

The Romans did the same thing to their coins when they needed more money to fight their extended wars. Sound familiar?

In 1965, after noticing the copper tinge to American coins, I would take my paper money, go to a bank and buy rolls of either dimes or quarters. I'd unwrap them, inspecting each coin. If the coin did not have a copper tinge, I kept it. All the coins with copper tinge on the edge (the debased coins) I returned to the bank. Then I bought more rolls of coins and continued my search for real silver coins. It was not rocket science. I did not need any financial education because there was no counter-party risk.

Gresham's Law essentially states that bad money drives out good.

That is all I was doing. I do not know why I was doing it. It just made sense to want real silver.

In 1972, I purchased my first gold coin in Hong Kong. It wasn't until 1974 that it became legal for Americans to own gold.

The good news is that, even today, for a dollar you can buy pre-1965 silver coins.

For about $20, you can buy a real silver dollar. And for about $1,500, you can buy a real gold coin.

If you are a beginner, I would not buy numismatic, rare collectible coins. That requires a lot of financial education and years of experience.

The best news is that everyone, rich or poor, can afford God's money.

James Rickards, a person I respect, predicts gold will eventually reach $10,000 an ounce. Others predict that gold will drop to $400 an ounce.

What you do will depend upon whom you believe.

I do not care. As I said, I buy gold and silver and will never sell for the seven reasons I've just explained.

On the other hand, you can always look at the words on U.S. money and trust in God. That is what everyone else is doing.

In Part 2: Fake Teachers and Part 3: Fake Assets,
I will explain how and I why I do not need money,
how and why I can buy what I want, and how and
why I keep buying more gold and silver.

For now, it is important to understand why
I own gold and silver and why I do not believe
the elites when they say, "Trust in God."

YOUR QUESTIONS... ROBERT'S ANSWERS

Q: Could the "1,000-piece puzzle" be called the GRUNCH Puzzle?
Scott J. – USA

A: You can call the 1,000-piece puzzle anything you like. My reason for calling money a 1,000-piece puzzle is to encourage you to become students of money, to search for your own answers to your own financial puzzle called "money and your life."

Real life is not like life in school. In real life, you do not memorize answers, take a test, and pass or fail. Real life is a life-long learning process. There are no right answers.

When you are really learning... you are learning throughout your life. There is no one special teacher to learn from. In real life, everything is your teacher. In real life, there is no such thing as one right answer. A right answer in one situation can be the wrong answer in a different situation. In real life you learn from everything, from your wins and especially from your failures. In real life, it is foolish to follow only one teacher, believe in only one philosophy, and live in a world of "I am right and you are wrong."

It is insanity to believe in someone just because he or she has a PhD or is a CEO... or is a rich person. A real student learns from everything and everyone. Life itself is your teacher and you are in a state of constant learning.

My wish is that, after completing this book, every reader goes on to find their own pieces to their own 1,000-piece money puzzle.

You can call it the "Grunch Puzzle" or you can call it "My Life's Puzzle."

Q: Why have the academic elites been taught to (legally) rip off the world through the engineering of derivatives? And if the elites are the puppets, then who are the puppeteers controlling them?

Jackson G. – USA

A: That's a great question—and one to which we may never know the truth.

The real answer is that people lie about money. Most people are just not honest with themselves or others and will say "I'm not interested in money." Yet deep down they desire, crave, and are often desperate for money. For most people, money squeezes the life out of their minds, bodies, and souls.

The real truth is that today money is survival. A thousand years ago, no one really needed money to survive. A thousand years ago, hunters could hunt for food and gatherers could gather what they needed to survive. They lived in caves or tents—and didn't have mortgage payments. They walked or rode animals and did not have a car payment or need to buy gas.

Today, people need money for food, shelter, transportation, education, and personal survival. Rather than tell the truth about the money—the truth being that money is essential for survival—people tell lies about money. Why? Because, in most cases, they can't handle the truth.

That is why people go to work at a job they hate and say, "I'm not interested in money."

People will say, "I'm not interested in money," yet resent the rich for having money. People will say, "I'm not interested in money," yet play the lottery hoping to win a million dollars.

People will say, "I'm not interested in money," yet will sue you for millions in court.

People will say, "I'm not interested in money," yet marry someone for money.

People will say, "I'm not interested in money," yet demand their kid get good grades in school, not because they want their child to learn, but because they want their kid to get a high-paying job.

So why do academic elites rip off the world? Because academics are not honest with themselves about their need for money. Academics get away with it because most people are not honest about money.

Q: How long do you think the general public will continue to accept the U.S. dollar even though its purchasing power continues to decrease? And what will it take to make people question the true worth of the U.S. dollar?

Leticia J. — Croatia

A: No one really knows. I believe in being prepared, which is why I own real gold and real silver, held outside the banking system.

Q: How can we protect ourselves from the elites? Is there hope or any form of protection?

TJ B. — United Kingdom

A: The best way to protect yourself from the elites is to own real gold and real silver.

Elites can control and manipulate everything that is human-made.

It is harder for the elites to control, manipulate, or destroy god's money. Gold and silver will be here long after the elites, you, and I are gone.

Q: How can people use fake money to their advantage?

Lincoln T. - USA

A: I use debt to create equity, fake money. With fake money I acquire assets that produce fake money. I use fake money to acquire real money, god's money—gold and silver. Please know that to do this requires real financial education.

Chapter Four

PRINTING FAKE MONEY
HISTORY REPEATS ITSELF

Printing fake money is not new.

The ancient and modern banking systems are built on printing fake money. Printing fake money is the way banks make money.

The reason banks make so much money is because, for thousands of years, the banking system has had a license to print money.

Banks are not the only organization with a license to print money. The stock market, bond market, real estate market, financial derivatives markets, and many other markets have licenses to print money.

Counterfeiters print *real* fake money.

You can print money too, legally, and you do not need a license.

LESSON

People who work for money… work for people who print money.

The Problem with Education

A bigger problem is that our education system does not educate students about printing money. Instead, the education system teaches students *to work for people who print money.* This is what's really behind the financial crises we face today.

August 15, 1971, was the start of the biggest money-printing expedition in world history. On that date, President Richard Nixon announced the U.S. dollar could no longer be traded for gold at a fixed rate.

In 1972, the year I flew behind enemy lines looking for gold, I did not know what I was doing—or why I was doing what I was doing. I was just curious, wondering what rich dad meant when he said, "Watch out—the world is going to change."

Looking back, I realize I was inadvertently witnessing the start of THE Greatest Financial Rip-Off in world history.

Centuries of Printing Money

Just as a reminder: Money printing is not new.

Most money-printing ventures have been tiny, isolated, regional, and limited to smaller countries.

A few cash heists have been monsters, world game-changers. A few giants have been:

1. **The Chinese** were the first to print paper money in AD 618. Marco Polo noticed Chinese paper money on his travels and the practice of printing paper money slowly spread to Europe.
2. **The Roman Empire**, faced with rising debts, fighting long distance wars, diluted their gold and silver coins with base metals, such as nickel and tin.
3. **American colonists** printed fake money to fight the Revolutionary War, as did the South, printing the Confederate dollar to fight the Civil War.

4. **Germany** printed trillions in fake money in the 1920s. Printing fake money led to World War II, the rise of Adolf Hitler, and the slaughter of millions of Jews and other innocents.

5. **Zimbabwe**, once the breadbasket of Africa, became the basket case of Africa after the leaders began printing money in the 2000s.

6. **Venezuela** is one of the richest oil countries in the world. In 2018, Venezuela is on the verge of bankruptcy and revolution, yet continues to print fake money.

LESSON

In nearly every example, the rich got richer and everyone else lost.

LESSON

The printing of fake money has never ended gracefully.

LESSON: THE PROMISE

In 1944, the U.S. dollar was made the *reserve currency* of the world at a conference of 44 nations in Bretton Woods, New Hampshire. That year, the United States, through the Bretton Woods Agreement, promised the world to back its dollar with gold. With that promise, the U.S. dollar became the first global money. The stage was set for the mother of all money printing, a global cash heist.

LESSON: TRADING WITH THE ENEMY

In the 1950s, former enemies Germany and Japan began selling Volkswagens and Toyotas in the United States. The more the United States imported, the more gold left the country.

LESSON: BROKEN PROMISE

In 1971, the United States broke its 1944 promise. The reason Richard Nixon broke the promise was to stop gold from leaving the United States. History has proven that Nixon was a liar, hence his nickname Tricky Dick. He also lied about why he broke his promise.

If Nixon had kept the dollar on the gold standard, the gold standard would have solved the problem of gold leaving America. The United States would have been punished for importing more than it was exporting, America would have had to start producing better products at better prices (aka capitalism), and gold would have flowed back to America.

Instead, the academic elites killed capitalism, factories were forced to close, and jobs left America for lower-wage countries.

The gold standard was broken so that the academic elites could print money—making themselves richer by ripping off the world. In Bucky Fuller's words: Grunch—Gross Universal Cash Heist.

LESSON: THE DOLLAR BECOMES DEBT

In 1971, the dollar morphed into an IOU from the American taxpayer. The United States began paying for Volkswagens and Toyotas with IOUs.

LESSON

Nixon promised taking the dollar off the gold standard was temporary.

LESSON

Nixon resigned before being impeached for the Watergate scandal. He did not keep his promise to put the U.S. dollar back on the gold standard.

The biggest money-printing operation in world history was underway—and it's still operating today. The rich are getting extremely rich and the poor and middle class are in trouble.

As Steven Brill writes:

> *Lately, most Americans, regardless of their political leanings, have been asking themselves some version of the same question: How did we get here? How did the world's greatest democracy and economy become a land of crumbling roads, galloping income inequality, bitter polarization, and dysfunctional government?*
>
> *As I tried to find the answer over the past two years, I discovered a recurring irony. About five decades ago, the core values that make America great began to bring America down.*

Dr. Fuller warned our class of this. Paraphrasing from the three times I studied with him, he said that the old-money rich began opening the doors to elite higher education to extremely bright students from the middle class and poor in the 1960s and 1970s. These elite Baby Boomer students became the puppets of the puppeteers, who are Grunch.

Brill is one of the extremely bright middle-class students of the 1960s who was among the chosen.

Others are Presidents Barack Obama, William Clinton, Secretary of State Hillary Clinton, and Fed Chairman Ben Bernanke and Chairwoman Janet Yellen.

Bucky Fuller was from the old-boy, American white aristocracy with inherited wealth. He was fourth-generation Milton Academy and fourth-generation Harvard. Fuller never graduated from Harvard.

Presidents John Kennedy, George H.W. Bush, George W. Bush, and Senator Mitt Romney, all graduates of Harvard and Yale, are from America's white aristocracy, inherited wealth.

Work Harder

Steven Brill came to the realization that his peers—the academic elites from middle class and poor families—did not have inherited wealth. Hence, they had to use the same grit and tenacity that made them academic elite scholars to become rich. They used that grit and tenacity to invade Wall Street, corporate America, and law firms.

Brill's realization was that it was these poor and middle-class academic elites who destroyed the American economy for fellow Americans from the poor and middle class.

Brill states:

> *"His peers entered corporate America and exported jobs overseas, rather than compete with low-wage countries. Lawyers took over law firms, serving only the very rich, rather than protecting the unprotected poor and middle class. Wall Street went to financial engineering, manufacturing fake assets, rather than create new real assets. Rather than focus on "American exceptionalism," the academic elites in education focus on social engineering, making sure everyone is equal and no one's feelings are hurt.*

> *While they focused on kids being equal, to protect their kids, insuring their kids climb to the top, they made sure their kids went to the same prep schools, which assured their kids entrance into the most elite universities.*

Simply said, their elite kids got the education the poor and middle class have no access to.

All in all, Steve Brill realized this about his hard-working, high-achieving peers:

> *They created a nation of moats that protected them from accountability and from the damage their triumphs caused in the larger community. ... Then, in a way unprecedented in history, they were able to consolidate their winnings, outsmart*

*and co-opt the forces that might have reined them in, and
pull up the ladder so more could not share in their success or
challenge their primacy.*

Fuller shared similar concerns in his lectures and in his book
Grunch. In *Grunch,* Fuller almost referred to President Ronald
Reagan as a "stooge," surrounded by and taking advice from
ambitious academic elites who ripped off America from the inside.

Global Money Printing

The year 1971 was the start of a global cash heist, a rip-off of the
wealth of the people of the world.

In 1983, futurist Buckminster Fuller's book *Grunch of Giants*—
again, Grunch standing for <u>Gr</u>oss <u>U</u>niversal <u>C</u>ash <u>H</u>eist—was a
prophetic and prescient warning of things to come and told of a
global cash heist that is going on and still goes on today.

In 1971, with the dollar no longer backed by gold, money
became invisible. People *could not see* the cash heist. Again, as Fuller
said, people do not get out of the way of things they cannot see
moving toward them.

It's Not All Bad

Printing money has not been all bad. Printing fake money has
done a lot of good. Billions of people working for fake money have
produced a functioning economy, new inventions, better housing,
advances in medicine, travel, consumer products, and technology.

These hard-working people have produced a better world in spite
of parasitic elites who suck the health and wealth out of the people
who make the world a better place to live.

The problem is that printing money has never worked. The cash
heist that began in 1971 will eventually fail. The party caused by
printing fake money is about to end. And the hangover—and it will
be a horrific one—is about to begin.

While the 1 percent has become very rich, billions have become poorer... or are about to become poorer.

Today, millions of American Baby Boomers—arguably the richest, luckiest, generation in history—are not looking forward to a glorious retirement. Millions of Baby Boomers are worried. Many know they will never retire. After working all their lives, many will live poor and grow poorer as they grow older. This is what happens when you work for and save fake money. The chart below tells the story:

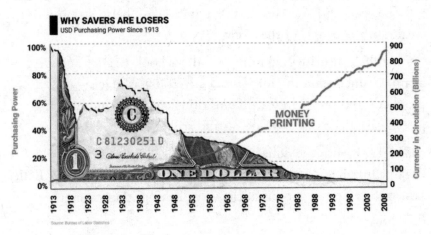

WHY SAVERS ARE LOSERS
USD Purchasing Power Since 1913

From the *Wall Street Journal*, June 23, 2018:

Time Bomb Looms for Aging America
"Americans are reaching retirement age in worse financial shape than the prior generation."

LESSON

The "prior generation," the WWII generation had a defined benefit (DB) pension plan—a *paycheck for life*. Financial education for the WWII generation was not necessary because DB plans had "professional management."

Then DB plans ended. The corporations that used to offer DB plans stopped because DB plans for their employees were too expensive.

Today, only a few Baby Boomers have DB plans, retirement plans that give them a paycheck for life.

Today, even Baby Boomers with DB plans are worried. The *Wall Street Journal* states, "Some public-sector workers are living with uncertainty as cash strapped governments consider pension cuts."

LESSON

The reason many DB pensions are in trouble is because they based their computations on a 7.5 percent return on their investments and that most Boomers would not live past 70. The good news is Boomers are living longer. The bad news is the markets have not always cooperated in delivering on projections.

Add this to the unsettling mix of facts and figures: 10,000 Baby Boomers are retiring every day.

The crisis will turn into financial disaster in 2026 when the first Boomers turn 80 and need more and more long-term health care … just when Social Security and Medicare go broke.

Boomers Have DC Plans—Not DB Plans

In 1974, as millions of Baby Boomers were entering the work force, Employee Retirement Income Security Act (ERISA) was introduced to reduce the cost of employees. A few years later, we saw the first 401(k) plan, also known as a DC, or defined-contribution pension plan.

Baby Boomers had to become "professional" money managers—without any financial education. This is the Baby Boomer crisis.

A DC plan is limited to the *contributions made* and the total benefit is only the amount in the plan at retirement. If there is nothing in the DC account, the Boomer is on his or her own… out of luck and, perhaps, out of money.

The *Wall Street Journal* continues to report:

> "Gains in life expectancy, combined with the soaring price of education, have left people in their 50s and 60s supporting adult children and older relatives."

Boomers are often called the "sandwich generation" for supporting both their parents and children.

Americans aged 60 through 69 had about $2 trillion in debt in 2017.

There are only 75 million Boomers. That is a lot of debt per Boomer.

> [Baby Boomers] have high average debt, are often paying off children's educations, and are dipping into savings to care for aging parents. Their paltry 401(k) retirement funds will bring in a median income of under $8,000 a year for a household of two.

> In total, more than 40 percent of households headed by people aged 55 through 70 lack sufficient resources to maintain their living standard in retirement. That is around 15 million American households.

> Households with 401(k) investments and at least one worker aged 55 to 64 had a median $135,000 in tax-advantaged retirement accounts in 2016. ... For a couple aged 62 and 65 who retire today, that would produce about $600 a month in annuity income for life.

> Market declines in 2000 and 2008 revealed the perils of do-it-yourself retirements, as many 401(k) participants cut back on contributions, shifted funds out of stocks and never put them back in, or withdrew money to pay bills.

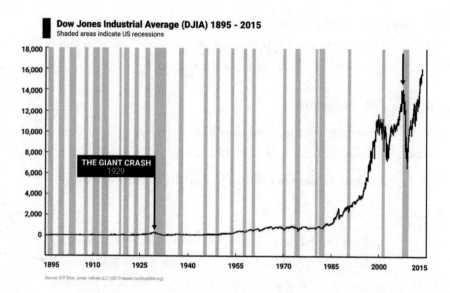

Dow Jones Industrial Average (DJIA) 1895 - 2015
Shaded areas indicate US recessions

THE GIANT CRASH
1929

Source: S7P Dow Jones Indices LLC | (2015 research.stlouisfed.org)

Arthur Smith Jr., 61 is still feeling the impact. He consistently saved in 401(k)-type plans with various employers over the past 35 years, he says. His 401(k) got hit hard in the market crashes, he says, in large part because he invested in individual tech stocks.

"We were allowed to pick our own stocks and I jumped on some high-risk ones," he says. His 401(k) lost about half its value early in the 2000s and lost half again in 2008, he says.

LESSON

When I was a kid in the 1960s, only gamblers invested in the stock market. In the 1960s, if people did invest, they invested in the bond market. Today, most Baby Boomers are gamblers in the stock market.

LESSON

One reason most Baby Boomers are in the stock market is because interest rates on savings and bonds are at historic lows. In search of "higher returns," many people have become gamblers and entered the stock market.

Take a look at the Dow Chart again. Notice where the chart is today. Once again, the Dow is at an all-time high, a high caused by fake money looking for returns on investment.

A $1.5 Billion Bonus

On the same front page of the *Wall Street Journal*, next to the article on Baby Boomers, read the headline:

Xiaomi Gives Its CEO a $1.5 Billion Thank You

The article starts:

> *Chinese smartphone maker Xiaomi Corp., whose valuation could soon register at $70 billion, gave its founder and chief executive a token of its appreciation: $1.5 billion in stock, no strings attached, in one of the largest corporate paydays in history.*

History Is Repeating Itself

History has proven that printing fake money never ends in prosperity. History is evidence that printing fake money always ends in poverty for those who work for fake money.

American Baby Boomers are the economy's canary in the coal mine. Once affluent American Baby Boomers are now worried about living in poverty. Boomers are canaries, sensing fake money's looming failure.

Historically—from the Chinese, the Romans, the German Weimar Republic, and Venezuela today—printing fake money has never produced a sustainable prosperity. Historically, printing fake money has always ended in either depression, revolution, war, or all of the above.

The year 1971 was the start of the world's largest money printing in history.

The question is: How and when will it end?

Real Financial Education should include how and why money is printed. Being aware of how money is printed increases the possibility of your financial survival.

YOUR QUESTIONS... ROBERT'S ANSWERS

Q: Why do you say it's God's money, if God didn't exist until we invented him? (I'm not anti-religion or against spirituality.) Why is that reason enough to own real money?

Jason C. – USA

A: Are you questioning the existence of god... or gold? I have no proof of god. I do have proof of gold.

I state gold and silver are god's money because I have started both a gold mine and a silver mine. The gold mine was in China, the silver mine in Argentina. Both were sold to the public via IPOs, Initial Public Offerings, on the Toronto Stock Exchange.

Before we could "go public" we had to prove we had found real gold and real silver. We had to physically verify there was gold and silver in the ground... and that our company had the legal right to own, mine, and sell the gold and silver. We also had to prove we had the right to sell shares in the company, via an IPO.

So, I know that real gold and silver were here when planet earth was created. I saw real gold and silver in the ground. That is why I state gold and silver are god's money. Gold and silver will be here long after fake money, government money, people's money, and people are gone.

I also know there is fake gold and fake silver. They are gold and silver ETFs, exchange-traded funds. ETFs can legally sell gold and silver they do not own. It is estimated that for every ounce of real gold an ETF has, the ETF may possibly sell a hundred ounces of fake gold. I know this because I have taken companies public. While taking companies public and getting them listed on stock exchanges, I learned that most paper assets sold on the stock exchanges are fake.

Q: How much gold should I own? Any tips on percentage of "portfolio"?

Bruno T. - France

A: Most financial experts recommend that 10 percent of your assets be in precious metals. I do not follow that formula.

In Part One: Fake Money, I wrote that gold is god's money and gold is an attractor of wealth. That means that I hold real gold because I believe real gold attracts real wealth.

In simple terms, if I want $10,000 a month in income, I hold $10,000 in real gold. I cannot prove it will work for you. I can only say that this belief works for us.

As the guru said to Kim and me many years ago: "Gold is the tears of god."

When Kim and I want more income, we simply buy more real gold. It works for us. If you do not believe that real gold attracts wealth, or do not believe in god... don't buy real gold.

Chapter Five

HOW MUCH MONEY ARE YOU PRINTING?

HOW TO TAKE CONTROL

Reminder: Printing money is not new.

Reminder: Printing fake money is the foundation of the banking system.

Understanding how money is printed offers you a better chance of doing well in a world of fake money.

LESSON: In understanding how money is printed, you will better understand why poor people are poor and how not to be one of them.

PRINTING MONEY #1: Printing cows

For thousands of years, money has taken many forms. Money has been beads, feathers, stones, animals, and pottery. One of the earliest and most important forms of money was cattle.

Cattle have been the foundation for modern money for thousands of years. Cattle are real money, even today. In fact, the word *cattle* means *property* of any kind, including money, land, and income.

When a person who had cattle needed to borrow money, he would take his cattle to the moneylender, borrow the money he needed, and leave his cattle as collateral.

When the person repaid the borrowed money, his cattle were returned.

The collateral system is still in use today. A synonym for collateral is *security*. The 2008 crash was caused when collateralized debt obligations (CDOs) and mortgage-backed securities (MBSs) failed.

Take notice of the words *collateralized* and *securities*. They represent the same purpose *cattle* did a thousand years ago. A thousand years ago, cattle were *real* collateral and real security.

The world economy nearly collapsed when fake collateral, in the forms of CDOs and MBSs, were proven to be fake.

How could so many highly educated, highly talented, and highly paid people believe fake collateral is real collateral? This is scary, very scary. What's even more frightening is that these same people—people who believed fake collateral is real collateral—are still running the show.

Can you imagine a banker a thousand years ago not knowing what a real cow was? Yet that is exactly what is going on today.

"All Hat, No Cattle"

Today, when people speak about the gap between the rich and everyone else, they are talking about the lack of collateral.

LESSON: One reason so many poor and middle-class people are poor is because they do not have any collateral. That would be like a rancher, going to the bank to borrow money, without any cattle to use as collateral.

My friends in Texas have a saying: "All hat, no cattle."

The world is filled with people who are "all hat, no cattle." They may live in big houses, drive nice cars, have kids in private school… but they have no collateral. A banker may loan them money for the house and the cars and issue them credit cards—a category of debt known as *consumer credit*—but *not* the credit to invest. Then they complain, "My banker won't give me a loan."

Bankers need real collateral. So do you.

Modern CDOs and MBSs are about *collateral* and *security*. The problem was that modern CDOs and MBSs were backed by fake collateral and fake security.

If you want to be more secure in the future, having *real collateral* is essential to *real security*. Real collateral and real security are what this book is about.

Financial Literacy:
In kind (adj), A financial term derived from the German word *kinder* which means *child*. The word *kindergarten* means, simply, a *garden of children*.

When a person left his cattle as collateral, the moneylender was paid *in kind* with the children of the cattle.

Calves, or *kinder*, were an early form of interest. Today, when a banker lends you money, the interest you pay your banker is today's modern form of *kinder*.

In kind means *like-for-like*. Calves-for-cattle, money-for-money... and an eye for an eye.

Interest is *in kind*. Or, another way to look at it: Interest is money having children—or money printing money.

Modern banks could not survive if they were not allowed to charge interest on their fake money.

Savings: You... Printing Money

When you save money in a bank, your money is printing money.

When you save money, the bank pays you interest, in kind, money for money. Again, the interest on your savings is your money printing money.

Credit Cards

When you use your credit card, you are printing money. There is no money in a credit card. The only thing behind a credit card is your good credit. Your good credit is the bank's collateral. In America, your credit is measured via a FICO score, a measurement of how creditworthy you are.

The difference is that when you use your credit card, *you are printing money for the bank*—money you have to pay back and, likely, pay interest (in kind) on.

Loans

When you borrow money for a car, home, or business loan, you are printing money. *You are printing money for the bank*, and the bank charges you interest on their newly printed money.

Whose Money Is More Valuable?

Think about these two examples of you printing money:

- You save money $1,000 in your savings account, and the bank pays you 2 percent interest.
- You charge $1,000 on your credit card, and the bank charges you 18 percent interest.

In both examples, you have printed money. The question is, whose money is more valuable: Your money? Or the money you printed for the bank?

Remember: Since 1971, the entire world money system has run on printing fake money.

Remember: People who work for money, work for people who print money.

In this book, you will learn to be the person who prints the money that people work for. But first, it is important to understand other examples of how money is printed.

PRINTING MONEY #2: The Fractional Reserve System

The world's banking system is built on the *fractional reserve system.*

The fractional reserve system has been running the world for thousands of years. The following is a simple explanation of the system.

Let's pretend that, a thousand years ago, you are a shop owner. You have 10 gold coins. You need to travel many miles through bad-guy country to buy goods for your store.

You go to a local "banker," often a goldsmith, who agrees to hold your 10 gold coins for safekeeping.

The "banker" issues you a piece of paper, saying you have deposited 10 gold coins with him. That piece of paper is a certificate of deposit (CD), a term still in use today.

You travel the hundred miles through bad-guy country with only a piece of paper, a CD, in your possession. Your gold coins are safe with your "banker."

You then buy new merchandise for your store, give your CD, your piece of paper, to the person who sold you the merchandise, and you head home.

The person who sold you your merchandise, goes to his "bank" and collects his payment in the form of gold from the CD on your gold.

After a while, you realize a piece of paper, a CD, is much more convenient than carrying around gold coins. You leave your gold with your banker and use your banker's CDs as paper money.

How the Banker Prints Money

People who need money go to a banker and ask for a "loan." The banker lends out nine of *your 10 gold coins.* The one gold coin he holds in his vault is the "fractional reserve." The banker only needs to hold 10 percent—or 1 of your original 10 gold coins—in his safe to meet the "reserve" requirement.

Money has now been printed. Ten coins have become 19 coins through the fractional reserve banking system. Your 10 coins are real money. The nine coins out on loan to borrowers are fake money. Fake money has been printed.

This is where it gets exciting. The person who borrowed nine of your 10 gold coins goes to his or her bank and deposits your nine gold coins. The person who borrowed those nine coins is now issued a CD for nine coins.

The banker holding the nine borrowed coins then lends out 8.1 of the nine coins to the *next* borrower.

This borrower takes his 8.1 coins and deposits them in his bank. That banker lends out 90 percent of the 8.1 coins to the next borrower... and on and on.

The Mandrake Mechanism

Do you get the picture? This is known as the Mandrake Mechanism, named after a comic-strip magician character named Mandrake. Mandrake could pull anything out of his hat—and your banker can pull money out of thin air.

In this simple example, the original 10 coins have now been expanded to 27.1 coins through the magic of the fractional reserve system of banking. The 27.1 coins are soon 2,710 or more coins through the magic of the fractional reserve system and the Mandrake Mechanism.

The fractional reserve system and the Mandrake Mechanism are how massive amounts of fake money are printed.

Mandrake Takes Over the World

Think about this: In 1971, the year Nixon took the dollar off the gold standard, *the world no longer needed the original 10 gold coins.* The Mandrake System of Magic Money took over the world.

Imagine billions of people borrowing and depositing billions of fake dollars in banks all over the world—as Mandrake magically pulls more and more fake money out of his hat.

After 2008, Mandrake the Magician had to pull over $1 quadrillion out of his "hat" to save his Magic World of Money from collapse.

How long can Mandrake keep pulling magic money out of his hat? That's the question.

Run on the Bank

If Mandrake's Magic wears off, a run on the bank occurs. Mandrake's Magic Show closes. A run on the bank is a panic and savers line up, demanding their money. The problem is… Mandrake does not have the money.

This is why American banks have a back-up plan: the FDIC, or Federal Deposit Insurance Corporation, which insures savings in banks up to $250,000. The problem is that the FDIC does not have enough money to cover a massive run on the bank.

If a panic does take place, the entire banking system can legally be shut down. Shutting down banks has happened many times in modern history.

If Mandrake's Magic Show does shut down, the amount of money a person can withdraw will be determined by automatic teller machines (ATM). Imagine going to your bank ATM and seeing a sign that says, "Your limit today is $100."

Trusting Mandrake's Magic Show

After rich dad explained fractional reserve banking and Mandrake's Magic Act to his son and me, we knew why "In God We Trust" was on our money.

Today, I prefer to trust God's money, *real* gold and silver. I do not trust in Mandrake's Magic Show—or what Bucky Fuller named Grunch, the powers behind a Gross Universal Cash Heist.

I trust gold and silver rather than the elites Mandrake hires to run his magic show, print our money, run our central banks, governments, banks, bond markets, and stock markets.

Always remember, gold and silver will be here long after you, I, the elites, and the cockroaches are gone.

Fake Gold and Fake Silver

Mandrake also produces fake gold and fake silver.

LESSON: Fake gold and fake silver. I do not invest in fake gold or silver, aka exchange-traded funds—paper gold and paper silver.

GLD and SLV are, respectively, gold and silver ETFs, fake gold and silver. I do not invest in ETFs because all ETFs are part of the fractional reserve system… aka Mandrake's Magic Show. For example, Mandrake can take one ounce of real gold turn it into 50 to 100 ounces of fake paper gold via the ETF. Printing ETFs and mutual funds are a part of Mandrake's Magic Show. Mandrake can print money, stocks, bonds, and even real estate.

Real Estate ETFs are called REITs, or real estate investment trusts. I love gold, silver and real estate. I do not invest in GLD, SLV, or REIT.

LESSON: This does not mean you should not invest in ETFs or mutual funds. These paper assets have certain advantages for different people.

In Part Three of this book, Fake Assets, I discuss who should invest in GLD, SLV, and REITs, and why I do not.

One reason I do not invest in ETFs is because they are derivatives and a part of the Mandrake Magic Show.

PRINTING MONEY #3: Derivatives

The global banking system is based on derivatives.

LESSON: What are derivatives?

I'll do my best to KISS… Keeping It Super Simple.

Derivatives from an Orange

Think of an orange. When you squeeze the orange, you get orange juice. The *orange juice* is a derivative of the orange. When you take the water out of the orange juice, you have *orange juice concentrate*, a derivative of both orange juice and the orange.

Derivatives from Oil and Uranium

Think of crude oil. Gasoline is a derivative of crude oil. Gasoline is much more flammable and volatile than crude oil. Other derivatives of gasoline are aviation fuel, jet fuel, and other refined oil distillates.

Uranium's atomic number 92 and symbol is U. Uranium is more abundant than silver. When you take derivative after derivative of uranium, it becomes unstable, toxic, and dangerous. Derivatives of uranium are used as nuclear fuel for reactors and weapons of mass destruction.

Derivatives of Money

Stocks are derivatives of a company. A mortgage is a derivative of real estate. And a bond is a derivative of money.

Then about 50 years ago, things changed.

Bucky Fuller said, they began playing games with money.

As Steven Brill quotes Martin Lipton, "We created a whole separate economic activity of trading pieces of paper—which accomplishes nothing."

In 1950, manufacturing made up 60 percent of corporate profits. Today it is about 25 percent. In 1950, the financial industry accounted for 9 percent of corporate profits. Today it is 30 percent.

In her book *Maker and Takers: The Rise of Finance and the Fall of American Business,* Rana Foroohar writes, "Wealth creation within the financial markets has become an end in itself, rather than a means to the end of shared prosperity."

Translation: "I got mine. Screw everyone else."

Her example of the "I got mine" attitude in America's financial industry is, "The top 25 hedge fund managers in America make more than all the country's kindergarten teachers combined."

RICH DAD RADIO INTERVIEW
WITH RANA FOROOHAR

Rana's interview on how greed runs America's financial industry can be accessed via this link:
http://youtu.be/VgZZnG7US14

Financial Engineering

Rather than create new assets, assets that produce real and lasting prosperity, financial engineering took over the business of money and created fake, toxic assets.

Around 2005, desperate for higher returns, the elites' financial engineers took ordinary financial derivatives such as home mortgages, found subprime borrowers, gave them loans they could not afford, and created a Frankenstein of financial monsters called mortgage-backed securities (MBSs) or collateralized debt obligations (CDOs), and sold them to the world as "securities"... aka *financial derivatives of financial derivatives.*

Warren Buffett called these financial derivatives of financial derivatives "financial weapons of mass destruction."

Steven Brill, in his *Time* article, has this to say about derivatives:

> [The elites] upended corporate America and Wall Street with inventions in law and finance that created an economy built on deals that moved assets around instead of building new ones. They created exotic, and risky, financial instruments, including derivatives and credit default swaps, that created sugar highs of immediate profits, but separated those taking the risk from those who would bear the consequences.

In 2008, those weapons of mass financial destruction exploded, and the world economy nearly collapsed.

Has Anything Changed?

In 2007, there were $700 trillion in derivatives.

In 2008, the financial weapons of mass destruction imploded, nearly bringing down the world economy.

In 2018, there are $1.2 *quadrillion* in derivates.

Why change? Mandrake's Magical Money Show must go on.

PRINTING MONEY #4: Inflation

Mandrake's Magical Money Show runs on inflation. If inflation stops, Mandrake's tent collapses and the show is over.

Mandrake's Tent Collapsed

Look again at the 125-year chart of the Dow.

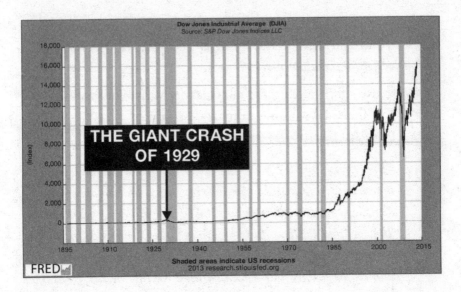

You can clearly see where and when tops of Mandrake's tents collapsed in 2000 and 2008.

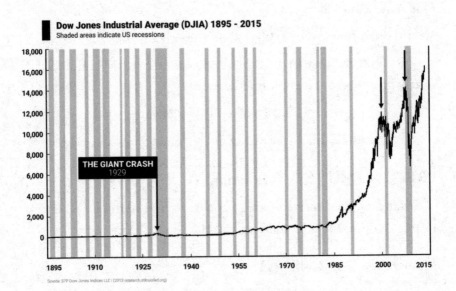

Don't the peaks look like the tops of giant circus tents?

You can also see where the Gross Universal Cash Heist began pumping air back into the Mandrake's tent.

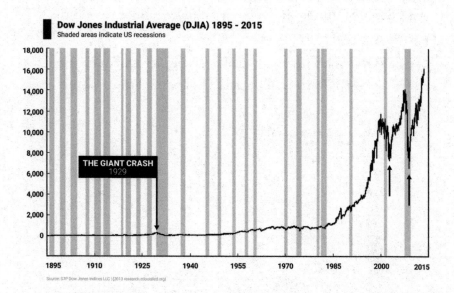

Dow Jones Industrial Average (DJIA) 1895 - 2015
Shaded areas indicate US recessions

THE GIANT CRASH
1929

Source: S7P Dow Jones Indices LLC | (2013 research.stlouisfed.org)

TARP and QE

Rather than call it printing money, the mega-elites—Federal Reserve Chairman Ben Bernanke and the U.S. Treasury Secretary Hank Paulson, former CEO of Goldman Sachs—came up with new names: the Troubled Asset Relief Program (known as TARP) and later, quantitative easing or QE.

I guess to them, it sounded more intelligent than to simply say "printing money."

I'd call it BS: blowing smoke.

Mandrake's Magical Money Act and the fractional reserve system had printed so much money that the tents of the world were deflating. The world was on the verge of a giant depression.

TARP and QE were required to keep Mandrake's tents from collapsing.

LESSON: Mandrake's Magic Act can only survive if there is inflation.

(Get it? Keep the tents inflated...)

LESSON: Without inflation, Mandrake cannot pay off the massive debt that printing money creates.

LESSON: With inflation, debt gets cheaper—because money gets cheaper—and debt can be paid back with cheaper dollars.

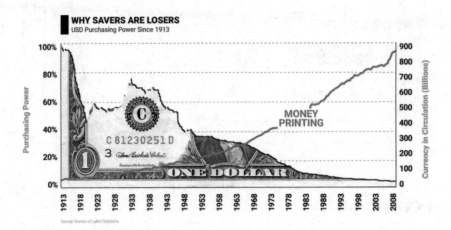

Inflation Is Better than Deflation

LESSON: If there is deflation, the debt becomes more expensive and that debt has to be paid with more valuable, more expensive dollars.

Deflation often leads to depression.

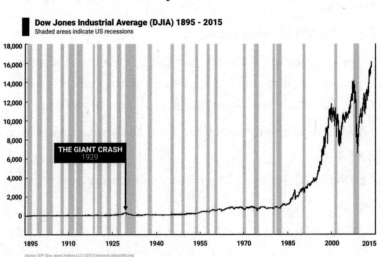

Inflation and Deflation

LESSON: With inflation, people spend faster. They are afraid prices will go up.

LESSON: With deflation, people do not spend. They wait for prices to get lower, which may lead to financial depression.

LESSON: This is why Mandrake's Magical Money Show requires inflation for the Mandrake Show to go on. Without inflation, Mandrake cannot pay for the last show.

LESSON: This is why the Fed and U.S. Treasury employed TARP and QE. They had to reinflate Mandrake's tents with trillions and quadrillions in fake money.

The Collateral Damage

Notice, again, the word *collateral*. The collateral damage from toxic derivatives, fake assets, fake collateral, was the innocent people of the world. And savers became losers.

The American Dream was taken away—not only from homeowners, but also savers as well.

When the markets crashed in 2008, banks dropped interest rates and begged people to borrow money.

Savers, in many cases retirees living on fixed incomes, became the biggest losers when the interest on their savings was cut—in some cases to below zero.

Without interest from their savings, savers began living off their principal, which diminished their savings.

Millionaires Were Rich

In 1970, a year after I graduated from college, savers could earn as much as 15 percent interest on their savings. Keeping the math simple, let's use $1 million.

$1 million x 15% = $150,000

A person could live on $150,000 in 1970.

After 2008, interest rates dropped, in some countries to below zero.

Savers were the biggest losers and millionaires became poorer.

Again, keeping the math simple and using $1 million in savings:

$1 million x 2% = $20,000

It is difficult for anyone in America to live on $20,000 a year, even if you are a millionaire. Millionaires living on interest from their savings are the new poor.

This forced many people into the stock market, hoping for higher returns on their money. The result: the stock market is blown into a bubble. Look at the 125-year chart of the Dow and you can see the stock market bubble burst after the 2000 and 2008 crashes.

Bitcoin and Cyber Money

In 2009, Bitcoin appeared… and cyber money begins to challenge Mandrake's Magical Money Show.

Mandrake does not like competition. Grunch will fight back against cyber money, the people's money. A few elites are defecting to cyber money.

LESSON: Inflation causes poverty.

Printing money makes some people richer. People feel richer when their house "appreciates" in value or their "net worth" increases because stock portfolio increased.

For millions, printing money makes them poorer.

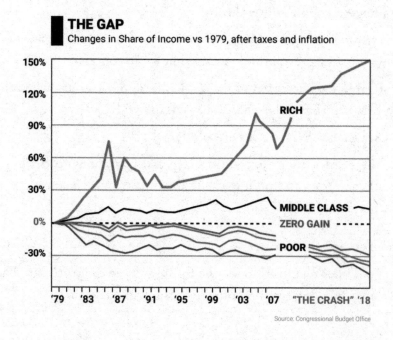

THE GAP
Changes in Share of Income vs 1979, after taxes and inflation

Source: Congressional Budget Office

A study by professors at Stanford, Harvard, and Berkeley found: Children's prospects of earning more than their parents fell from 90 percent to 50 percent in just 40 years.

A separate study found that incomes for the top 1 percent of earners rose 31.4 percent from 2009 to 2012. Yet, incomes for the bottom 99 percent crept up only 0.4 percent.

Tent Cities

Tent cities are springing up all across America, especially in some of our most prosperous cities: San Francisco, Seattle, and Honolulu.

Many who are living in tents have jobs. They just cannot afford a house. In 2018, there were approximately 550,000 homeless people in America.

You Say You Want a Revolution

Historically, when the gap between the rich and everyone else grows too wide, revolutions occur. That is my concern.

Revolutions occurred in Russia, Cuba, and Venezuela when the gap between rich and everyone else got too wide.

Are we headed for a new revolution?

The Beatles' song "Revolution" expresses my thoughts better than I can. You can find it on YouTube (www.youtube.com/watch?v=BGLGzRXY5Bw).

Can You See the Future?

Dr. Fuller taught us to see the future by studying the past. And here are some charts and photos that can help us do that.

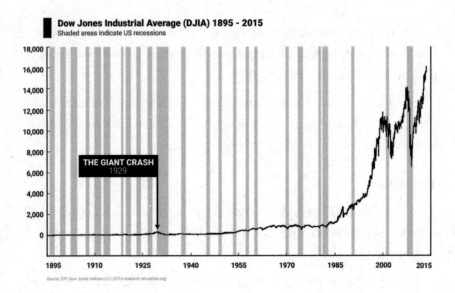

Dow Jones Industrial Average (DJIA) 1895 - 2015
Shaded areas indicate US recessions

THE GIANT CRASH
1929

Source: S7P Dow Jones Indices LLC | (2013 research.stlouisfed.org)

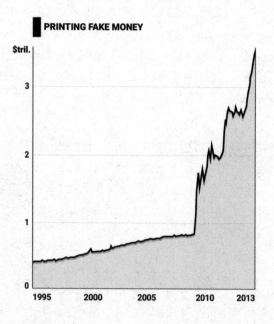

PRINTING FAKE MONEY

What Happens When a Country Prints Too Much Money?

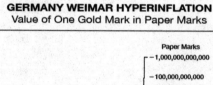

GERMANY WEIMAR HYPERINFLATION
Value of One Gold Mark in Paper Marks

Paper Marks

- 1,000,000,000,000
- 100,000,000,000
- 10,000,000,000

"However enormous may be the appearant rise in the circulation in 1922, actually the real figures show a decline." –Prof. Karl Eister

- 1,000,000,000
- 100,000,000
- 10,000,000

"In proportion to the need, less money circulates in Germany now than before the war," –Prof. Julius Wolfe

- 1,000,000
- 100,000
- 10,000
- 1,000
- 100
- 10
- 1

1918   1919   1920   1921   1922   1923

dollarvigilante.com

Today, America appears to be following
the 1918-1923 Germans into hyperinflation.

When inflation fails, many countries have suffered hyperinflation, often fueled by a hyper-printing of money. The following are pictures of hyperinflation in Germany during the 1920s. As you look at these photos, you may understand why *I do not save fake money.*

Source: Getty Images / Albert Harlingue/Roger Viollet
Stacks of banknotes in the basement of a bank at the time of the Mark devaluation in 1923

Source: Getty Images / Universal History Archive
Hyperinflation in Germany post WWII has a woman using banknotes to start a stove

Source: Getty Images / Corbis
German children in 1923 playing with money in the streets—billions in fake, worthless money

Source: Getty Images / ullstein bild
Money which became worthless in the Weimar Republic in 1923 was burned

This hyperinflation led to the rise of Adolf Hitler, WWII, and the murder of millions of innocent people.

Source: Getty Images / H. Miller
Victims of the Buchenwald concentration camp

Printing money has never produced a sustainable prosperity. Printing money has always caused poverty for those who work for money.

The year 1971 was the start of the first global "money printing." Today, the entire global banking system runs on printed money. How long can the U.S. and the world continue to print fake money?

Is History Repeating Itself?

I believe it is.

In the following chapter, I will explain why I own real gold and real silver.

YOUR QUESTIONS... ROBERT'S ANSWERS

Q: What happens then when bubbles burst? Does the money just disappear?

Chris G.- Greece

A: Yes and no. When a bubble bursts some money is transferred from winners to losers. Most of the losers are average investors who drank the Kool-Aid of "invest for the long term." Sometimes investing for the long term works and sometimes it doesn't.

When money changes hands from winners to losers, money is not really lost. The loser lost but money did not really disappear. It just changed hands.

That is why so many experts say you do not lose money if you do not sell. These experts base that upon the fact that you still have the shares of stock.

I disagree. Let's say, I buy 100 shares of a stock at $20.

$$100 \times \$20 = \$2,000$$

The market crashes the next day. The stock is now worth $2 a share.

$$100 \times \$2 = \$200$$

In this example money did disappear. The investor lost $1,800.

The investor calls his or her financial advisor and says, "I lost $1,800."

The financial advisor replies, "You will only lose when you sell. That is why you invest for the long term. The share price will go back up."

That is a lie. In this example, at that moment in time, money was lost. It disappeared from the investor's asset column.

Q: What would happen if everyone demanded to get their money from the bank when there's a bank run? Would the banks be able to lend money to anyone?

Manual A – Mexico

A: It depends. In a panic, people do interesting things. So, it is difficult to predict what might happen.

After the crash of 2008, millions of people lost trillions. The rich did not lose because the U.S. government "bailed out" the biggest banks.

Savers lost because banks printed trillions of fake dollars, causing the value of a saver's savings to go down.

In the next crash, if everyone wanted their money at once, banks may do the opposite of a "bail out." Banks may pull a "bail in." A "bail in" occurs when a bank takes a saver's savings, convert's savings into bank stocks (equity) and the saver's money is frozen in the bank. Again, savers lose and the rich win.

In his book *The Road to Ruin*, Jim Rickards is predicts an "Ice Nine" event. An Ice Nine event means the entire system of money and banking is frozen. That is why Jim Rickards recommends keeping some money, as well as gold and silver, outside the banking system.

Q: I find it difficult to keep my mind open to the truths exposed by you and others. I read, listen, think… but I know I'm defaulting to denial. How can I become more open to accepting reality?

Jana V. – USA

A: You are demonstrating you have an open mind. When you are aware, your mind is open to new thoughts and ideas. Congratulations.

Q: How do you find out if the news in the media is fake or real?

Rohit M – India

A: Always consider the source of the news. In this book, I list sources I have interviewed on Rich Dad Radio. Most interviews are 40 minutes long. You will learn a lot in 40 minutes, listening to people who have done the real thing in the real world of fake money.

If you are getting your information from stock brokers, real estate brokers, insurance brokers, always remember rich dad's warning: "The reason they are called 'brokers' is because they are broker than you."

Q: Isn't the real problem the central banking system in my country, the Federal Reserve?

Jon K. – USA

A: It depends upon who you ask. I believe there are many problems. The Fed and the system of central banks are definitely one of the many problems.

I believe the real problem is the lack of financial education in our educational system. If an individual had real financial education, this financial crisis we are in would not be a problem. This crisis would be an opportunity to become really rich… which is why I wrote this book and my other books.

This reminds me that the Chinese symbol for crisis is made of two words: *danger* plus *opportunity.*

I write for people like you, people who want to see the opportunity in the danger.

Q: Is a Roth IRA account a fake or real asset?

Ivan K. – USA

A: It depends. A Roth IRA is a tax-advantaged vehicle. Although tax-advantaged, not all IRAs are assets. In a crash, IRAs can also crash, becoming a liability.

Q: Why is the graph that shows the U.S. stock market so negative—or isn't it? I see big opportunities there for people if they bought stocks…

Lukas D. – Germany

A: Great question. The graph may be positive or negative, depending on the person looking at the graph. For a person investing for the long term, a crash may become a crisis. For a person who can "short" a market, a crash may be an opportunity.

Again: Crisis = Danger + Opportunity

Q: Isn't money just a medium of exchange? So this long-term value is not so important. Isn't it everybody's own fault if he saved his money in U.S. dollars, because they also could have bought stocks?

Danny W. – Japan

A: I agree. By the end of this book, you will learn you will not even need money, much less save it. The real value of real financial education is to become rich—with or without money.

Q: Why do people not see what the banks and the government are doing until it is too late?

Victor R. – Singapore

A: As the saying goes, "You cannot catch fish in clean water."

The purpose of this book, and all the Rich Dad books, is to allow you to see what most people cannot see.

Q: Will Bitcoin become the dominant global currency?

Benny S. - Israel

A: I doubt it. Yet, blockchain technology will change the world.

Chapter Six

EIGHT PHILOSOPHICAL REASONS WHY I OWN REAL GOLD AND SILVER

WHAT ARE YOURS?

Notice, again, that I say I *own* real gold and silver. I do not say "I invest" or "I trade"—I'm saying that I own real gold and silver. There are eight reasons for the differences between *owning, investing,* and *trading* anything.

REASON #1: Trust

I do not trust fake money. And I do not trust myself. I know I do not know everything. I do not have all the answers. I cannot predict the future, but I know I must prepare for the future.

I do not trust the elites who run our governments, banks, or Wall Street. I do not trust anyone who prints fake money.

I own gold and silver because I trust real gold and silver. I trust God's real money.

Real gold and silver have been here since the Earth was formed. Gold and silver were here before the cockroaches and will be here long after the cockroaches are gone.

Gold is atomic number 79. Silver is atomic number 47.

In God's money… I trust.

REASON #2: Gold and silver are not investments

I do not own gold and silver to make money. Gold and silver are insurance, a *hedge* against the stupidity of the elites and myself.

I have insurance on my car in case someone hits me or I hit someone. Gold and silver serve a similar purpose.

I do not trust the elites. They believe they know everything. They believe they are always right. In their minds, they do not make mistakes. They will never admit they are wrong. If they make mistakes, they are paid bonuses. If they make mistakes, we pay for it.

Gold and silver are insurance against the elites. And their mistakes.

Steven Brill writes:

> *[The elites] were able to consolidate their winnings, out smart and co-opt the forces that may have reined them in, and pull up the ladder so more could not share in their success or challenge their primacy.*
>
> *By continuing to get better at what they do, by knocking away the guardrails limiting their winnings, aggressively engineering changes in the political landscape, and by dint of the often unanticipated consequences of their innovations, they created a nation of moats that protected them from accountability and from the damage their triumphs caused in the larger community.*

TRANSLATION: The elites are above the law. They have no guardrails. They have the money to hire the best elite attorneys, from the same elite schools they attended, to battle lower-paid government attorneys from less prestigious law schools. They have the power to do what they want without being held responsible for what they do, or how many people's lives they damage. Their privileged education and success have turned them into despots.

DEFINITION:

despot (n). A ruler or other person who holds absolute power, typically one who exercises it in a cruel or oppressive way.

Gold and silver are insurance against the greed, corruption, ignorance, and incompetence of elites who have become despots.

REASON #3: Real gold and silver have no risk

The price of gold and silver will go up and down—because the value of our fake money is going up and down.

Before 1971, gold and silver prices were relatively stable. Today, when gold or silver prices go down, I buy more. I want God's money.

When person invests in a stock or in real estate, they expect an ROI, a *return on investment*. They expect a return because they are taking a risk. When a person saves money in a bank, they expect a rate of interest, because saving money in banks is extremely risky, especially when elites are printing money.

Take a look at the following chart:

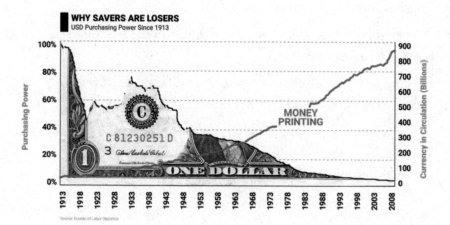

WHY SAVERS ARE LOSERS
USD Purchasing Power Since 1913

MONEY PRINTING

Source: Bureau of Labor Statistics

When I purchase a gold or silver coin, I do not expect an ROI because I am not taking a risk. Gold and silver are God's money. Always remember, the price of gold or silver will go up or down because the value of our fake money is going up or down.

When I purchase real gold or silver, I purchase them forever. I never plan on selling. Just as Warren Buffett holds stocks forever, I purchase gold and silver forever.

I know some of you are saying, "But I want to spend money." Or, "I need money." That is why most people are not rich. They need fake money to survive and they love spending fake money. I love spending fake money too. I love nice cars, clothes, homes, and food. But after Vietnam, even when I had no money or job, I never sold my real gold and silver.

Banks Are Not Safe

I'll repeat that: Banks are not safe. Banks are risky. I use banks to store short-term cash, my operating capital. I do not hold real gold and silver in banks. I do not hold my long-term wealth in banks. Banks are just too risky. Banks can be shut down—with your money, gold, and silver locked inside.

People's Money: Cryptocurrencies

Bitcoin came on the scene in 2009, just as the banking system was on the verge of collapsing.

One giant advantage of cryptocurrencies and blockchain technologies is trust and security outside the banking system.

As cryptocurrencies evolve, the power of the banking system— Mandrake's Magical Money Show—will lose its grip on the financial freedom of the world.

Reducing Risk

To reduce risk even further, my gold and silver are held in different safe-haven countries. Legally. Far, far, away. The gold and silver are held in private vaults, not in bank vaults. That is to make sure I am not tempted to get my hands on my gold and silver, and to thwart the possibility of someone forcing me to go to my local bank and get my gold and silver.

I must protect gold and silver because gold and silver are my cattle, my collateral.

If you are not yet flying around in your private jet, you may want to keep your real gold and silver in a fireproof safe, away from your home.

I am not flying my gold around in a private jet, yet, but I do have several private vaults far away from banks and my home.

How to Make a Lot of Money

In the coming chapters you will learn how to make money and then convert gold and silver into savings outside the bank. As long as you are making a lot of money you will be less tempted to spend your gold and silver.

Fake money is risky. Gold and silver have no risk, because they are God's money.

James Rickards, author of *Currency Wars, The New Case for Gold*, and *The Road to Ruin,* has run the numbers comparing ounces of gold to government money. His computations state that if the U.S. dollar were to go back on to the gold standard, gold would rise to $10,000 an ounce.

Other experts are calling for gold to drop below $400 an ounce.

Who do you think is right?

REASON #4: Affordability

I began collecting silver coins in 1965. I was 18 years old. That was the year the U.S. government began *debasing* our silver coins. Again, *debasing* means mixing cheaper base metals, such as copper and tin, into the silver.

After 1965, all U.S. "silver" coins had a copper tinge around the edge.

Patrick, a classmate of mine and the class nerd and brain, began researching the reason for the copper tinge. He found out that silver was getting expensive. Silver coins had to be made more cheaply. Silver, being an industrial precious metal, was being used in the growing electronics industry, medical industry, and as a purifier of toxins.

Today, the uses of silver in industry keep growing.

Patrick and I began collecting real silver coins for ¢10 and ¢25.

Today, almost everyone in the world can afford to buy real silver coins. Real silver dimes are still available, for about $1.50 each. Anyone who cannot afford a $1.50 dime has other problems.

Today, a silver U.S. eagle runs about $20. Today, I would rather save a dime, a silver ¢10 piece, or a $20 U.S. eagle than a modern U.S. dime or dollar.

Again, the reason there is no interest on real gold and silver is because there is no risk. Banks pay you interest on your savings because banks are risky, due to the fractional reserve banking system and the Mandrake Mechanism.

Look again at what has happened to government money versus gold. Note that in the chart on the following page gold is represented by the straight line, at 100—reflected here as a constant in terms of purchasing power. Also note (referencing bottom right of that same chart) that all currencies have lost 97–99 percent versus gold over 100 years.

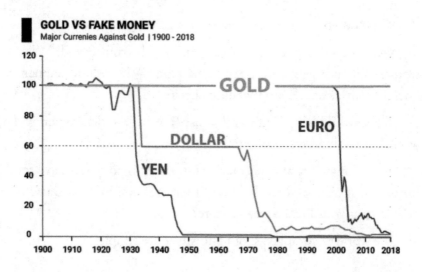

GOLD VS FAKE MONEY
Major Currenies Against Gold | 1900 - 2018

Which is riskier: Saving government money or saving gold and silver?

If you must have fake money quickly, real gold and silver are liquid. You can trade them anywhere in the world for fake money.

REASON #5: Complexity vs. Simplicity

In 1972, the year I purchased my first gold coin for approximately $50, the world was simple. Today, the world is complex and getting more complex.

In 1972, my Corvette had a simple push-button radio. My condo had a simple lock on the door.

Today, I need instructions on how to use the radio in my Ferrari. A simple lock will no longer keep thieves out of my house. Thieves can steal anything I own, even my identity, from anywhere in the world.

In 1972, nuclear war was the threat. Today, cyber war is happening every day.

Let's pretend a 15-year-old hacker from some obscure country figures out how to cut off the electricity to New York City, London, Tokyo, and Beijing. Just for kicks.

What do you think would happen to the world?

What would happen if money could not be transferred? What would happen if people stopped being paid? What would happen if Social Security checks and welfare checks stopped?

What would happen if banks closed? What would happen if the world's stock markets crashed?

It is estimated that supermarkets in the United States have food for only three days. What happens if tens of thousands of starving people rush your local Safeway store?

The world is complex. Gold and silver are simple.

The 5 Gs

To be a realist, it is important to be both a pessimist and an optimist.

I am optimistic about the future. I am also a pessimist about the future.

Being a pessimist, I prepare for the future with the 5 Gs. They are:

1. **G**old and silver
2. **G**rub: food for at least six months
3. **G**asoline: I invest in oil wells and have gasoline I'd need to get out of town.
4. **G**round: I have safe properties with food and water, away from cities.
5. **G**uns and ammo: Both guns and ammo serve as protection *and* currency.

Counter-Party Risk

Fake money has counter-party risk. That means it cannot be money on its own.

Think about the example I gave in a previous chapter. Let's say a friend borrows $100 from you and he give you an IOU. There is now counter-party risk. In this example, your IOU is only as good as your friend, who is the counter-party in this example. If your friend is a flake, your IOU is not worth the paper it is printed on.

That is what happened in 1971. The U.S. dollar was an IOU, a promissory note from the government. The counter-party is the U.S. government. The U.S. dollar is only as good as the integrity of the U.S. government.

Millions of people have lost everything when the government that was issuing their money went bankrupt. It has happened many times throughout history.

The same is true for a stock certificate. If the company issuing the stock disappears, the stock certificate is not worth the paper it is printed on.

Repeating this very important point: All fake money has counter-party risk.

Gold and silver have no counter-party risk. If gold and silver have a counter party, it is God.

Warning

Do not purchase numismatic coins—rare coins. Most coin dealers have them and would love to sell you rare, collectible coins, because they can name their price.

Unless you are an expert in rare coins, stick with ordinary gold and silver coins, such as U.S. Eagles, Canadian Maple Leaves, Chinese Pandas, Australian Kangaroos, and South African Krugerrands.

If you are a beginner, KISS: Keep It Super Simple.

Simple to Complex

It was the elites that took simple and made things complex. They added layer after layer of counter-parties and counter-party risk. The elites took a simple mortgage and turned it into a MBS, a mortgaged-backed security, a financial derivative of derivatives, layers upon layers of counter-parties. They have not stopped building these ultra-complex financially engineered Frankenstein's monsters. Why stop?

Repeating Steven Brill's words:

> [The elites] created an economy built on deals that moved assets around instead of building new ones. They created exotic, and risky, financial instruments, including derivatives and credit default swaps, that produced sugar highs of immediate profits but separated those taking the risk from those who would bear the consequences.

REMINDER: Warren Buffett called these derivatives, "financial weapons of mass destruction."

When these derivatives went off in 2008, the *political elites* (including a few elite lawyers) such as the Clintons, Presidents George H.W. and George W. Bush, Fed Chairmen Alan Greenspan, Ben Bernanke, and Janet Yellen, and President Barack Obama, bailed out the *financial elites* working for Mandrake's Money Show. They still run the show. They believe they are God.

The Bitcoin Threat

That is why cyber money, people's money, is such a threat. Many cryptocurrency miners and developers are driven by an intense desire, a passion (and in some cases a hatred) to bring down Mandrake's Magical Money Show and the invisible leaders Fuller called the Grunch of giants.

I love simplicity. That is why I love real gold and silver. God is the counter party for gold and silver.

REASON #6: What is real money?

The following are the definitions of real money.

1. Medium of exchange—readily acceptable for financial transactions

2. Unit of account—value is measurable
3. Store of value

God's money: Gold and silver coins fit all three categories. The prices of gold and silver go up and down because the value of government money is going up and down.

Government money: Fiat currency fails as a store of value. Fiat currency is fake money because it can be printed, because of the fractional reserve system of banking, and Mandrake's Magical Money Show. Fiat money loses value the longer you hold it. That is why savers are losers.

People's money: The jury is still out on cyber money. Yet, I am certain that cyber money and blockchain technology will be the money of the future.

REASON #7: Buying gold and silver coins is easier and less expensive than buying gold and silver mines.

For a number of years, I worked with Frank, a man about my father's age, whose niche was to find old gold and silver mines, rehab them, and take them public through an IPO. As I've stated earlier, as soon as our mine went public, the Chinese government took it.

While I am grateful for the years Frank and I worked together and I learned a lot about how the stock market works, I've come to realize that buying gold and silver coins from reputable dealers is a lot easier and less expensive than buying old gold and silver mines.

REASON #8: Gold... the tears of God

Years ago, Apple Computers ran a magazine ad that featured a group of Hindu holy men. The headline on the ad was "Holy Icons." The head "guru" was a white guy, not someone of Asian ethnicity. The ad featured Apple's new Macintosh computer and the guru's honey business on the Hawaiian island of Kauai. The ad was clever, meaningful, and memorable.

A few years later, I was invited to a seminar, featuring the same head guru, Gurudeva. When it came time for questions, most questions were on enlightenment, spirituality, peace, or happiness. The guru was wearing a lot of gold—gold glasses, a large gold earring, gold bracelets, and a gold necklace. Since I was raised a Methodist, and Methodist ministers did not wear much (if any) gold, I raised my hand and asked, "Why do you wear so much gold?"

The kindly guru smiled and said, "Because the tears of God are made of gold."

"What?" I gasped. In the Methodist church, those would have been words of heresy, words of the devil.

I sat there, in silence, my mind struggling with the guru's words.

Sensing I was struggling with the thought of God's tears being made of gold, he said, "The tears of God—gold—attract wealth."

When I asked what he meant by "gold attracts wealth," the guru replied, "Let's say you want to attract $1,000 a month into your life. Then you should own $1,000 of real gold."

"And if I want $1 million a month, then I own $1 million in gold?"

The guru, sensing my greed overtaking my spirituality, just smiled and said, "Why don't you start with $1,000, and see if what I say works for you. Gold does not work for everyone. There are conditions on God's generosity."

The year was 1986 and Kim and I were not making much money. Finding an extra $1,000 for gold was tough, but Kim and I did it. Every month, we purchased some gold and silver and have never stopped.

Does Gold Attract Wealth?

I cannot prove gold attracts wealth. I can only tell you what we did and how it worked.

For example, if we wanted to increase our income from $5,000 a month to $10,000 a month, we would acquire $10,000 in gold coins and forget we bought the gold. A few months later, it seemed more wealth *did* come in, without us really noticing the increase. If the price of gold went down, we purchased more gold, and we kept doing it. Today we must have private vaults in far away, safe-haven countries. We do not need a private jet and private runways to hide our gold... yet.

Whenever Kim and I are asked, "Will gold attract wealth for me?" we reply with the guru's reply: "Why not try it yourself, and see if gold, God's tears, works for you? God is generous, but there are conditions on God's generosity."

Spiritual Lesson on Gold: While the tears of God are made of gold, the question each of us need to ask ourselves is, are God's tears tears of joy or tears of sadness?

Much of the world's gold in storage is from tears of sadness. Many Swiss bankers helped the Nazis store their gold, stolen from the Jews murdered by the Nazis.

When I was standing in the Andes, looking at ancient Inca gold mines, I was reminded of my history lesson on how the Spaniards, led by Francisco Pizarro, murdered thousands of natives just for gold. Much of that gold remains in storage in Spain.

Spiritual Wealth

For much of human existence, wealth has been stolen.

The English plundered the world using the technology of large wooden ships, metal swords, cannons, rifles, and black powder against indigenous, under-defended people—and stole their wealth.

The Spanish, Dutch, Portuguese, and the French did the same.

Early Americans stole land from the American Indians, using the technology of horses and rifles.

Americans were one of the last major world powers to finally outlaw slavery, the gaining of wealth via the blood, sweat, and tears of slaves from Africa.

The Japanese joined Italy and Germany—using the technology of oil, internal combustion engines, airplanes, ships, tanks, cannon, machine guns, and rockets—in an attempt to conquer the world.

The Cold War was a war that threatened the end of the world using the technology of atomic energy. Today's elites are using the power of sophisticated education, the law, and derivative finance to steal the soul of the world today.

The Invisible Technology

All the previous heists in history were visible.

Indigenous people could see European ships and attackers— before they were raped, murdered, enslaved, and before their wealth was stolen.

American Indians could see horses and rifles before they were killed and had their land stolen. Many native Americans took horses and rifles to fight back.

In World War II, people could see the attacking planes, tanks, and ships running on petroleum, the new world resource.

During the Cold War, pictures of rising mushroom clouds permeated the consciousness of the world.

Invisible Money

On August 15, 1971, President Richard Nixon did more than take the dollar off the gold standard. He made money invisible.

On that date, many Americans were watching the TV show *Bonanza* when Nixon interrupted the telecast to make his announcement. Obviously, most people did not get the message because people could not *see* what Nixon was announcing.

Ever since 1971, our education system has been a case of the blind leading the blind.

I was not watching *Bonanza* on that day. I would have remembered, because I did not particularly care for Tricky Dick. In the 1950s, my poor dad and I met Nixon when he was vice president visiting Hawaii as he campaigned for President Dwight Eisenhower.

I *do* know where I was on August 15, 1971. I was at Camp Pendleton in California in an advanced weapons class, preparing to go to Vietnam.

On January 3, 1972, I was on my way to Vietnam—as destiny would have it—to meet a real teacher, a tiny Vietnamese woman, behind enemy lines, who was selling real gold. My real financial education about real money—real gold, God's money—had begun.

Today, people without real financial education are blind. They cannot see the cash heist, they cannot see how their labor and their lives are being stolen via the very money they work for.

Millennials vs. Boomers

Recently I listened to a group of millennials who were struggling with student loan debt and blaming the Baby Boom generation for ripping them off. Little did they know millennials and Boomers are actually in the same boat. Without real financial education, how could they know? How can they know the very education they cherish—and went into debt to acquire—is ripping them off?

Tears of God

The question is: are today's tears of God tears of sadness, sorrow over our larcenous education system?

DEFINITION:

Larceny is the wrongful taking and carrying away of the personal goods of another from his or her possession with intent to convert them to the taker's own use.

The American education system—the most expensive educational system in the world is corrupt. Perhaps that is why even massive amounts of money spent cannot change the fact that that educational system produces the worst results in the Western world.

Steven Brill writes in his book *Tailspin*:

> *The world's richest economy [the U.S.] continues to have the highest poverty rate among the 35 nations in the Organization for Economic Cooperation and Development (OECD), except for Mexico. (It is tied in second to last place with Israel, Chile, and Turkey). ...*
>
> *Among the 35 OECD countries American children rank 30th in math proficiency and 19th in science. ...*
>
> *Nearly one in five of America's children live in households that their government classifies as "food-insecure," meaning they are without "access to enough food for an active, healthy life.*

Today, I can still hear the guru's words: "The tears of God are made of gold."

As I accumulate my gold, I check in with myself—I check in with my spirit—asking myself, *Is my gold from God's tears of sadness—or from God's tears of joy?* Most importantly, *Am I doing what God wants done?*

We have all heard stories about people who acquired their wealth via ill-gotten means.

The spiritual lesson here applies to anything. It is not your money, wealth, or power that matters. What matters is how you acquired that money, wealth, and power.

The Fall of Fake Money

How much longer will fake money be allowed to steal the wealth of the people of the world is anyone's guess.

I don't think the Grunch of giants—Mandrake's Magic Money Show—can go on much longer.

I believe that is why people's money—cyber money and blockchain technology—are here. Blockchain is much more trustworthy than Mandrake or the Giants of Grunch... or our education system.

No matter what happens in the future, gold and silver will always be God's money.

ABOUT PART TWO:
FAKE TEACHERS

In **Part Two: Fake Teachers,** you will discover how our education system is ripping off billions of people, all over the world. Without real financial education, few people can see the real world of invisible money.

In **Part Two: Fake Teachers,** you will find out how the education system blinds you to riches found in the world of invisible money.

In **Part Two: Fake Teachers,** you will learn how to find real teachers—real teachers who can teach you to see the invisible world of real money the invisible world fake teachers cannot see.

YOUR QUESTIONS... ROBERT'S ANSWERS

Q: You state that Bitcoin is a threat to those who print fake money. Can you elaborate on the fact that the fake money system continues to tolerate it?

Joop P. - The Netherlands

A: The Fed and Bitcoin miners have a lot in common. Both manufacture money. That is why cryptocurrencies are a threat to the Central Bank monopoly on fake money.

Q: Do the rich benefit from employees who have little or no financial education?

Samuel S. - Australia

A: I do not know if anyone benefits from poorly educated people. We all pay for financial ignorance and incompetence in one way or the other. Unfortunately, it is the poor who pay the highest price.

Q: What if the government tries to outlaw private gold ownership and confiscate gold as it did in the 1930s and extend it to silver? Would this make the case to own cheap numismatic Morgen and Peace dollars?

Richard K. — USA

A: I am not a financial advisor. I do my best to educate and I share what I've learned, what I do and what I do not do. You must decide for yourself what is best for you to do.

Q: Don't you think that if you'd add fake politicians that would explain why we have fake money and fake teachers and, by extension, fake assets?

Juan T. - Spain

A: Aren't all politicians fake? Do we ever know their real agendas? I often ask myself why anyone would want to be a politician.

Q: Without revealing too much, what are the criteria you use when you're looking for places to store your precious metals?

Christopher R. — Russia

A: I asked my friends who hold money in private vaults. When I decided to hold assets overseas outside the United States, I asked my attorneys to find attorneys who specialize in moving money offshore... legally. Then I interviewed the attorneys and traveled to the country and interviewed the custodians of the vaults.

There are many people in the business of holding assets outside the banking system.

I would encourage you to be cautious and careful and to take your time finding reputable people and organizations.

PART
TWO

FAKE TEACHERS

When I was nine years old
I asked my poor dad, the head of Education
for the island of Hawaii,
when I would learn about money.

His response:
"We don't teach about money in school."

That's when I went in search of a real teacher.

– RTK

INTRODUCTION

PART TWO

**What made the three wise men wise?
What makes a teacher real?**

How can teachers and parents teach you about money
when our schools have not taught them about money?

– RTK

Introduction to Part Two

FAKE TEACHERS

The story of *Rich Dad Poor Dad* is a story about two teachers—two great teachers.

My real dad was an academic elite much like Dr. Fuller, who attended Harvard, and Steve Brill, who graduated from Yale. My dad, my poor dad, was a straight-A student in high school and his class valedictorian. He completed a four-year undergraduate program, graduating with his bachelor's degree in two years from the University of Hawaii. He then went on to Stanford University, University of Chicago, and Northwestern University for his advanced studies, ultimately earning his PhD in education.

My rich dad never completed high school. His dad passed away when he was 13 years old, and he took over the family business. In spite of his lack of formal education, he grew the business into a statewide hotel and restaurant operation.

In the 1960s, rich dad took a bold step and purchased a small hotel on Waikiki Beach. Using that hotel as his base of operations, he began to assemble smaller pieces of beachfront property adjacent to his hotel.

Today, when I look at the Hyatt Regency on Waikiki Beach, I know that it was rich dad who started small and "assembled" small plots of beachfront land into the large tract of land that the Hyatt Regency sits on today.

In 2016, the whole property sold for $756 million.

The Story of Rich Dad Poor Dad

The story of *Rich Dad Poor Dad* begins in 1956, when I was nine years old and in the fourth grade. I was growing up in the sugar plantation town of Hilo, Hawaii, a beautiful town far, far away from the bright lights of Waikiki Beach. Our family had moved from Honolulu to Hilo when I was seven. When I was nine, we moved from one side of Hilo to the other side of town. At the age of nine, I was in a new school with new classmates.

The first thing I noticed about my new classmates was that they were rich. Many were *haole,* is a Hawaiian word often used to describe white people. The rest were Asian-American, like me. Most of my "white" classmates were children of the owners of the sugar plantations and businesses like the car dealership, the meat-packing company, the two largest grocery stores, and the banks. The Asian-Americans were children of doctors and lawyers. I was the child of a school teacher.

My classmates were great. They were friendly and welcoming. I knew they were richer than me because most had new bicycles, they lived in big homes on a private island, their parents belonged to the yacht club and the country club, and they had vacation homes either at the beach or on their ranches in the mountains.

I had a used bicycle that my dad bought for $5. I did not know what a yacht club or country club was. Crossing the bridge to the private island where many of my *haole* classmates lived was like crossing a bridge into another world. I could not believe the size of the homes. When I was invited to their "second homes," I could not believe the beauty of the beach homes or the homes on their ranches.

Our family lived in an older house that we rented, two blocks from my new school, next to the Hilo Library. The land our home was built on is a parking lot today.

I had never felt poor, until I went to a school with rich kids.

That is why, when I was nine years old, I raised my hand and asked my teacher, "When will we learn about money?"

Caught off guard and flustered by my question, my teacher, an older woman near retirement, stammered for a while, then finally replied, "We don't teach money in school."

There was more to her reply than simply her words. It was the tone, the energy behind her words that communicated her message. For a moment, I felt I was back in Sunday School. I sensed my teacher was really saying, "Don't you know that 'the love of money is the root of all evil' and 'Money is filthy lucre'?"

In Sunday School, I was taught that filthy lucre was a financial temptation from the devil.

Not satisfied with her answer, I asked again, "When will we learn about money?"

Still a bit flustered, she said, "Go ask your father why we don't teach money in school. After all, he is the head of education."

Poor Dad's Response

My father just chuckled when I told him about the upset in class. He was smiling when he said, "Son, never ask a teacher a question he or she cannot answer. Teachers must know all the answers. They are not trained to say, 'I don't know.' You embarrassed her."

"But why doesn't she know anything about money?" I asked.

"Because teachers do not need to know anything about money."

"Why is *that*?"

"Because teachers have job security. They cannot be fired—even if they are bad teachers. Teachers have a government retirement pension and health care. That is why they do not need to know anything about money. And best of all, teachers have all holidays and summers off—with pay."

Still confused, I asked, "But why, Dad? Don't we all use money?" I followed those two questions with this statement: "I just want to know why my classmates are rich, and why we are not."

"Son," my dad replied, a bit more seriously, "You love baseball? Don't you?"

"Yes. I love baseball."

"Would you ask your teacher about the game of baseball?"

"No. She doesn't know anything about baseball."

"And she doesn't know anything about the game of money either."

"But why not?" I persisted. "Why do my classmates have more money than us? Shouldn't she be teaching me about money, so I can be rich like my classmates?"

Shaking his head, my dad replied, "You love fishing, don't you?"

"Yes."

"Would you ask your teacher about where to catch fish?"

"No," I replied.

"And she knows nothing about money." My dad said, "If you want to get through school, don't ask your teacher questions about subjects they know nothing about. If you are in math class, ask your teacher math questions. If you are in science class, ask your science teacher science questions. If you do that, you will do well in school. If you make your teachers look stupid, they will make you look stupid."

The Real Reason We're Not Taught about Money in School

My dad then said, "The main reason money is not taught in school is because teachers can only teach what the government allows us to teach."

"You teach what the government tells you to teach?" I couldn't believe what I was hearing.

My dad nodded and said, "Even as superintendent of education, I have little control over what is taught in school."

"So how do I learn about money?" I asked.

My dad chuckled again. And, after pausing to think a moment, he suggested, "Why don't you talk with Mike's dad?"

Mike was my best friend. "Why Mike's dad?" I asked.

"Because he is an entrepreneur."

"What is an entrepreneur?" I asked.

"Someone who owns a business," replied my dad. "Entrepreneurs do not have a job. An entrepreneur's job is to create jobs."

"And what are you? Aren't you an entrepreneur? You have hundreds of teachers working for you."

"That's correct. But I did not create the school system. I am a government employee, just like all the other teachers. Employees and entrepreneurs are very different people."

"What's the difference?" I asked. I was nine years old and his words, the distinction he was making between the two, made no sense to me. I had heard the word *employee*, but I had never heard the word *entrepreneur*.

Poor dad was happy to explain. "Our school system trains people to be employees. Employees do not need to know about money. That is why there is no financial education in our schools," he said.

"Entrepreneurs must know about money. If the entrepreneur does not know about money, employees lose their jobs and the entrepreneur is often out of business."

That was the answer I was looking for. I knew I could be an employee. I did not know if I could be an entrepreneur. And if I wanted to be a successful entrepreneur, I had to know about money.

A few days later, I rode my bicycle to Mike's house, where his dad had his office in his home, and asked if he would be my teacher.

And that is how, where, and when the story of *Rich Dad Poor Dad* began.

Is Education Important?

In the 1960s, when I was kid growing up in Hilo, Hawaii, education was not that important. Hilo was a sugar plantation town. There were plenty of high-paying jobs, even for those who did not finish high school. The plantation paid great wages to drivers of the large cane trucks, giant field crane operators, and heavy-equipment operators in the sugar mill.

On top of that, the plantations paid workers a paycheck for life, which meant they did not need a retirement plan. With a paycheck for life, who needed financial education or a college degree? Many plantation workers made more money than school teachers.

The plantations provided company housing, had their own hospitals, healthcare facilities, doctors, and nurses. The plantations paid their workers well, took great care of them and their families... which is why a great education was not essential.

That all changed in 1994, the year the last plantation in Hawaii shut down. The owners moved their sugar plantations to lower-wage countries in South America and Asia.

The owners, my classmates' parents, got richer, but the workers were poorer.

Honoring a Great Teacher

In February 2018, I returned to Hilo for the 60-year reunion of our fifth grade class. Imagine that: a group who met as ten-year-olds was still holding regular class reunions.

The reason for our reunions was not about our class or our classmates, but to honor our fifth grade teacher, Mr. Harold Ely, one of the greatest teachers in our lives.

It was Mr. Ely's inspiration that kept me reaching for my dreams, although I failed high school English twice because I could not write. If not for Mr. Ely's early inspiration I might have dropped out of high school. If not for his early inspiration, I would never have been accepted into the U.S. Merchant Marine Academy and sailed the world. It was in his fifth grade class that I was inspired to follow the great explorers in history—Columbus, Magellan, Cortés, and Cook—and follow a path that led me to the academy, a very tough school. My dream was to sail into Tahiti, which I did in 1968, while a student at the academy.

Today, I am best known as a writer and I continue to travel the world, following in the footsteps of the great explorers. None of that would have happened without the inspiration of a great teacher in the fifth grade.

The most important lesson Mr. Ely taught our class was to stand up after falling down, and that falling down and standing up made us stronger. He also taught us never to let anyone rob us of our dreams.

Electronic Welfare

In 2018, while attending this reunion, I had time to do something I had not done in years: wander around the town of Hilo. I had not been in Hilo since the plantations left Hawaii.

In store windows everywhere, I saw signs welcoming EBT. The acronym EBT stands for Electronic Benefits Transfer, a government welfare system that replaced paper food stamps. EBT is a system that allows a recipient to authorize a money transfer from their federal government account to a retailer to pay for products received. The EBT program has been in use in all 50 states since 2004, as well as Washington D.C., Puerto Rico, the Virgin Islands, and Guam.

Stopping in a small food store, I asked the retailer about EBT cards. He said, "Many people cannot survive without EBT" but that, in most cases, EBT alone was "not enough to get a family through the month."

He went on to tell me that at the start of every month, EBT cards are electronically replenished at midnight. Recipients line up in the evening, and rush in at 12:01 a.m, to purchase food and supplies. In many ways, EBT is a reflection of America and the world today.

Tying this back to education, begs these questions: Will going back to school get people off EBT? Will going back to school bring back high-paying jobs?

A Million Dollars in Debt

Here's an article from *The Wall Street Journal*, May 25, 2018:

> *DRAPER, Utah—Mike Meru, a 37-year-old orthodontist, made a big investment in his education. As of Thursday, he owed $1,060,945.42 in student loans.*
>
> *Mr. Meru pays only $1,589.97 a month—not enough to cover the interest, so his debt from seven years at the University of Southern California grows by $130 a day. In two decades, his loan balance will be $2 million.*
>
> *He and his wife, Melissa, have become numb to the burden, focused instead on raising their two daughters. "If you thought about it every single day," Mrs. Meru said, "you'd have a mental breakdown."*

So here's a question: If Mike Meru went back to school, would more education solve his million-dollar problem?

Here are a few stats from the Department of Education:

- 101 people in the United States have $1 million or more in federal student loan debt.
- The number owing at least $100,000 has risen to around 2.5 million.
- In 2018, the number one asset of the U.S. government was student loan debt, currently at over $1.5 trillion.

This means that, for millions of young people, student loan debt is their biggest liability.

Here's another question to think about: does a college education provide financial education?

Will Education Make You Rich?

From *The New York Times*, also on May 25, 2018, emphases mine:

> *A Walmart employee earning the company's median salary of $19,177 would have to work for more than **a thousand years** to earn the $22.2 million that Doug McMillon, the company's chief executive, was awarded in 2017.*
>
> *At Live Nation Entertainment, the concert and ticketing company, an employee earning the median pay of $24,406 would need to work for **2,893 years** to earn the $70.6 million that its chief executive, Michael Rapino, made last year.*
>
> *And at Time Warner, where the median compensation is a relatively handsome $75,217, an employee earning that much would still need to work for **651 years** to earn the $49 million that Jeffrey Bewkes, the chief executive, earned in just 12 months.*

Steven Brill cites the research in his book, "Incomes for the top 1 percent rose 31.4 percent from 2009 to 2012: but crept up a barely noticeable 0.4 percent for the bottom 99 percent."

Let's look again at these charts again ...

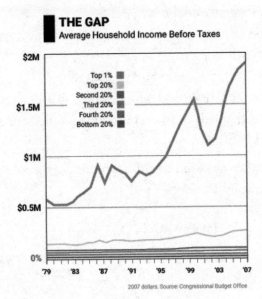

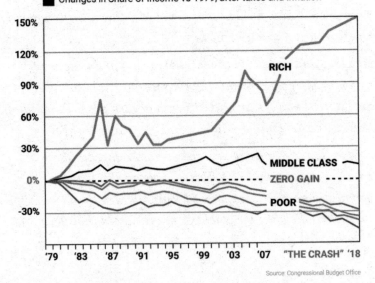

Will more education solve this problem?

Subprime Education

In 2008, the world economy nearly collapsed due to subprime real estate mortgages. In 2008, the Federal Family Education Loan (FFEL) program was unable to lend money to students due to the collapse of subprime mortgages.

In 2010, President Barack Obama eliminated FFEL and required all new student loans to be "direct loans." Private lenders begin offering private student loans to students independently from the government programs.

In 2012, student loan debt surpassed the $1 trillion mark, as well as credit card debt. As of 2018, federal student loan debt is the number one asset of the U.S. government.

The way I see it, the United States went from subprime mortgages for poor people to subprime education for poor students. Subprime education loans are *the worst-of-the-worst* loans. At least a subprime mortgage can be forgiven via bankruptcy. Most subprime education loans can never be forgiven.

Are schools ever going to teach real financial education? Without real financial education, education will always be subprime.

Inflation

In an earlier part of this book, I wrote about inflation. Without inflation, the banking system, Mandrake's Magical Money Show, and Grunch's cash heist will not work.

A few reminders:

- Without inflation, Mandrake cannot pay back the money that was printed.
- When there is inflation, people spend faster, afraid prices will keep rising.
- If there is deflation, people stop spending, waiting for lower prices.

- The banking system must produce inflation, or the economy collapses.
- Inflation steals from the poor and middle class.
- The people who can least afford inflation pay the highest price: they pay with their lives.

The New York Times ran this piece on June 30, 2018:

San Francisco Is So Expensive, You Can Make Six Figures and Still Be 'Low Income'

In the latest sign of the astronomical cost of living in parts of California, the federal government now classifies a family of four earning up to $117,400 as low-income in three counties around the Bay Area. …

The "low income" designation allows people to qualify for affordable housing and a variety of government programs. …

The average [San Francisco-area] household that receives [housing] assistance makes just $18,000. …

The median home price has climbed above $1 million. …

The second highest [low-income] threshold is in Honolulu. …

The New York City area, where a family of four earning up to $83,450 is classified as low-income, came in at No. 9.

That pesky question again: Will more education solve this problem?

More from *The New York Times* …

This was the headline:

Lesson of the Blue Wave Primaries? We're All Struggling Now

The article starts with the story of Alexandria Ocasio-Cortez, a 28-year-old bartender and Democratic Socialist, who beat long-time incumbent Joseph Crowley in the Democratic primary.

The article was about why socialism is gaining in popularity, and promoted a new book, *Squeezed*, on the causes driving a socialist agenda.

> Squeezed: Why Our Families Can't Afford America *examines the deteriorating fortunes of the middle-class—the teachers who sustain themselves with second jobs as Uber drivers; the young adjunct professors on food stamps; the unemployed 50-year-olds with few prospects; the junior lawyers far from the Wall Street partner track, carrying heavy student loan debt, whose work is already being automated.*

The New York Times article continued:

> *If you live in a place where a master's degree won't permit a lifestyle that looks much different from an office clerk's—if, in fact, it means you moonlight in a cubicle you despise and eating lentils for dinner in the Rubbermaid TakeAlongs you brought from home—it follows that you will be less likely to think of yourself as a member of the privileged elite to which you have been told you belong and more inclined to find affinity with the broadening numbers of the more obviously oppressed, and vote accordingly.*

Ocasio-Cortez ran on a platform of free Medicare and tuition-free public college and trade school. She won with that message.

Here's that question again: would free college educations solve the problem?

And, if the government gave all deserving people $1 million, would the $1 million make them rich?

If millions of dollars made people rich, why are 60 percent of former NBA players broke within five years of retirement? Why do most lottery winners fail to use that financial windfall to secure their financial future? We've all heard the stories of lottery winners who could have been set for life… but are broke.

Let's take this to a higher level. Why is America, the richest country in world history, so deeply in debt?

And, my favorite question: why is there no financial education in our schools?

There are many reasons, a number of answers, many excuses, and many solutions… none of them easy. The issue continues to be sidestepped and ignored—another can kicked down the road—and we wonder why we see the problem of growing income inequality.

In Part Two, Fake Teachers, you will learn how to spot fake teachers from real teachers. As my poor dad explained, most teachers know nothing about money, so how can they teach you about money?

But it's not only school teachers who know nothing about money. Many financial experts know little about money. Most have never really studied the subject of money. Most are not rich, and yet they get paid for being financial educators. Many financial experts make the subject of money confusing, using jargon and words most people do not understand—jargon and vocabulary that make them seem smart and you stupid. They are not real teachers. They are financial con artists.

Make the Invisible Visible

Since money became invisible in 1971, the most important thing I can do is do my best to make real financial education visible.

When you can "see" invisible money, then you can decide for yourself what is real and what is fake financial education.

As always, I will do my best to KISS: Keep It Super Simple. But even when it's simple, real financial education not easy. If it were easy, everyone would be rich.

As my rich dad said, "It is easier to give a man a fish… than to teach a man to fish."

That is why socialism grows in popularity in America, the richest country in the history of the world.

Many people would rather be given fish—because being given a fish is much easier than learning to fish. And shouldering the responsibility for their financial future.

Real learning and real education require much more than just memorizing the right answers. That is not real life. In fact, in Part Two, Fake Teachers, one thing you will learn is how going to school keeps people poor, even academic elite students like my poor dad.

If you want to be given fish, this book is not for you. If you are willing to learn to fish, read on.

Chapter Seven

WHAT MADE THE THREE WISE MEN WISE?

THE VALUE OF LIFELONG LEARNING

I n Sunday School, I learned an important life's lesson. It was a lesson from the Three Wise Men.

My Sunday School teacher was a great teacher. One reason for that, I'm sure, was that she loved teaching kids. During one class, she asked us:

"What made the Three Wise Men wise?"

Naturally, I said, "They had money. They came bearing expensive gifts. They were rich *and* wise men."

Obviously, that was not the answer she was looking for. After a few other students attempted their answers, she smiled and said: "What made them wise was their lifelong search for great teachers."

Pausing for a moment to let that thought sink into the minds of kids below the age of 12, she continued: "They were wise men, rich men because they never stopped learning. They kept seeking new knowledge, knowledge from great teachers."

"So, they were lifelong students?" asked the class brain, a girl.

"Yuck!" said one of the boys. "I hate school. I hate learning."

Nodding and just listening for a while to the different responses from her Sunday School students, the young teacher smiled and said:

"As you go through life, always remember the lesson from the Three Wise Men and what made them wise."

It was then I understood the wisdom of my poor dad, a very wise man. He had encouraged me to seek a new teacher in my rich dad, another wise man. He was wise enough to know that the teacher I was seeking would not be found in the school system.

Prep School Education: Unfair Advantage

In his *Time* magazine article "How My Generation Broke America," Steven Brill writes:

> In 1964, I was a bookworm growing up in Far Rockaway, a working-class section of Queens. One day, I read in a biography of John F. Kennedy that he had gone to something called a prep school. None of my teachers at Junior High School 198 had a clue what that meant, but I soon figured out that prep school was like college. You got to go to classes and live on a campus, only you got to go four years earlier, which seemed like a fine idea. It seemed even better when I discovered that some prep schools offered financial aid.

Steve Brill toured three prep schools and chose Deerfield Academy, in western Massachusetts. Brill continues in his book *Tailspin*:

> Deerfield has changed but then it was almost completely a place for well-rounded rich kids. [The headmaster] had only recently decided to tinker with the mix a bit by adding a few scholarship boys, including some Jews like me, and even a few African Americans.

> I got the message the first week when one of the kids in our dorm, who lived on Park Avenue, asked where I lived. When I said Queens, it didn't register, so I explained that if he had ever flown out of Kennedy or LaGuardia airports he'd been to Queens. (A relative of his in our class knew where Queens was because his family owned the Mets, who play there.)

You might recall that Donald Trump is from Queens. He often speaks about his difficulties doing business in Manhattan because he was from Queens and not Park Avenue.

Kings Point, the U.S. Merchant Marine Academy I attended, is just past Queens on Long Island. My roommate Ed Peterson and I would clip dollar-off coupons from milk cartons and to be able to afford tickets to Mets baseball games.

My Classmates Went to Prep Schools

Four of my classmates in Hawaii went on to prep schools. They were rich kids whose parents could afford prep schools. At the age of 12, most of my classmates went on to attend Hawaii Preparatory Academy, a beautiful boarding school on a ranch about an hour from Hilo.

When I asked my dad if I could also attend Hawaii Prep, he said:

"I am not rich. I cannot afford to send you to prep school. Besides, it would not look right if the superintendent's son went to a private prep school."

Future President Barack Obama was a smart poor kid who went to Punahou School, a private prep school for rich and smart kids in Honolulu. As you may know, Obama went on to Columbia and Harvard Law School, much like Steven Brill went on to Yale and Yale Law School… with other poor kids who were being groomed to become today's academic elites, today's leaders.

Fuller and Education

Bucky Fuller often spoke about education and inequality in education. He was fourth generation Milton Academy, a prep school, and fourth generation to attend Harvard University. He never finished Harvard (though he was enrolled there twice) but did attend the U.S. Naval Academy, sister school to the U.S. Merchant Marine Academy.

Entrepreneurs and Education

Fuller noticed that many of America's great schools were started by entrepreneurs, many robber barons like John D. Rockefeller, J.P. Morgan, Cornelius Vanderbilt, James Duke, and Leland Stanford. I have heard that Fuller called Harvard "J.P. Morgan's School of Accounting" and the University of Chicago, "John D. Rockefeller's School of Economics." Duke University, Stanford University, and Vanderbilt University are named after the great entrepreneurs.

Fuller's concern was the mission or the purpose behind the entrepreneur's philanthropy and interest in higher education. He said the entrepreneurs were looking to train employees to run their empires, not really to educate the best and the brightest.

While Fuller attended Harvard, he never graduated. He spent the money his family gave him for Harvard on partying and women. When he failed to show up for tests, Harvard had to ask him to leave, twice, for the same problem.

Brill Agrees

Kennedy, Bush, Trump, and Romney came from the class of inherited, multi-generational wealth. They came from families who could afford the best education, starting with prep schools, private tutors, standardized test prep, and tutors to get them into the best universities.

Brill recounts a meeting while still in prep school with R. Inslee Clark Jr., the dean of admissions at Yale. After a brief interview, Clark assured Brill he would be admitted to Yale. Brill did not need to apply anywhere else. Brill states: "What I didn't know then was I was part of a revolution being led by Clark, whose nickname was Inky. I was about to become one of what come to be known as Inky's boys and, later, girls."

This group of alumni vetters who interviewed prospective students were urged not to "hesitate to admit a lad with relatively low academic prediction whose personal qualifications seemed outstanding, rather than a much drabber boy with high scholastic predictions."

One Yale alumnus objected. He had this to say about letting in non-white poor kids.

> *Let me get down to basics. You're admitting an entirely different class than we're used to. ... You're talking about Jews and public school graduates as leaders. Look around this table. These are America's leaders. There are no Jews here. There are no public school graduates here.*

That alumnus lost, and non-white kids from public schools began to be admitted to Yale and other brand-name schools.

It is this same group of extremely bright students from the poor and middle class that run the world today. Today they are Barack Obama, Bill Clinton, Hillary Clinton, Ben Bernanke, and others.

These are the new elites who did not come from wealth. These are people had to work very hard to get into the best schools and gain their wealth.

This the theme of Brill's angst:

> *Many of the most talented, driven Americans used what makes America great—the First Amendment, due process, financial and legal ingenuity, free markets and free trade, meritocracy, even democracy itself—to chase the American Dream. And they won it, for themselves. Then, in a way unprecedented in history, they were able to consolidate their winnings, outsmart and co-opt the forces that might have reined them in, and pull up the ladder so more could not share in their success or challenge their primacy.*

TRANSLATION: They very smart, hard-working, driven poor and middle-class kids won the American dream, then changed the laws and the financial system so others could not follow their success. The only way the ordinary person can gain their status is to become one of them, starting with the right prep school.

Brill comments on the end of democracy.

As a result of their savvy, their drive and their resources (and a certain degree of privilege, as these strivers may have come from humble circumstances but are mostly white men), America all but abandoned its most ambitious and proudest ideal: the never perfect, always debated and perpetually sought after balance between the energizing inequality of achievement in a competitive economy and the community-binding equality promised by democracy. In a battle that began a half-century ago, the achievers won.

TRANSLATION: "To hell with democracy. I got mine." This is why socialism is growing in America. That is why I saw so many signs in Hilo welcoming EBT cards. This is why a relatively intelligent dentist can be over $1.2 million in debt and not know how he and his wife can earn enough to pay it off. This is why student loan debt is the American government's greatest asset, over $1.5 trillion and growing. And this is why America is now a debtor nation, printing more and more money to pay off the debt printing money creates. America is much like a person who uses his credit card to pay off his other credit cards. This is why there is no financial education in our schools.

Financial stupidity is very profitable for people who know how to print fake money.

The Good News

It was my good fortune my poor dad could not afford to send me to a private prep school. It was due to my realization I was poor (at least, relative to my elementary school classmates) that I wanted to learn about money. It was the wisdom of my poor dad, who suggested I follow in the footsteps of the Three Wise Men and go in search of my teacher.

Apprenticeship: Real Teachers

At the age of nine, I became an apprentice to my rich dad. Apprenticeship is one of the oldest methods of real education. Apprenticeship works because most apprentices learn from real teachers, not fake teachers. For example, in medieval days, if you wanted to learn to be a blacksmith, you learned from a real blacksmith.

About two to three days a week, after school, I would go to my rich dad's office, and work for free. His son Mike and I did things such as pick up trash, tidy the office, and other tasks a nine-year-old can handle. After about an hour, rich dad would bring out his *Monopoly®* game and we'd play. Rather than just throw the dice and move the playing pieces, rich dad would teach us, asking us to think before we made a move and explaining different age-appropriate financial strategies for nine-year-old kids.

As we grew older, our apprenticeship tasks become more about business and investing, yet we always ended playing *Monopoly*, receiving financial education for our free labor.

On a regular basis, rich dad would take his son and me to see his "green houses," as represented in the *Monopoly* game. We went from apprenticeships, to learning via playing *Monopoly*, to doing the real thing and learning from rich dad's real "green houses." In 1966, at the age of 19, I returned to Hilo from school in New York to see rich dad's big "red hotel"—a hotel, literally—right in the middle of Waikiki Beach.

When people ask me what I do today, I say, "I play *Monopoly* in real life."

Today, my wife, Kim, and I own over 6,500 "green houses," rental houses, and several "red hotels," as well as golf courses and oil wells.

As fate would have it, rather than go on to prep school with my rich classmates, I followed my poor dad's advice and went in search of real teacher.

If my poor dad had been rich, I might have gone to a private prep school and never really learned how to be rich.

YOUR QUESTIONS... ROBERT'S ANSWERS

Q: You say that the financial system is rigged, and I agree with you. But how exactly can "normal" or average people benefit from this, too? Is there a way to turn this game around?

Glenn B. – Germany

A: I am often asked: "What do you say to the average investor?" My reply is, "Don't be average."

Q: How can we have any faith in—or rely on—the banking system? In general... or in a crisis?

Jeffrey T. – Malaysia

A: There is a difference between the words *faith* and *trust*. I have faith the banks are greedy, focused only on self-interests. I do not trust the banking system to take care of its clients, crash or no crash.

Q: Are you positive on the long-term prospects of the United States? What alternative life and investing areas of the world would you suggest?

Wendell M. – USA

A: The United States is the greatest, richest country in modern history. I am blessed to be born an American, which is why I fought in Vietnam, to serve my country.

The problem is that the world is changing. And I am afraid that our leaders, our education system, and most people are not changing fast enough.

That is why I appreciate those who read my books, listen to The Rich Dad Radio Show and attend our seminars. I am not saying I have the answers, or that I am right. I am saying, we all need to be more aware and vigilant, and prepare to change.

Q: What leads you to believe that cryptocurrencies are less fake than the fake money we already use? You do realize that most of the money we have in circulation is electronic and not printed, right? Is that cybercurrency... vs. cryptocurrency?

Roberta N. - Mexico

A: I am not an expert on cryptocurrencies. I do understand that blockchain technology is the real technology. Blockchain technology is more trustworthy than human beings.

Money is dependent upon trust, so I trust blockchain technology more than I do human beings.

Q: I live in Ethiopia. Is fake everything affecting every economy in the world? My country is growing fast, but it has lots of weird financial systems.

Semegn T. — Ethiopia

A: Ethiopia, as well as the continent of Africa, is very rich. That is why the Europeans colonized Africa, centuries ago. The problem is that the Europeans installed a poor education system and the result is a rich country on a rich continent with rich people... who struggle financially.

Q: Why does our money say "In God We Trust"? Is it something that instills the truth that gold is God's money but put on the fake money to trick us?

Benny J. — India

A: Glad to see other people asking the same questions I've asked. What do you think the answer is? Why would a government state "In God We Trust"? Why not "In Government We Trust"?

More importantly, who or what do you trust?

Chapter Eight

GOING BACK TO SCHOOL

FIGHTING WHAT'S FAKE

O n January 3, 1973, our plane landed at Norton Air Force Base in California. There were approximately 200 servicemen on board, returning from Vietnam. I was the officer in charge of the 16 Marines from the carrier.

The first thing we all noticed were the large crowds of anti-war protestors waiting for us. After my 16 men had gathered their bags, I shook their hands and wished them well as they headed home. We had all served together for one year in Vietnam.

The chanting from the protestors was growing louder as the returning troops approached the gate. I could feel the fear and see the tension in my men's faces as we headed toward the gate. In many ways, facing American anti-war protestors was more frightening than facing the Viet Cong in Vietnam.

I knew I had to say something before we walked through the protestors. Stopping one last time just before the gate, I said to the young men, "Remember, this is what we fought for. We fought for the freedom of speech, their right to call us baby-killers, rapists, and murders." The young men nodded their heads, we exchanged salutes and exited the gate, pushing through the spitting and shouting crowds. I never saw any of those men again.

Poor Dad's Advice

I was fortunate to be assigned to Marine Corps Air Station, Kaneohe, Hawaii, less than an hour from my dad's house on Oahu. I had about a year and a half left on my contract with the Marine Corps.

After welcoming me home, my dad, my poor dad, asked what my plans were. He wanted to know if I was planning on making the Marine Corps a 20-year career, fly for the airlines, or return to Standard Oil in San Francisco and sail as a third mate on their oil tankers. I told him that I had a year and a half to think about my future.

Being an educator, he suggested I get my master's and, possibly, my PhD, as he had done. A few months later, I was accepted into night school in the University of Hawaii's executive MBA program.

Rich Dad's Advice

My rich dad was glad to see me.

After showing him my gold coin and telling him about flying behind enemy lines looking for gold, all he said was, "You're nuts."

When I asked him for suggestions on my future, he said, "Learn to invest in real estate."

When I asked him why, he said, "You need to learn to use debt as money."

Rich dad and I talked at length about President Nixon and his decision to take the U.S. dollar off the gold standard. He was explaining what he meant in the letter he sent me in Vietnam, when he wrote: "Watch out… the world is going to change."

He suspected the dollar was going to be 100 percent debt, forever. Nixon, or the powers that be, would not put the dollar back on the gold standard. When it was backed by gold, the dollar was about 80 percent debt, 20 percent gold.

"What does that mean?" I asked.

His answer? "It means money is debt. It means money can only be created by creating debt. It means, the U.S. Federal Reserve Bank and the U.S. Treasury will encourage everyone to get into debt. If people do not get into debt, our economy will not grow."

Rich dad had done very well financially, using debt when the dollar was backed by gold. In 1973, he suspected he would become even richer, now that the dollar was 100 percent debt.

He was also concerned. Sitting with him in his Waikiki office in my Marine uniform, he asked, "Do you have a credit card?"

"Yes, I do," I said. "I was issued one on the base."

Rich dad silently nodded his head. "They issued you a credit card?"

"Yes. All officers were issued one. The Base Exchange wants us to use credit cards when we shop."

"Interesting," said rich dad, smirking.

"Why?" I asked.

"That is how money is created. There is no money in your card. You don't need money in the bank. Money is created out of thin air, the moment you charge something on your credit card."

I saw silent for a moment. Things were starting to make sense. I asked him, "Is that why you wrote, 'Watch out... the world is going to change'?"

Rich dad nodded his head and said: "Millions of people are about to have their lives changed, using credit cards. Millions will buy houses and cars, using debt. Millions will work harder and grow poorer because they never learned to use debt."

I asked rich dad, "And is that why you want me to take a real estate course, to learn how to use debt as money?"

Rich dad, paused, thinking for a while before he answered: "Real estate will always be the basis of wealth. Real estate is like gold and silver. The word *real* is derived from Spanish. *Real* in

Spanish means 'royal.' Royalty, throughout history, has always valued land, gold, and silver."

He continued: "If you learn to use debt as money, and buy royal estates with debt, as I have, you will become a very rich and smart man." He added, "If you use debt to buy liabilities, you will join the millions upon millions of poor and middle-class people who will spend their lives working for the 'royals' who own the banks, working for fake money to pay off their debt."

I sat quietly, thinking about being a criminal for owning a gold coin. I was now thinking about using debt to buy real—*royal*—estate.

Then I asked, "What if I choose to stay out of debt? What if I live debt-free?"

Rich dad smiled and said, "For most people, that is the smarter choice. If you do not want to learn to use debt as money, stay out of debt. Debt is very dangerous. Debt is like a loaded gun. Debt can both kill you and protect you."

I knew rich dad had more to say, so I asked, "And what happens if I choose to learn to use debt as money?"

Rich dad smiled and said, "You see this hotel we are sitting in? Do you think I could afford a million-dollar hotel using my savings?"

All I could do was shake my head, a silent "No."

"I paid less than $1 million for this hotel on Waikiki Beach. If the government keeps printing money, what do you think it will be worth in 10 years?" rich dad asked.

"I don't know," I replied.

"If you keep working hard, paying taxes, and saving money, do you think you will be able to afford this hotel in 10 years?"

I really did not know what to say... or how to answer his question.

"Do you think your fellow Marine pilots, who get jobs flying for the airlines, will be able to afford this hotel in 10 years?"

Again, I did not know what to say.

Rich dad continued: "And the Japanese tourists are arriving in droves. They have money. They are buying Waikiki and the rest of Hawaii. Do you want to work for the Japanese? Do you think you can afford Waikiki real estate in 10 years? Do you think you can afford a beach front home in Waikiki in 10 years?"

Rich dad's lesson was sinking in. I asked, "Will you teach me to invest in real estate?"

Rich dad shook his head saying: "I invest in real estate. I don't teach real estate. Besides, I am a student always... always taking real estate courses." He told me, "If you want to be a professional investor, you too must be a student, a lifelong learner. Using debt as money is a dangerous and risky game. If you are not willing to be a lifelong learner, don't use debt to buy real estate."

I had to think about that. I hated school. The idea of being a lifelong learner was not appealing to me.

Sensing my resistance, rich dad asked, "As a pilot, aren't you always taking flying lessons?"

I nodded, then replied, "Constantly. I've been flying for five years, and we're constantly taking more advanced flying lessons, more difficult lessons."

Rich dad said, "Investing in real estate is no different. I am always taking lessons. I am always a student. That is why I own this hotel on Waikiki Beach today." He added, "It's just like *Monopoly*. When you and Mike were tiny kids, I owned tiny green houses. Today, I own red hotels. If I did not study and take courses constantly, I would not be sitting here on Waikiki Beach."

After a long silence, I said, "I'll sign up for a real estate course."

Rich dad smiled, and the meeting was over.

My MBA Program

I now had two dads to listen to. My poor dad suggested I get a master's and my PhD. My rich dad suggested taking real estate courses.

Signing up for the MBA program was easy. The Marine Corps had an officer in charge of advanced education. All I had to do was go to his office and sign up.

The Marines did not have real estate investment courses, so I had to search for those courses on my own. The Marines had stock market investment classes, but no real estate classes. I wanted real estate courses because I wanted to learn to use debt as money.

In less than two months, I was enrolled in the University of Hawaii's MBA program. Twice a week at night and all day on Saturday, I would finish flying and go back to school.

I never liked traditional school, but I loved flight school. In flight school, we had real teachers, real pilots. We took classes and we flew. The more skilled we got as student pilots, the better our instructors got. We knew they could fly because we flew with them. Our instructor pilots were like Mr. Ely, my fifth-grade teacher. They were teachers who inspired students to learn, to become smarter.

Advanced weapons school was even more exciting. Flying an aircraft with weapons was actually flying a very different aircraft. The tactics and strategies are different for combat pilots. Our advanced weapons instructors had just returned from Vietnam.

When we fired weapons, machine guns, and rockets from our aircraft, our instructors shot first... just to show us they could do what they were teaching us to do. If we missed, the instructors did not flunk us. They simply said, "Take it around. Do it again." And we did. Again and again, many times until we could fly and shoot as well as our instructors. That is why I loved flight school. I loved flight school because our instructors were real teachers, preparing us for a real war.

In the classroom, I was not enjoying the MBA program. I felt like I was back in high school. One night, my frustration hit a boiling point.

"Have you ever been a real accountant?" I asked the accounting teacher.

"Yes," he replied. "I have a degree in accounting."

"That is not what I am asking you," I said tersely. "I know you have a degree in accounting, but have you ever been a real accountant... in the real world?"

After an extended pause, the teacher admitted, "No, I haven't. I am a graduate assistant. I have a bachelor's degree in accounting. I am going for my master's."

"I can tell," I replied.

"Are you an accountant?" the teacher asked me.

"No, I'm not," I replied.

"So why did you ask me if I am a real accountant?"

"Because I can tell you don't know what you're talking about. You're teaching from a textbook, not real life."

The Apprentice

My real-life accounting experience began as an apprenticeship to rich dad. I was not an accountant, yet I had worked with rich dad's real accountants for years. I could tell our instructor was teaching from theory, not reality.

The United States was still fighting in Vietnam and Marines were not too popular on college campuses. Me sitting in class and giving the instructor a hard time was not improving my popularity.

"Are you planning on becoming an accountant?" the instructor asked.

"No," I replied. "I plan on being an entrepreneur. I plan on hiring accountants. So, I need to be able to ask accountants intelligent questions."

"And what question do you want to ask me?"

"I just asked you an intelligent question: Are you a real accountant? Do you have any real-world accounting experience?"

The teacher just stood there dazed, like a deer in the headlights.

Time was up, and the class ended.

Marketing Class

I was looking forward to taking the marketing class as part of the MBA program. The class catalogue promoted a respected marketing guru. So, I signed up, excited about learning from this expert.

Again, it was a disappointing experience. Again, I asked the same question: "How much real-world experience do you have?"

The guru was proud to tell us that he owned a bicycle shop that our class would visit and get some "hands-on" learning.

The bicycle shop was less than 1,500 square feet. It was tiny. For two Saturdays, our class "studied" in his bicycle shop.

The guru was not teaching us marketing. He was teaching us merchandising, how to display bicycles on stands, accessories on shelves, and clothing on racks.

I had learned more about merchandising by working hands-on as rich dad's apprentice, in the gift shops in his hotels and restaurants.

The guru was not teaching us marketing, because he had only one store. He was teaching us advertising—how to place ads in local papers and magazines.

I learned more about real marketing working for free, marketing rich dad's chain of hotels and restaurants.

I did buy a bicycle. The guru could *sell...* which is a part of the marketing process. He offered our class a special student discount, and many of us bought new bicycles.

When I told my rich dad about my new bicycle and my lightweight marketing instructor and his tiny store, he just laughed and said, "Your marketing instructor is very smart. He teaches marketing to the entire university where he is a guru. He invites students and faculty to visit and study his bicycle shop. And guess what? You and your classmates buy bicycles. That guy is a brilliant marketer."

It was a great bicycle. I rode that bike almost every day, up and down the flight line on the Marine Air Base. My instructor was a real marketing guru.

A Real Estate Seminar

One night while watching television, an infomercial came on promising to teach students how to buy real estate for "nothing down."

A few days later, I was one of about 300 people attending a "free seminar" in a beautiful Waikiki hotel ballroom. The "upsell" was a real estate course, and I paid $385 for a three-day weekend course.

About two months later, the instructor arrived from California and the three-day class began. It was my first seminar, as opposed to a school or classroom setting.

My poor dad believed in school. He did not attend seminars, which he thought were rip-offs. Granted, some are. But so are some schools.

My rich dad only attended seminars. He said he liked seminars because they were "short and specific." He attended only to learn more about a specific subject he was interested in. He was not there for the degree, or the alphabet soup of advanced degrees. Many corporate and government employees and licensed professionals displayed these designations—MS, PhD, JD, MD, CFP—as badges of honor.

Warren Buffett is a college graduate. He makes no secret of that, yet he does not display his college diploma in his office. He does, though, proudly display his certificate from a Dale Carnegie public speaking course. For him, learning to speak without his knees shaking and his voice quivering has proven priceless when raising billions of dollars from investors.

A *Real* Real Estate Teacher

There were about 30 students, out of the 300 who showed up for the free introductory seminar, who signed up for the three-day course. The instructor was impressive. He was dressed casually, but well. He didn't wear a tie, but his sport coat, slacks, and shoes looked expensive. He looked, to me, like a real real estate investor.

Ask anyone who has been in the military about the importance of grooming and appearance. Most military personnel wear their uniforms with pride. They are well-groomed with their shoes shined.

The instructors in the MBA program looked like teachers. They did not look prosperous. They looked cheap, scruffy, and frumpy—like well-dressed hippies, which many were.

Our real real estate instructor began by showing slides of his real real estate investments and the financials on each property. He shared with us how much he made, his financing, and the challenges he had to overcome.

He also showed us properties on which he lost money, told us about the mistakes he made, what he learned, and how his mistakes made him smarter and richer.

He was real. He was not there to sell real estate. He wasn't teaching us to sell bicycles.

And he was transparent. He showed us his audited personal financial statement. He did not need to teach to support himself. And although he was paid a fee to teach, he did not need the money. He was there to teach.

And so the class began. For three days we went into real deals, real problems, real challenges, and the real crooks he had met in his 24-year career as a *real* real estate investor.

He taught us to see what most amateur real estate investors do not see. He taught us how he talks to sellers, bankers, and investors about money.

On the last day, he was teaching us how to negotiate a "nothing down" deal, an investment where he puts up none of his own money.

By the end of the third day, the class was in overdrive—really pumped up. I had a better understanding why rich dad often said, "You do not need money to become rich."

The last two hours were spent on review and asking and answering questions. Just before the class was to end, the instructor said, "Now the class begins."

Perplexed, the students wanted to know why he said the class was beginning… just as it was ending.

The instructor replied, "This class begins when you enter the real world. Your assignment is to find 100 potential investment properties in 90 days. Write a one-page analysis of each of the 100 properties. Then decide which of the 100 is the best investment. You do not have to buy anything. If and when you find a great investment, you will find the energy and enthusiasm to buy it, even if you have no money."

The class of 30 students broke into smaller groups of three to five, all promising to complete the assignment in 90 days.

As you might guess, *real life* got in the way off getting rich. I suspect only three out of the 30 completed the assignment. Which also gives us an insight into human nature. Getting rich takes work and discipline.

At the end of 90 days, I knew which of the 100 properties was the best of the best. It was a 1-bedroom, 1-bath condominium on the beach on the Island of Maui.

The developer had gone bust. The bank was dumping the project. The price of the condo was $18,000. All I needed was 10 percent down. The bank would finance the rest.

Immediately, I got out my credit card and charged the $1,800.

It was a "nothing down" deal. It was 100 percent debt financed. And it cash flowed a positive $25 a month.

It was an "infinite return" investment because I had nothing—none of my own money—in the investment, and I still made $25 in net cash flow from 100 percent debt.

A few days later, I dropped out of the MBA program.

"You can't do that here."

Today, no matter where I go in the world people say to me, "You can't do that here."

They are right. *They* may not be able to do an infinite return deal, but other people can.

The primary reason "people cannot do that" is because they went to school or their parents went to school.

If you look at the diagram on the following page, depicting the Higher Levels of Teacher, you will see how going to school keeps many people poor.

How to Tell the Difference between Real Teachers and Fake Teachers

Fake teachers teach via lecture and books. Real life is a classroom.

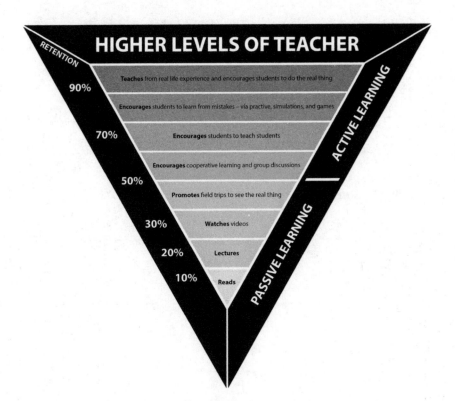

Real teachers teach from real-life experience, from their mistakes, and encourage you to do the same.

PERSONAL EXERCISE:

List three fake teachers you've had in your life and the subjects they taught:

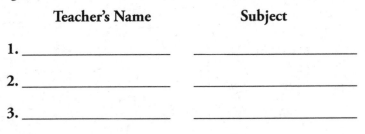

Teacher's Name	Subject
1. _____	_____
2. _____	_____
3. _____	_____

List three real teachers in your life and the subjects they taught:

Teacher's Name	Subject
1. _____	_____
2. _____	_____
3. _____	_____

What lessons did the real teachers teach you?

1. _____

2. _____

3. _____

YOUR QUESTIONS... ROBERT'S ANSWERS

Q: What is the one word or phrase you would use to convey the value of your experience in the Marine Corps?

Marco C. – Italy

A: Great question. When I was in high school, I knew I was in trouble. I was a surfer. I was flunking out of school. I was a screw-off and a clown. I did not want to grow up and "go to school, get a job, work hard..." etc., etc., etc.

When I was in high school, I wanted my freedom.

Many of my high school friends who chose to live free, living the life of surfers, wound up in jail, became addicts, or died young. One committed suicide, one died in a motorcycle crash, and two in car wrecks, driving drunk.

So, although it sounds counterintuitive, I chose to go to a military school and join the Marine Corps... if I wanted to be free.

Sunday school taught me that "The word became flesh." The words the Academy and the Marines made real, or "became flesh" for me, are: mission, duty, honor, courage, respect, discipline, and code.

For most people, especially those in the corporate world, those words are only words—lip service, corporate speak, a punch lines that never became real, never became flesh. If those same words do not become flesh, the words *job security, paychecks,* and *retirement* become more important than real freedom.

That is why I am grateful for the Academy and the Marine Corps. Those words become real, became flesh, became me... became my spiritual strength. And real spiritual strength is essential to real financial freedom and, most importantly, real personal freedom.

As rich dad often said: "You do not have personal freedom until you have financial freedom."

Q: How do you think your rich dad was able to predict the future at a time of such economic uncertainty?

Adonis K. – Greece

A: Rich dad taught his son and me that "Entrepreneurs must pay attention to the future... because your competition is the future."

Andy Grove, founder of Intel, had this to say about the future of business: "Only the paranoid survive."

Chapter Nine

HOW TO CATCH A LOT OF FISH

SEEING THE INVISIBLE

R ich dad often said, "You cannot catch fish in clean water." He also said, "You can only catch fish in muddy water."

In an earlier chapter, I wrote, "It is easier to give people fish... than to teach people to fish."

Why? Because learning to fish is hard.

All real learning is hard. Think about the game of golf. In theory, golf is an extremely simple game. Unlike a baseball, the ball in golf is not moving. Yet, golf is one of the hardest games in the world to play, much less master. To become a Tiger Woods, a Rory McIlroy, or a Phil Mickelson requires superhuman dedication and sacrifice. Talent alone is not enough.

The same is true with the game of money.

Prosperity has made many people soft, weak, and lazy. This is not only true for Americans. You can see it all over the world. It is most noticeable in the rampant corruption in government, business, sports, politics, and even religion. Today, every child gets a trophy. Everyone is entitled. Students need safe rooms—rooms and spaces where they are safe from ideas that challenge, or threaten, sensitive beliefs. And as the gap between rich and everyone else grows wider—and everybody wants to get rich—many actually believe they are entitled to be rich. It is understandable. As rich dad said:

Money is a drug. Without financial education, people become addicted to money. Money makes them happy. Money solves their problems. Money heals their pain. Today, billions are addicted to the "quick fix," the "temporary high" of money. The problem is, the "highs" become "lows," and the addicts goes back to work to feed their addiction. Addicts will do anything to feed their addiction.

When Nixon took the dollar off the gold standard in 1971, monetary corruption, like a drug, spread worldwide. And, as rich dad warned, "Corrupt money creates corrupt people."

Corruption in Paradise

Politics is a dirty game. My poor dad was an honest man. Climbing the government ladder to success disturbed him. When he got to the top, as a member of the governor of Hawaii's cabinet, he could not tolerate the corruption.

Rather than tolerate the corruption, my dad resigned and ran against his boss, the governor, a Democrat, in the 1970 gubernatorial race.

I was in flight school in Pensacola, Florida, when my dad called and told me he was going to run as a Republican for lieutenant governor. He said, "I doubt we can win, but I could not live with myself if I did not run."

He handed the phone to my mom and we discussed her fears and concerns. She was worried about my dad's job security and money. She said, "The Republicans promise they will find Dad a job in California. Maybe even as a professor at Stanford University."

Dad was in his early 50s and mom in her late 40s. They had a lot of life ahead of them. When the conversation was over, I wished them well and to be strong as they entered the dirty world of politics. The governor was an ex-police officer and it was common knowledge that his friend, also an ex-police officer, was allegedly the head of organized crime in Hawaii.

When my dad lost the election, as expected, the governor informed my dad he would never work in Hawaii government again.

My mom and dad were crushed. The game of politics was far nastier than they had imagined. Friends they thought were true friends, turned against them, spreading lies and untruths about both my mom and dad throughout the campaign, accusing Dad of being corrupt.

Mom died of a broken heart two months after the election. She was only 48 years old. Not surprisingly, the job in California promised by the Republicans never materialized. My dad took early retirement and used his retirement savings to purchase a national ice cream franchise, a business that failed in less than a year. My dad was not a businessman, and he died a broken man, 21 years after the election, in 1991.

The Truth Comes Out

In 2015, James Dooley, a former investigative reporter for a local paper, *Honolulu Advertiser*, published the book *Sunny Skies, Shady Characters: Cops, Killers, and Corruption in the Aloha State.*

The book starts with singer Don Ho and lists by name the cops, killers, and the corruption in Hawaii. He includes the names of governors and the trustees of Kamehameha Schools, one of the richest schools in the world. Dooley writes about the relationships between the courts, political leaders, labor leaders, TV shows like *Hawaii Five-0* and *Magnum PI*, and the Japanese, Hawaiian, Chinese, and Italian Mafias. He even lists a few bodies found buried in shallow graves.

James Dooley wrote about the very corruption my dad could not stomach. He even named some of my classmates and my dad's former friends.

I met with Dooley in Hawaii to thank him for writing the book—and to tell him I wished my dad were alive to have read it.

When I asked him how he was still alive after naming names, he smiled and said, "Corruption is so rampant today it's a part of life, and people don't care."

President Barack Obama was the first and only U.S. President from Hawaii.

This is a good time to remind readers that I have no political or religious affiliations or agendas. Like my two dads, I detest corruption, laziness, and the entitlement mentality. Another take on this topic: *Forbes* magazine once called Hawaii "the People's Republic of Hawaii."

Don't Change the World ... Change Yourself

President John F. Kennedy credited Edmund Burke (1729–1797) for this quote, although there is some dispute as to its actual origins: "The only thing necessary for the triumph of evil is that good men do nothing." I think you'll find those who agree that, today, many good people are doing very little.

During the three summers that I studied with Bucky Fuller, he often spoke about the Mafia being an integral part of American politics. And President Kennedy's brother Robert Kennedy, while U.S. attorney general, courageously took on Jimmy Hoffa and the Teamsters Union, accusing them of colluding with the Mafia.

Robert Kennedy was assassinated in 1968 after winning the California Democratic presidential primary. Jimmy Hoffa disappeared, his body never found.

Let's Get Together

Many people say, "Let's get together and change the world."

That sounds good as a sound bite, but it's not realistic. Today there is too much fake news. Today, news is designed to infuriate, not educate; its goal is to polarize, not unite. The same is true in our schools.

Today, the world is too fractured. There is too much hate. Too much animosity. Too much raw violence. Millions of people all over the world are migrating, not for financial reasons but to run away from crime, murder, and rape.

Like Hawaii, corruption is an accepted part of life. Law and order are breaking down globally. American cities are patrolled by paramilitary troops in armored vehicles, much like cities in Iraq and Afghanistan. Are American cities on the verge of becoming war zones? Is this the end of the American Republic?

Rather than change the world, it may be best to change yourself.

One of the many reasons our world is corrupt is because our money is corrupt. Without real financial education in our schools, people cannot see Fuller's cash heist, they cannot see how their money and their lives are stolen via the money they work for.

As rich dad said, "You cannot catch fish in clean water. You can only catch fish in muddy water."

The reason the gap between the rich and everyone else is growing is because, without real financial education, the fish—the people—are swimming in muddy water. This is why and how the academic elites who run our legal system, banks, and Wall Street are catching a lot of fish.

Rich Dad Poor Dad, published in 1997, used some of the

illustrations and diagrams rich dad developed to teach his son and me to see through muddy water. If you've read *Rich Dad Poor Dad*, you may remember some of those illustrations.

If you read my second book, *Rich Dad's Cashflow Quadrant*, you may remember this diagram of the quadrant.

Since rich dad did not graduate from high school, he used simple diagrams to teach us new ideas. He believed "a picture is worth a thousand words."

The following are some of the pictures he developed so his son and I could see through muddy waters.

Nouns and Verbs

Rich dad, although simple man without much education knew the difference between nouns and verbs.

He taught his son and me that in the world of money, you cannot tell if a *noun* is an asset or a liability without *verbs*.

For example, a house can be either an *asset* or a *liability*. You cannot tell if a house is an *asset* or a *liability* without the verb *flow*, as in examining how the cash flows in and out of it.

The reason Kim and I named our game *CASHFLOW*—one word instead of two—was to turn two words into one word.

Rich dad also said, "Since academics know very little about money, nouns without verbs… make little difference."

To entrepreneurs, the words **cash flow** are life itself. Cash flow is as important as **blood flow** is to the human body. Could you imagine a doctor, observing blood gushing out of a patient's wound and pouring on to the operating room floor, saying, "Yes, that is blood …" and not doing anything?

That is what our academic elites are doing to our government and our people. *We the People* and our country are hemorrhaging, as the academic elites, via our educational system, get richer and richer … as they keep the people and our government bleeding.

What Is Financial IQ?

Rich dad said, "IQ is a measure of a person's ability to solve problems." In the world of academics, IQ measures a person's ability to solve math, writing, and science problems. In the world of auto mechanics, a person's automobile IQ is his or her ability to fix a car.

Rich dad said, "Financial IQ is a person's ability to solve money problems. Financial IQ is measured in money."

When I completed my three-day real estate course, I was able to solve an $18,000 problem without money. So, according to my rich dad, my financial IQ was $18,000.

Financial IQ can go up if the person practices. Today, I would say my financial IQ is about $100 million. A $100 million problem would push the limits of my financial IQ.

Sobering Statistics

The Washington Post reported on May 25, 2016, the following:

> *The Federal Reserve surveyed more than 5,000 people to determine whether their personal situations were improving along with the economy. The results ... [included] this one telling statistic: About 46 percent of Americans said they did not have enough money to cover a $400 emergency expense.*

Translation: 46 percent of all Americans have a financial IQ of less than $400.

KISS: Real Financial Education Is Simple

Rich dad kept things simple. Or, as they say, KISS: Keep It Super Simple. He said there were six foundational words to real financial education. They are:

1. Income
2. Expense
3. Asset
4. Liability
5. Cash
6. Flow

If you read *Rich Dad Poor Dad* or played *CASHFLOW*, you may recognize these as the words on a financial statement: income, expense, asset, and liability.

Income and expenses are tracked on the P&L, the profit and loss statement. Assets and liabilities are listed on the balance sheet. And cash flow is illustrated through the statement of cash flow.

Rich dad often said, "My banker has never asked me for my report card. My banker has never asked me what school I went to. My banker has never asked me for my GPA." He emphasized, "When I talk to my banker, my banker wants to see my financial statement. My financial statement is my report card in the real world."

Academic Confusion

When you look up the words *asset* and *liability* in a dictionary, the definitions are:

> Asset (*n*): a useful or valuable thing, person, or quality.

> Liability (*n*): the state of being responsible for something, especially by law.

Here are some lessons:

- Without the verb *flow*, in *cashflow*, the water is muddy, confusing.
- In 2008, millions of people worldwide lost their homes because they thought their homes were an asset.
- Millions lost their homes because the academic elites created fake assets, known as mortgage-backed securities (MBSs) and credit default swaps.
- A little financial education would have protected millions of people from the crimes of academic elites running our legal, banking, financial, and educational institutions.
- If a house is cash flowing positively, with money going into your pocket, then the house is an asset.

- If a house causes cash to flow out of your pocket, the house is a liability.
- In 2008, millions of people found out their homes were liabilities.

Muddy Waters

Today, I hear schoolteachers say to students, "Your education is an asset. Get a high-paying job."

Today, I hear real estate brokers say to first-time homebuyers, "Your house is an asset."

Today, I hear financial planners tell clients, "Your 401(k) is an asset."

Yet, if you clear the water and can see where the cash is flowing, you will know the truth.

Follow the Money

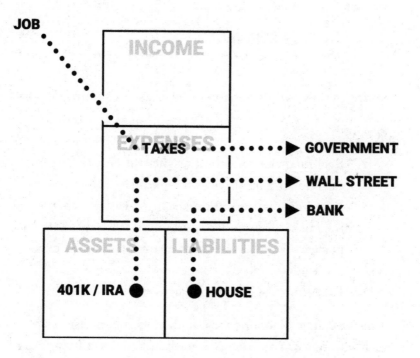

The middle class is the asset for the government, Wall Street, and the banks. Compare the cash flow of the middle class to the cash flow of the rich.

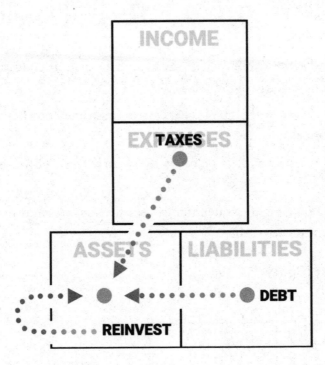

Notice the cash keeps flowing into the asset column of the rich.

LESSONS

- Real financial education teaches the rich to keep the cash flowing into the asset column.
- Fake financial education keeps the cash flowing out of the pockets of the poor and middle class and into the pockets of those who print fake money, the pockets of the academic elite.
- Fake financial education keeps the water muddy.

If the cash flow diagrams are not clear to you, please get together with one or two friends and discuss the cash flow patterns. Discussion is a great way to learn.

The three-day real estate course taught me to do this:

INCOME

$25

EXPENSE

ASSET   **LIABILITY**

Condo ⟵——— Debt ($18,000)

A cash flow of $25 a month is not a lot of money. Yet, $25 was a transformation in the way I thought about money. Once I was able to earn $25 from 100 percent debt, I was free. I knew that if I kept practicing, I would never need money again. I would never have to say "I can't afford it" ever again.

Infinite Return

Using 100 percent debt to produce $25 is an example of an infinite return. It is money for nothing... money created from financial intelligence.

It is printing money. An infinite return can be achieved from anything. It does not have to be real estate.

STOCKS

Let's say I purchase 100 shares of a stock for $1 per share. I have invested $100 invested.

The price of the stock rises to $10 per share. My 100 shares are now worth $1,000.

I sell 10 shares at $10 and receive my original $100. My 90 remaining shares are free once I have recouped my initial investment.

Net transaction:

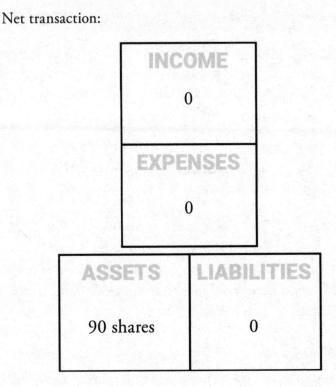

The dividends from the 90 shares of stock are income... and infinite return is achieved.

BOOKS

I may spend a year writing a book. It costs about $50,000 to edit, print, and publish the book.

The book goes out for licensing to book publishers all over the world. Let's say I receive offers from 30 countries for $10,000 per license.

$300,000 from sale of international licenses come in, and after the $50,000 in expenses is recouped, $250,00 in net income from international rights is realized. In addition, royalties from every book sold come in from all over the world.

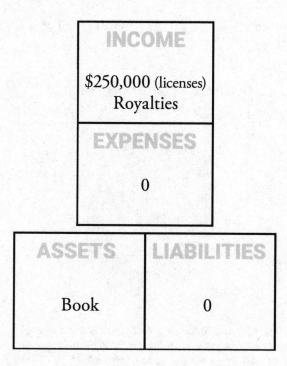

The asset—the book—creates income via royalties... for an infinite return.

BUSINESS: The Rich Dad Company

The Rich Dad Company began in 1997 with $250,000 raised from investors. In 2001, $750,000 was returned to investors. All profits from that point forward were infinite return.

Infinite Possibilities

Once a person understands the power of infinite returns, then almost anything can be an asset. The possibilities are infinite. The water is clear.

When I present financial education via pictures someone always asks, "If it is so easy, why isn't everyone rich?"

First of all, the drawings make it simple. Doing it is not so easy, yet—with practice—it does get easier.

The primary reason why most people are not rich is because they went to school.

"All coins have three sides" – Rich Dad

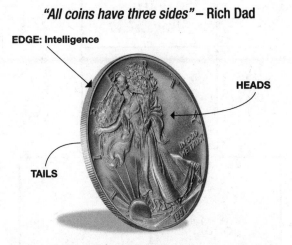

EDGE: Intelligence

HEADS

TAILS

"The test of a first-rate intelligence is the ability to hold two opposed ideas in the mind at the same time, and still retain the ability to function."
—F. Scott Fitzgerald, 1936

Why People Are Not Rich

1. In school, students are taught that mistakes make you stupid.
   In real life, making mistakes makes you richer.
   God designed humans to learn from their mistakes.

2. Cheating means asking for help.
   In school, students take tests on their own.
   Asking for help is cheating.
   In real life, business and investing are team sports.
   The rich have teams.
   The average person does not have a team. The average person has a financial advisor, stock broker, or real estate broker giving them advice. And very often, that "advice" is a sales pitch, not financial education.

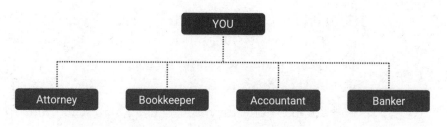

3. Good grades mean you are smart.

   In real life, my banker has never asked for my report card. My banker does not care what school I went to or what my GPA was.

   In real life, my banker wants to see my financial statement.

INCOME STATEMENT

Income
Expenses

BALANCE SHEET

Assets	Liabilities

The third financial statement is the statement of cash flow. The *CASHFLOW* game is one of the only games that teaches players to control their cash flow and increase their financial IQ.

Since it's likely that the majority of all high school and college graduates do not know what a financial statement is, much less use one, most people have a tough time getting loans to buy investments.

In 1996, Kim and I created the *CASHFLOW* game so people could learn to speak the language of money.

The power of the *CASHFLOW* game is people can teach people without having to go to school.

Today, there are thousands of Cashflow Clubs all over the world.

4. Get out of debt.
   In real life, debt makes the rich richer.

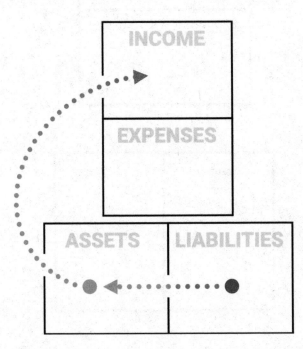

In 1971, money became debt.

Bankers love debtors because debtors make bankers richer.

The richest people in the world know how to use debt to make money.

The *CASHFLOW* game is one of the only games that teaches players to use debt as money and get richer.

If you make mistakes using debt when playing *CASHFLOW*, you make mistakes with play money.

5. Taxes are patriotic.
   The American Revolution had its origins in a tax revolt, the Boston Tea Party, in 1773.
   In real life, the rich don't pay taxes.

The Cashflow Quadrant keeps the waters clear:

TAX PERCENTAGES PAID PER QUADRANT

If you would like to learn more about taxes, please read Rich Dad advisor Tom Wheelwright's book *Tax-Free Wealth*.

You will find that tax laws throughout the world are similar. The rich, on the B and I half of the quadrant, pay less in taxes legally.

As Tom Wheelwright explains in his book, the tax laws are incentives from the government. If you do what the government wants done, the government offers tax incentives.

For example, if I rent a home for myself I receive no tax break. If I provide rental houses for others, the government offers me many tax breaks because I am doing what the government wants done. If I have a job in the E-quadrant, I receive no tax breaks. If I provide thousands of jobs, like Amazon, cities offer massive tax breaks, hoping Amazon will move to their city.

In other words, people in B and I quadrants do what the government wants done. They receive tax breaks for doing it. Those in the E and S quadrants, do not do what the government wants done. They do not receive tax breaks.

Muddy Waters

Real financial education does not have to be confusing. It can be very simple. A child can understand real financial education. I did.

I also knew simple does not mean easy. Yet rich dad's simple diagrams were my mental guides, much like navigational stars in the sky.

Without real financial education in our schools, millions become the fish that the elites trap in their nets and webs of lies. Without real financial education, millions go to school, get a job, pay taxes, save money, buy a house, and invest in the stock market.

Muddying the waters is the educational system's insistence on punishing students for making mistakes and taking tests on their own. That may be a great way to train students for the E and S quadrants, but not entrepreneurs who will operate in the B and I quadrants. Entrepreneurs know they must make mistakes and learn from their mistakes and that business is a team sport.

To compete in the world economy, every country needs more visionary entrepreneurs like Steve Jobs, Bill Gates, Mark Zuckerberg, Michael Dell, Richard Branson, Henry Ford, Walt Disney, and Thomas Edison... bright young men who never finished school.

In the next chapter, you will learn who your best real teacher is.

YOUR QUESTIONS... ROBERT'S ANSWERS

Q: How does Grunch continue to operate without the public catching on?

Mari J. – Canada

A: Fantastic question. Grunch is too big to see because Grunch is everywhere. Grunch is like looking for air. Grunch is your corner bank, your financial planner, your education, your credit card, your taxes, your job, your mortgage, your politicians, police, military, food, medical care and on and on.

Grunch is impossible to see because Grunch is money, and money is everywhere, in everything—and invisible.

A core theme of this book is: "You can't catch fish in clean water."

In the real world of business and investing, the word used for seeing in dirty water is *transparency*. In the real world of money, transparency is a very, very important word.

The purpose of *financial literacy* is to empower the mind to see what our eyes cannot see, via words. The purpose of *financial education* is to empower our ability to see in dirty water, aka transparency. And one reason why the latest crashes have been so big and severe is due to a lack of transparency.

The Rich Dad Company is dedicated to empowering people to see in dirty water... because without real financial education in our educational system students leave school financially blind.

Q: How big will the next crash be?

Stephen B. – United Kingdom

A: The next crash, in my opinion, will make the crash of 2008 look tiny. Since 2008, the banking and derivative risks have only grown exponentially. In 2008 there were $700 trillion in derivatives. Today, there are $1.2 quadrillion in off-balance-sheet derivatives… which means the average person cannot see. *Off-balance sheet* means *murky waters. Off-balance sheet* means no transparency.

In Part Three, Fake Assets, I will go into Dark Pools and Dark Money.

Q: Are you saying that, since 2008, the water has only gotten murkier?

Artur N. – Estonia

A: Yes… deeper, darker, and more dangerous.

You can listen to an interview with Nomi Prins on Rich Dad Radio about *dark money* and the *new normal,* how the central banks are running our world—*not the politicians.* Listening to Prins on Rich Dad Radio, you will "see" a dark and murky world that very few people will ever see.

Q: What do you think needs to happen to end the corruption we see in the government?

The too-big-to-fail banks and global monetary regulators? Is it even possible to put an end to it?

Simon J. – Thailand

A: Rich dad often said, "Grow up. The world will always be filled with greed, corruption, and incompetence. That is why real financial education and a smart team are your best protection from the real world.

Rich dad also said, "Greedy people are smarter and more clever than government bureaucrats. That is why you need to protect yourself from smart crooks and incompetent bureaucrats. That is why your financial education is essential to your financial survival."

Q: Do you think our generation will see the day that the subject of money is taught in schools?

Rafael R. – Peru

A: I doubt it. Unfortunately, most academics fall into the government bureaucrat category. By the time schools start teaching financial education, the smart and the greedy will have created new financial products, as they did financial derivatives in the 1980s.

We all know academics are out of touch with the real world of money. That will never change.

The good news is that this makes life easier for people like you, people who seek, read, and learn from real teachers from the real world of money.

There is a new book, *The Case against Education: Why the Education System Is a Waste of Time and Money* by Bryan Caplan.

Bryan Caplan writes from the point of view of a real college professor. Caplan argues that the primary function of education is not to enhance students' skill but to certify their intelligence, work ethic, and conformity—in other words, to signal the qualities of a good employee.

It's a very good book, especially for parents who worship at the altar of higher education.

At least for now, it seems that students will still leave school financially blind due to lack of transparency, deeply in debt, and searching for a job in dirty water.

Chapter Ten

WHY MISTAKES ARE YOUR BEST REAL TEACHERS

USING MISTAKES TO GET SMARTER

I wish I could say getting rich was easy. I wish I could say I was a "boy wonder," a natural entrepreneur. I wish I could say I was always joyous and happy, that I got along with everyone.

I wish I could say everyone I met and did business with was an incredible, smart, generous, honest, law-abiding citizen of highest integrity, ethics, and morals. But I can't.

The journey from poor to rich and from employee to entrepreneur was a journey of very high highs and very low lows. It was a journey meeting wonderful people and horrible people. Oftentimes, that was the same person: a person who was wonderful in one instance or situation and horrible the next. A person who was honest to your face, then stabbing you in the back, ripping you off, lying, cheating, and stealing as soon as you signed the contract.

And I have met the best of people who were consistently great— no matter how good or bad things got, no matter how much money we made or lost.

I wish I could say the same about myself.

Human Beings Being Human

This is not to say I am perfect and wonderful. I am not on the shortlist for sainthood. The point is, none of us is a god. We are all human beings, which means we are humans... *being human*. We all have strengths and weaknesses, a good side and a dark side. We are not God. We are not perfect. We don't know all the "right" answers, which means we are not always "right."

And most importantly, being human means that we all make mistakes.

A baby learns to walk by falling down. Next, the child learns to ride a bicycle by falling off the bicycle.

Then they go to school and are taught, "Making mistakes makes you stupid." That is insanity.

The Problems of the World

When you look back at human history and your own history, it is easy to see that most of the problems of the world and our personal problems begin with the need to be "right." Wars, violence, arguments, murder, and hate grow very deep roots in the human need to be "right."

The Insanity of Being Right

The other side of being "right" is the fear of being "wrong." In our society, admitting you made a mistake is a sign of weakness. In our society, making mistake means you are stupid. In our society, the need to be right is killing us. The fear of being wrong, looking stupid, amplifies the insanity of being "right."

Before we can have peace on earth, humans need to step back, take a deep breath, and rethink the *psychosis,* the *duality* of "right" and "wrong." I use the word "duality" because "right" cannot exist without "wrong." Right and wrong are joined at the hip. When someone says something is "right," they are simultaneously saying something is "wrong."

Three Sides of a Coin

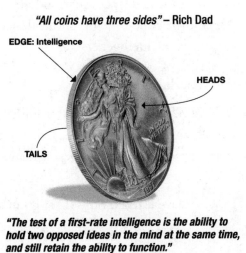

"All coins have three sides" – Rich Dad

EDGE: Intelligence

HEADS

TAILS

"The test of a first-rate intelligence is the ability to hold two opposed ideas in the mind at the same time, and still retain the ability to function."
—F. Scott Fitzgerald, 1936

I use the example of a three-sided coin as a metaphor for real intelligence. I say "real intelligence" because whenever we see life through the prism of "right and wrong," we become less intelligent.

One of Bucky Fuller's generalized principles—principles that are true in all cases, no exceptions—is, "Unity is plural, at minimum two."

In other words, the concept of "one" does not exist. In the real world of planet Earth, two is the minimum, not one. For example, the concept of *up* cannot exist without understanding *down. In* cannot exist without comprehending *out. Smart* cannot exist without *stupid. Left* would not exist without *right. Rich* would not exist without *poor.* And *man* could not exist without *woman.*

An important quote from F. Scott Fitzgerald (1896–1940) that I often refer to is:

> "The test of a first-rate intelligence is the ability to hold two opposed ideas in mind at the same time and still retain the ability to function."

TRANSLATION: The moment you operate from the concept of "right and wrong," your intelligence is cut in half. This is why standing on the edge of the coin—seeing both sides rather than taking sides—increases your intelligence.

Learning through Mistakes

In his book *Mistake Mystique,* Buckminster Fuller, one of the greatest geniuses of our time, describes how current educational and religious practices as well as parents keep students cut off from learning. Paraphrasing…

Fuller: Humans have learned only through mistakes.

Translation: If you are not making mistakes, you have stopped learning.

Fuller: Mistakes are sins only when not admitted.

Translation: God designed humans to learn by making mistakes. You become a "sinner" when you ignore the lesson God wants you to learn via your mistake.

Fuller: Witnessing the mistakes of others, the preconditioned crowd reflexively says, "Why did that individual make such a stupid mistake?"

Translation: Today, society believes people who make mistakes are stupid.

Fuller: So effective has the non-thinking group's deceit of humanity been, it now says, "We knew the answer the whole time."

Translation: We are smart. We know the right answers. Don't make mistakes. All you have to do is memorize the right answers we give you, and you will be smart like us.

Fuller: This means not yielding unthinkingly to "in" movements or crowd psychology.

Translation: Think for yourself.

Fuller: In love-generated fear for their children's future lives—in days beyond their survival—parents train their children to avoid making mistakes lest they be put at a social disadvantage.

Translation: Parents, out of love and a desire to prepare their children for life when they are gone, teach students not to make mistakes so they can be accepted socially.

Fuller: It's only at the moment of humans' realistic admission to selves, of having made a mistake, are they closest to that mysterious integrity governing the universe.

Translation: When a human being admits to making a mistake, they are tuning into God. God becomes their real teacher.

Fuller: God speaks to each of us directly. God speaks only through an individual awareness of truth and our most spontaneous emotions of love and compassion.

Translation: God does not punish people for making mistakes. Humans do.

When mistakes are made, God speaks to us individually through love and compassion. When you make a mistake, seek the truth and be kind and loving to yourself. When someone else makes a mistake, treat them as God would treat them—then they can learn God's lesson from the mistake.

When Fuller spoke of God, he was not referring to a religion or a human god. Fuller referred to God as "that mysterious integrity governing the universe."

You're Going to Fail

I remember, like it was like yesterday, the day I stopped being an employee and became an entrepreneur.

On that day, the paychecks stopped and I was on my own. No more job security, no more benefits, no more paid vacations, no more medical benefits, and no more pension plan.

On that day, I had three employees who needed job security, a steady paycheck, medical and dental benefits, paid vacations, and a pension plan. They earned more than I did.

On that day, I was working for the Xerox Corporation in downtown Honolulu. As I left the Xerox offices, heading across Bishop Street, the main street in downtown Honolulu, to my new office, the Xerox receptionist Elaine smiled and said, "You're going to fail, and you will be back."

Elaine had seen many hotshot salesmen like me leave and do just that: fail and return to Xerox.

I smiled and said to Elaine, "I may fail—but I will never be back."

First Big Mistake

One big piece of advice from my rich dad was, "You cannot know what you do now know." In other words, be very aware of the mistakes you will be making.

Rich dad also said, "Upsets are the first signs that you do not know what you need to know."

Things were going fine in my first business, my nylon and Velcro® surfer wallet business. The problem was, as it is in most start-ups, money was going out and nothing was coming in. There were production problems after production problems. Legal problems after legal problems. Employee problems after employee problems. Cash flow problems after cash flow problems. Problems most of my employees are not aware of.

Raising Capital

I went to my rich dad to borrow $100,000. He threw me out of his office, calling my business partners "clowns."

After convincing my poor dad that the nylon wallet business was set to take off, he took a second mortgage on his house and loaned the business the $100,000. He said he would rather give me the money while he was alive than after he was dead. It was all he had. After losing the election, he still did not have a job.

Happy to have bought us some time, I took the check to Stanley, our CFO, one of the business's three employees. I remember asking Stanley, "Will this $100,000 solve the problem?"

Stanley smiled and nodded. Three days later, Stanley had cleaned out his desk and was gone—with the $100,000.

The $100,000 had solved the problem... his problem. He repaid himself the money he had loaned the company.

Even after launching a number of successful new products, including one product that was the #1 product in the sporting goods industry in 1978, the company eventually folded. And I was left with my dad's $100,000 loan to pay back.

As Elaine the receptionist said, "You will fail—and you will be back."

I did fail. But I never went back to Xerox. A $100,000 loss at the time was the biggest in my life. I wish I could say $100,000 was my biggest mistake, but there were bigger, more expensive mistakes coming.

As Fuller said, "Mistakes are great—the more I make the smarter I get."

Stanley turned out to be a crook, yet he helped me become a rich man.

Three Sides to a Coin

When I stood on the edge of the coin, on one side was Stanley and a loss of $100,000. It was a painful, horrible, and miserable lesson. It took nearly 10 years to pay back the money Stanley stole.

On the other side of the coin were God's lessons, God's blessings. Because it was my father's house on the line, I could not stop. I could not declare bankruptcy. The thought of losing my dad's house was my motivation, my inspiration for not quitting. I knew I needed to keep going.

The blessing was that my younger brother, Jon, realizing how much I had f***** up, jumped in with a new partner and we rebuilt the business. It was the rebuilding of the business that made all of us smarter, better, wiser entrepreneurs. Through the love and compassion of my younger brother, God was teaching me what I needed learn.

My mistake was my real teacher.

As I've said, I wish I could say getting rich was easy. I wish I could say I was a boy wonder, a natural entrepreneur. But I can't.

Customized Mistakes

I often think a book on all my screw-ups would be the best, most beneficial book I could write. It would be a giant, multivolume set of books. But my mistakes are my mistakes. Your mistakes are your mistakes. In other words, my mistakes are customized to me. Your mistakes are customized just for you.

The most important thing I can do is encourage you to make your own mistakes and learn from them.

Unfortunately, making mistakes in our society is frowned upon. Our society wants us to listen to "smart people," memorize their "right answers," and not make mistakes. If you make mistakes, you will be punished.

Rather than punishment, I have found that Fuller's ways of learning from mistakes starts with first admitting you made a mistake and then using love and compassion to learn God's customized lesson, just for you. Then mistakes will make you smarter.

An Important Lesson

From Sunday School, I learned "lead us not into temptation."

In today's dysfunctional society, the temptation is to:

1. **Pretend** to never make mistakes. People like to pretend they are perfect. These people treat mistakes like cats covering up their mess in kitty litter, pretending the kitty litter is clean.

2. **Lie**. I remember President Bill Clinton saying, "I did not have sexual relations with that woman." Having sex is not a crime. On December 19, 1998, he was impeached for lying under oath.

3. **Make excuses**. Excuses are like air fresheners: although the bathroom may smell good, you can still smell the lie.

4. **Blame** is really two words: "be" and "lame." Someone who blames is a wimp not willing to take responsibility and learn.

5. **Go to court.** Sue the person who caught you in the lie. Keep the lie going for years. This has happened to me twice. I was sued after discovering people I trusted were cheating, lying, and stealing.

6. **Go big or go home.** Rather than cut their losses, people will double down or "bet the ranch," hoping to win back all their losses. They go big and most go home broke.

I suspect many Ponzi schemes are created when the promoter keeps lying and raising more money, robbing Peter to pay Paul, to cover their mistakes, their losses. I suspect that is what happened to Bernie Madoff, promoter of the largest Ponzi scheme—$65 billion—in American history. He could not admit he had lost investors' money, so he kept raising more and more investors... and kept losing.

Bernie Madoff should be running the U.S. government, the biggest Ponzi scheme in world history.

LESSON: LEAD US NOT INTO TEMPTATION.

It is better to be loving and compassionate to yourself and admit you made a mistake, than to punish yourself and others for their mistakes. Then you may learn what God wanted you to learn, even if you did not like the lesson.

In real life, simple apologies are better than lawsuits—and less expensive.

If more of us treated mistakes in a loving and compassionate way, I think we would have a more peaceful, prosperous, and intelligent world.

Mistakes Are the Key to Success

Thomas Edison changed the world by making mistakes. He reported failing 3,000 times before inventing the electric lightbulb.

Henry Ford went bankrupt before Ford Motor Company became a success.

And Jeff Bezos' Amazon-offshoot zShops failed.

Larry Ellison struggled for years and was on the verge of bankruptcy and mortgaging everything before Oracle took off.

Fred Smith received a failing grade in business school for his business plan which today is FedEx. Colonel Sanders had to reinvent himself many times and found himself broke at age 65 before KFC succeeded.

Higher Levels of Teacher

Take another look at the diagram of the Higher Levels of Teacher on the following page. You will see the difference between real and fake teachers.

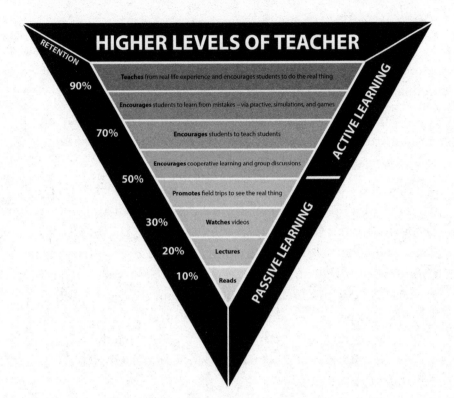

Fake teachers teach from the bottom of the Higher Levels diagram. Real teachers teach from the top. The biggest difference of all lies in the second line—simulating real experience. In real life, that is called *practice*.

Practice is how a person makes his or her mistakes before doing the real thing.

My rich dad had his son and me "practice" by playing *Monopoly*. Then he took us to see his real green houses, which would one day become a huge red hotel.

Kim and I designed the *CASHFLOW* game so that people could learn by making mistakes with play money.

When you learn in the real world from a stockbroker, financial planner, or real estate broker, you "do the real thing" with real money—your money.

The Power of Practice

Tiger Woods did not become the greatest golfer in the world without practicing, making millions of mistakes, and hitting millions of practice golf balls.

George Clooney, the actor, did not become a famous moving star until after he kept practicing, showing up, and interviewing for smaller parts.

And in his book *Outliers,* author Malcolm Gladwell states no band in history practiced more the Beatles. Gladwell also wrote that talent alone is not sufficient to guarantee success. The difference is hours of practice. He cites a survey of violinists at a Berlin academy that found that those musicians who were likely to become music teachers had practiced roughly 4,000 hours in the course of their career. Good performers, meanwhile, had practiced around 8,000 hours. Elite, world-class performers, on the other hand, had all practiced upward of 10,000 hours since first picking up the instrument.

If a person practiced four hours a day, it would take nearly seven years of practice to become world-class.

The Beatles played up to eight hours a night for years before becoming successes.

Doctors, lawyers, and dentists do not call their business a business. Professionals call their business a practice. They practice on you.

Translation: Real teachers practice what they teach. Fake teachers do not.

That is why my first real estate teacher encouraged us to look at 100 properties over 90 days before buying anything. He was a real teacher.

My accounting teacher was not a real accountant. He had no real-life experience. He required us to listen to him talk, memorize his answers, take his tests, and not make mistakes. He was a fake teacher.

"You're Fired!"

In today's world, people who make mistakes are fired.

At The Rich Dad Company, everyone works as a team and is encouraged to own their own businesses—and to make mistakes.

The only time anyone at Rich Dad is fired is if they lie about making a mistake.

As Fuller said, "Mistakes are sins only when not admitted."

People Teaching People

Again, Kim and I designed the *CASHFLOW* game so people could teach people. Many of the deals in the game are real deals— deals Kim and I worked on. Many of them failed.

It frustrates me when someone says to me, "I played your game once. It was fun."

The people who gain the most value from the game are those who play it at least 10 times and then teach 10 people. As the saying goes, give and you shall receive.

A better saying is, teach and you will learn.

Many CASHFLOW Clubs meet regularly, play the game, hold classes, compare real deals and real investments, cooperate, teach, and learn from other.

There are rules. Rules like no "pitching deals" to members or dating members. As you know, money and sex can interfere with real learning.

Learning can be fun and profitable if the rules, morals, ethics, and laws are followed.

The beauty of CASHFLOW Clubs is not how much money you make. As Gladwell argues, it's the number of hours you practice. If you join a CASHFLOW Club, your most important job is to practice, learn, teach, and support others as they learn. There are no guarantees, but I suspect if you commit to learning and teaching you will see those efforts deliver a solid ROI.

Real Assets

One of your most important assets is good people, people who are honest, law-abiding, moral, ethical, and generous with their knowledge, experience, and wisdom. These are people who love learning, practicing, doing the real thing, and learning from their mistakes.

As Gladwell found, real learning requires thousands of hours or practice. The good news is that, rather than try to get rich quick, if a person keeps learning, keeps practicing, keeps learning from their mistakes and the mistakes of others, real financial success is in their real future.

LESSON: Mistakes are the key to real success.

Why Losers Keep Losing

Rich dad often said, "The fear of losing creates more losers."

One reason why the study of economics does not work is because economists, the academic elite, believe that when it comes to money, people are rational. We all know that's not true. When it comes to money, people are *not* rational. Yet our academic elite economists, such as former Fed Chairman Ben Bernanke, do not know this. They actually believe people will work hard, pay taxes, live below their means, pay their bills, save money, and avoid debt.

That may be why Ben Bernanke, the most powerful banker in the world earned only $199,700 in 2013. He thinks everyone thinks like him. Most entrepreneurs would not work for that amount of money, which is why employees and entrepreneurs are so different.

Money is a crazy subject. People do crazy things for money, even kill a loved one, deal in drugs, sell their body, marry for money, or work at a job they hate.

The Subject of Risk

Nobel Prize winners found out some interesting things about people and money. One thing I found particularly interesting had to do with the subject of risk. They found:

The more a person avoids financial risk the greater financial risks they take.

Risk-averse people fall into four distinct categories.

The Worker: Often, a risk-averse person will work three low-paying jobs.

That is why so many people have a full-time job, then drive for Uber, and take a job on the weekends. Earning more money in the E and S quadrants means moving into ever higher tax brackets and sacrificing time with family, the people they love the most.

The Gambler: A risk-averse person will play the lottery, bet on the ponies or sporting events, or go to Las Vegas and pretend to be a high-roller.

Although everyone knows these "gambles" are built on losers, many risk-averse people hallucinate about "getting lucky."

The Student: The reason student loan debt is the U.S. government's number one asset is because there is a quasi-religious belief in education, that a good education can be salvation from the harsh cruel world.

When I ask most people, "What did school teach you about money?" all I get back is a blank stare. Or they say, "I learned about economics."

Bad news: economics is not money. Economics is based upon the belief that people are rational when it comes to money. Besides, economics is a soft science, not subject to the rigors of a real science, political manipulation, or greed and fear.

The Criminal: Many honest, risk-averse people become petty criminals. They work for cash, so they do not have to pay taxes.

They may sell a few recreational drugs on the side, hack into databases and steal identities, or earn a few dollars in the online sex trade.

The Investment Classes

When I speak to these types of risk-averse people about taking investment classes, they often say, "Investing is risky."

An example I have heard used to describe economists Daniel Kahneman and Amos Tversky's findings is:

> *A person needs to feed his family. He is given two choices to hunt wild game. One path has lots of wild game… but because it has lots of game, there are lions who feed on the game. The second path has no game. The game is all gone. Because there is no game, there are no lions. The risk-averse person will take the second path.*

Going to School

Most students are taught by teachers who have chosen the second path.

Revisiting Fuller's words from his book *Intuition*:

> *In love-generated fear for their children's future life in days beyond their own survival, parents train their children to avoid making mistakes lest they be put at a social disadvantage.*
>
> *Mistakes are sins only when not admitted.*
>
> *[God] speaks to each of us directly—and speaks only through our individual awareness of truth and our most spontaneous and powerful emotions of love and compassion.*

The next time you or someone else makes a mistake, don't punish them. Treat yourself and others as God would treat you. Treat them and yourself with love and compassion.

Babies would never learn to walk if they did not fall. Humans would not be flying to distant planets if hundreds of inventors, such as the Wright brothers, had not risked crashing.

And I would not be a rich man today if I had listened to Elaine, the receptionist at Xerox, who said I would fail and return to Xerox. After I failed, I got stupider, borrowed $100,000 from my poor dad, then handed the money over to Stanley, who ran away with it.

If I had not made so many stupid mistakes—many much bigger than $100,000—and learned from them, I would not be a rich man today.

The key to learning is being humble, being willing to say, "I screwed up." Then seek wiser men and women and learn from them. That is true learning.

Origins of Education

The word "education" comes from the Latin word *educere*, which means to draw out.

Unfortunately, our school system does not draw out. It puts in. In many cases, fake answers from fake teachers, teachers who punish students for not repeating those fake answers on fake intelligence tests, and then implanting (by force and threat) the insane idea that "mistakes make you stupid."

Today, millions of students leave school deeply in debt, searching for high-paying jobs that are rapidly disappearing, having learned little about money, terrified of making mistakes, angry and living in fear of failing.

Many of their parents and grandparents are in the same boat.

The Fear of Failure

The fear of failure is a powerful human emotion. The fear of failure is a three-sided coin, with heads, tails, and the edge of the coin.

Fake education involves only one side of the coin. Real education requires each of us to stand on the edge of the coin and see both sides.

On One Side of the Coin...

For most people, the fear of financial failure paralyzes them, keeps them small, poor, and obedient. They often work at jobs that kill their spirit—a little more every day they go to work. A few turn to crime and violence in order to survive.

Fake education causes people to be fearful of failing. The fear of failing also causes many to become cocky, arrogant, and greedy. Many of these people believe they are better, smarter, and richer than others. They often look down on people they feel are not as smart, attractive, or rich as they are.

The Other Side of the Coin

For a few people, the fear of failing financially inspires them to learn, to become real students, and to seek real teachers. Mistakes are not failure. For this person, mistakes are real learning experiences. Each failure—although painful—is a lesson in humility, for only through genuine humility, does a person learn.

Fake education causes a person to be cocky and arrogant, with a fixed mindset of, "I am right. I never make mistakes."

Real education, on the other side of the coin, inspires people to make mistakes, to be humble, and to learn from their mistakes. For this person, mistakes make them smarter, richer, more generous, and a more *human* human being.

Real education inspires sharing, generosity, love, and compassion for other people, our planet, and ourselves. Real education promotes love and compassion because real education teaches. We are all human beings, and real human beings make mistakes.

Real teachers have made mistakes. Fake teachers have not.

Lesson: Mistakes are God's real teachers.

YOUR QUESTIONS... ROBERT'S ANSWERS

Q: When buying gold and silver, how do you know who to trust?

Cameron R. – USA

A: "Let the buyer beware" is true even when buying real gold.

Lately, there have been many instances of fake or "salted gold" being sold. "Salted gold" is gold that contains impurities—base metals like nickel and tin added in the bar.

Salting gold is the same trick the Roman government used as the Roman Empire collapsed.

Recently, China rejected a large shipment of gold bars from the United States because the bars were salted, not pure. The bad news is, those gold bars are still floating around the country.

The way I find "reputable" dealers is by asking innocent, conversational questions.

1. How long have you been selling gold and silver?
2. Why do you deal in gold and silver?
3. May I talk to one or two of your customers?
4. Do you recommend rare coins for beginners?
5. Where should I store my coins?
6. What is the difference between 999 gold and 9999 gold?

The dealer's answers to those general questions should give you some insight into the wisdom, experience, and the soul of the gold dealer.

Again, when buying anything, the real answer is always:

"Let the buyer beware."

Q: What's your best advice for finding and choosing good and trustworthy partners? What things do you look for in employees, in advisors, in partners?

Marshall B. – Argentina

A: That is the multimillion-dollar question. A business partnership is like a marriage partnership. If you find the right partner, life is heaven. If you find the wrong partner, it can be hell.

The good news is that all of my bad partners have led to great partners. For example, I met every one of my good advisors as a result of bad advisors.

The two most important questions to ask when looking for a great partner are:

1. "Am I a great partner?"
2. "What do I have to do to become a better partner?"

Q: Why is it bad to buy real estate using equity instead of debt? I know that banks give debt not equity. I want to understand the shortcoming and benefits connected to equity, as you have outlined with debt.

Stanley P. - Poland

A: An important question…to which I offer five answers:

1. I do it for the challenge.
   Buying one property with 100 percent cash is easy.
   Buying 100 properties with 100 percent debt is hard.
2. Debt is dangerous.
   There is less risk using cash. There is a lot of risk using debt. If you want to use debt to invest, please take real investment seminars.
3. After 1971, the U.S. dollar became debt.
   Most people become poorer working for dollars (equity/cash). The challenge was to become richer acquiring assets, increasing income, and reducing taxes—using debt.
4. I wanted to live my life in the B and I quadrants—the Business and Investor quadrants—of the CASHFLOW Quadrant.

People in the E (Employee) and S (Specialist of Small Business Owner) quadrants use debt to become poorer.

People in the B (Big Business) and I (Investor) quadrants use debt to become richer.

In 1972, I took my first real estate seminar. In 1972, I learned to transform debt into equity. Without financial education, most people turn equity into debt.

5. The Infinite Return
    The goal of the B and I quadrants is to achieve an *infinite return* on every investment.

    An *infinite return* is the ability to make money without using any of your money.

    An *infinite return* is a sign of very high financial IQ.

    Financial IQ measures the size of financial problem a person can solve.

    Financial IQ is measured in dollars. For example, a survey found that the average American cannot solve a $400 money problem. That means they have less than a $400 FIQ.

    A person who knows how to turn *debt* into *equity* can solve very large financial problems. On the flip side, a person who turns *equity* into *debt* can cause very large financial problems.

Chapter Eleven

HOW GOING TO SCHOOL KEEPS PEOPLE POOR

BUCKING AN OBSOLETE SYSTEM

"**Y**ou can't do that here."

I have heard that statement a thousand times.

No matter where I am in the world, every time I explain my rich dad's lessons on money, debt, and taxes—and what I do in real life—people always say, "You can't do that here."

And that person is right. *They* can't do what I do. But I can. And I do. And I can do it virtually anywhere in the world. That is the power of real education.

In other words, real education empowers people. It empowers them to do things others can't. And, in many cases, things they thought might never be possible for them.

Fake education keeps people poor, small, limited, and tethered to tiny filaments of life, limited by limiting thoughts.

"I Can't"

The most destructive words a person can use are the words "I can't."

Especially when those words are tied to money: "I can't afford it."

What Causes Poverty?

When it comes to the cause of financial poverty, it is those few, short words—"I can't afford it"—that keep people poor... and keep people small.

If a person cannot change those words into the question "How can I afford it?" they will always live in financial poverty, no matter how much money they may make.

I Wish

The other day, a friend's wife asked me, "Where are you going this year?"

I said, "This year I will be in Australia, Japan, Africa, and Europe."

She replied, "I wish I could do that... but I can't afford it."

Which takes me back to the opening thought of this chapter: wherever I am in the world, when I explain how I use debt and taxes to get richer, someone always says, "You can't do that here."

As you know, when one finger points forward, three fingers point back. These statements—challenges, charges... whatever you choose to call them—are as much about the person making the statement as they are about me.

And that is the problem with going to school. Without real financial education, most people spend their lives saying things like:

"I can't afford it."

"You can't do that."

"I wish I could do that."

Education Creates Poor Dads

Rich Dad Poor Dad is really about my poor dad. My poor dad is a metaphor for the inadequacy, obsolescence, and delusion of modern education's inability to prepare students for the real world.

I have asked millions of people, countless times, "What did school teach you about money?"

The answer is usually a blank stare, or statements like "I studied economics," or "I learned to balance a checkbook."

Sorry, but economics and balancing a checkbook are not the same as learning about money.

Every time I ask what someone learned in school about money, it is meant to be a spear directed into the heart and soul of modern education.

My People Are Destroyed

As I learned in Sunday School, Hosea 4:6 (NIV): "My people are destroyed from lack of knowledge. Because you have rejected knowledge, I also reject you as my priests; because you have ignored the law of your God, I also will ignore your children."

I am not selling religion. I am quoting ancient wisdom.

Those who direct our modern educational system need to look into a mirror and ask themselves:

> *What knowledge am I rejecting?*
> *What subjects are we not teaching?*
> *Why do so many people hate school?*
> *Why do so many people say going to school was a waste of time?*
> *Why is the subject of money not taught in school?*
> *Why are the priests of education—the teachers—paid so poorly?*
> *Why are so many students leaving school crippled with student loan debt?*

Those questions are reflected in my poor dad, a great man who dedicated his life to public education and, unfortunately, an educational system that failed him.

"You Can't Do That Here."

A few months ago, I was invited to speak at a local church, where I did my usual talk on debt, taxes, and why the rich are getting richer. Asking for questions at the end, an irate parishioner, raised his hand and said, "You can't do that here."

I pointed out to him that the church was less than five miles from my house and I assured him I was doing what I said I was doing. Right here. And then I reaffirmed to those in the audience that what I was doing—here—was being done by the rich all over the world. That is why the rich are getting richer.

The person who asked the question stood and said, "I am a medical doctor. I have the best financial advisors, and I know you cannot do what you say you are doing."

Having gone through this fire drill all over the world, I asked, "What do you invest in?"

"I am a medical doctor in private practice. That is why I have an IRA. I have millions in savings, and I own my house and a vacation condo, free and clear."

"Is that it?" I asked.

He nodded his head and waiting for my answer.

"You're right." I replied. "You can't do what I do… but I can."

Rich Dad's CASHFLOW Quadrant

The medical doctor is obviously a highly educated man. As a private practitioner, he operates out of the S quadrant, the small business, self-employed quadrant. He also invests from the S quadrant, and he pays taxes out of the S quadrant, the quadrant that typically pays the highest percentage in taxes.

And he is right. He cannot do what I do.

Changing Quadrants

In 1973, the year I signed up for an MBA program, I was in school, preparing to find a job in the E quadrant, as an employee.

That same year, 1973, I signed up for a real estate course, a seminar to learn to be a professional investor, in the I quadrant.

The reason most people cannot do what I do is because they went to school to be in the E or S quadrants and are passive investors, not professional investors.

A medical doctor telling me I cannot do what I do is as ludicrous as saying to me, "You cannot fly because I cannot fly."

The reason I can fly is because I spent five years in flight school, flying professionally, and flying in Vietnam.

I can do what I do financially because I went to school in the B and I quadrants. The education is different for different quadrants.

The Power of Education

Real education should empower you to do anything you want to do.

If you want to become a doctor, go to medical school. If you want to be a pilot, go to flight school.

If you want to learn to be rich… where do you go? That is the power of real education.

The problem is that most people leave school, disempowered. Many leave the educational system hating school. When they run into something they cannot do, they say, "I can't do that." Just like the limiting thoughts that trigger statements like "I can't afford that" or "You can't do that." Rather than seek real education and real teachers, they close their minds—and their options.

Is Education Obsolete?

The second part of this book—**Part Two: Fake Teachers**—is the most important part of this book ... because there is nothing more important than education.

There would be no need for **Part One: Fake Money** if our educational system were functional.

There would be no need for **Part Three: Fake Assets** if education were real.

If our educational system offered and delivered real financial education and real spiritual education, our leaders would not get away with printing fake money or selling fake assets.

That is why Part II is the most important part of this book.

There is nothing more important than real education—academic, professional, spiritual, and financial education. All are important today.

Disempowering Education

The reason people challenge me saying "You can't do that" is because our educational system is designed to keep people powerless.

As stated earlier, most of our greatest universities were started by and funded by robber barons, men like John D. Rockefeller, Cornelius Vanderbilt, Leland Stanford, and Cecil Rhodes.

Their interest in education was fueled by their need to find the best and brightest students, educate them, and train them to work for *them*—employees who would do their bidding, but entrepreneurs or innovators who would compete against them.

As Bucky Fuller said, the reason the robber barons founded the country's greatest universities was to look for the best and brightest minds, and teach them to be Es (executive employees) or Ss (specialists such as lawyers and accountants) who would work for the rich, but not *be* a rich person in the B or I quadrants.

That may be why our greatest entrepreneurs like Bill Gates, Steve Jobs, Michael Dell, and Mark Zuckerberg dropped out of great schools. Apparently, they were not receiving the education they needed: education for the B and I quadrants.

Changing Quadrants

Today, millions of people are stuck in jobs they hate or jobs that don't pay enough—or both. They know they need to change. The problem is, they are afraid of changing. And they do not know how to change. Their education, or lack of education, keeps them stuck... afraid of failing, afraid of changing.

When I explain the differences between the four quadrants, I see many people who want to change. The problem is, to be able to change quadrants, from the E-and-S side to the B-and-I side requires real spiritual and real financial education.

That is why most people remain paralyzed, like my highly educated poor dad. After my poor dad challenged the governor of Hawaii and lost the election, he was unable to stand back up. It was the first time in his life that he had failed. His education had trapped him in the E quadrant. He was unable to change quadrants, even though he was unemployed. He bought an ice cream franchise to get into the S quadrant and failed. He was not an entrepreneur. He could not get out of his E-quadrant education and mindset. He could not change.

Invisible Poverty

Schools teach people to be poor with a term known as *invisible poverty*.

Schools reinforce *invisible poverty* by:

1. Punishing students for making mistakes
2. Teaching that mistakes make you stupid
3. Memorizing answers rather than learning by making mistakes
4. Decreeing that there is only one right answer that the teachers have
5. Delineating right versus wrong, rather than the concept of three sides to every coin
6. Lacking real financial education
7. Viewing cooperation as cheating
8. Taking tests on your own
9. Making it unacceptable to ask for help
10. Never saying, "I don't know"
11. Not helping others
12. Grading on the bell curve, where there are smart people and stupid people

The Crisis

Bucky Fuller was a futurist. In the opening statement to his 1982 book *Critical Path*, he writes:

Twilight of the World's Power Structures

"Humanity is moving ever deeper into crisis—a crisis without precedent."

Being a futurist, he was not talking about a crisis in 1981. He was warning of the crisis we are facing today, the crisis the Class of 1981 Baby Boomers would face the 21st century.

Accelerating Acceleration

Fuller was warning of a phenomenon he called *accelerating acceleration*. Accelerating acceleration would occur when humanity transitioned from the Industrial Age to the Information Age.

Prior to his death in 1983, the futurist predicted there would be a new invention that would radically change the world before the end of the decade.

In 1969, a decade prior, the foundation of the Internet, known as the ARPANET, was released to the world.

The Advanced Research Projects Agency Network was an arm of the U.S. Defense Department. Its initial purpose was to link computers at Pentagon-funded research institutions over telephone lines.

In 1989, with the invention of the World Wide Web by Sir Tim Berners-Lee, the world transitioned from the Industrial Age into the Information Age, and *accelerating acceleration* began.

Education, however, has not changed. Education remains frozen in time.

Repeating the lesson from Sunday School, Hosea 4:6 (NIV): "My people are destroyed from lack of knowledge. Because you have rejected knowledge, I also reject you as my priests; because you have ignored the law of your God, I also will ignore your children."

In the 21st century, billions are being destroyed from lack of knowledge.

And as Fuller warned in *Critical Path*:

"Humanity is moving ever deeper into crisis—a crisis without precedent."

Speaking to our class in 1981, he explained the reason why billions of people were in trouble. "Change in the Information Age is invisible," he said. "People do not get out of the way of things they cannot see moving toward them."

Rich dad was making a very similar statement when he said "money became invisible" in 1971 when Nixon suspended the convertibility of dollars into gold.

In *Critical Path*, Fuller writes:

Because of my driving conviction that all of humanity is in peril of extinction if one of us does not dare, now and henceforth, always to tell only the truth, and all the truth, and to do so promptly—right now.

Talking to Parents

After Fuller passed on, I have warned parents of education's failure to prepare their children for the real world, warning of education's reinforcement of "invisible poverty."

I mention that schools:

1. Punish students for making mistakes
2. View cooperation as cheating
3. Make you take tests on your own
4. Discourage you from asking for help
5. Discourage you from helping others
6. Grade on the bell curve

Nearly 100 percent of the time the parents say, "I know education is in trouble. But not in my child's school. My child's school is doing a great job. My kids are happy, they have fun, they cooperate, and they love their teacher."

Or they say, "My children are very bright. One is in a great law school and the other is in graduate school working on his PhD. Both will have good, high-paying, secure jobs."

As Fuller warned, "People do not get out of the way of things they cannot see."

Sunday *New York Times Book Review*, July 15, 2018

"BARELY AFLOAT IN AMERICA"

This is an excerpt by Robert Reich, U.S. Secretary of Labor from 1993 to 1997. Concerned about the changes in employment that are on the way, Reich writes:

I'm not just referring to big-brained robots taking over civilization from us smaller-brained humans, but the more imminent possibility they'll take over our jobs.

It's already happening. Robots and related forms of artificial intelligence are rapidly supplanting what remain of factory workers, call-center operators, and clerical staff. Amazon and other online platforms are booting out retail workers. We'll soon be saying goodbye to truck drivers, warehouse personnel, and professionals who can do whatever can be replicated, including pharmacists, accountants, attorneys, diagnosticians, translators, and financial advisors. Machines may soon do a better job than doctors at scanning for cancer.

This does not mean a future without jobs, as some doomsayers predict. But robots will almost certainly push down wages in all the remaining human-touch jobs (child care, elder care, home health care, personal coaches, sales, and so on) that robots can't do because they're not, well, human. Even today, with technology having already displaced many workers, there's no job crisis. … Instead we have a good jobs crisis. … Today's typical American worker earns around $44,500 a year, not much more than what the typical worker earned in 1979, adjusted for inflation. Nearly 80 percent of adult Americans say they live from paycheck to paycheck, many not knowing how big their next paycheck will be.

I offer this warning to parents: in the Information Age—because change and money are invisible—without real financial education, how can parents know what schools have (and have not) taught their children?

All most parents know is what they were taught in school. They do not know what was missing from their education.

That is why most parents I talk to say, "My child is in a good school."

Without real education, the gap between the rich and everyone else will grow, even if kids do well in school.

If the gap between rich and poor grows, the probability of civil unrest and revolution grows as well.

Human Assets and Liabilities

As we grew older, rich dad made his son and me aware of *human* assets and liabilities—not just financial assets and liabilities.

Rich dad drew the following diagram for his son and me.

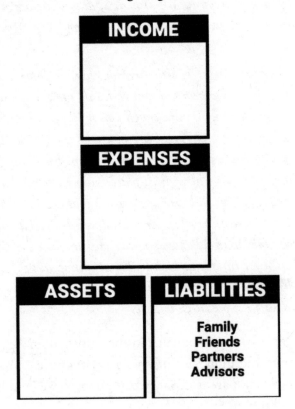

Rich dad then said, "Your greatest assets are people. So people are your greatest liabilities."

When a parent says these words to me—"I know education is in trouble, but my child goes to a great school"—I draw the same diagram of human assets and liabilities.

Once the class had an idea of how a financial statement works—especially assets putting money in their pockets and liabilities taking money from their pockets—I would then show them rich dad's balance sheet of people.

I would ask the class to look at the financial statement and discuss who are assets and who are liabilities in their lives today and in the future.

Discussions are awkward at first. No one wants to label anyone a liability.

Yet, as the discussions progressed, a few truths start to come to the surface.

As truths begin to be told, I hear statements such as:

- "My son dropped out of school, and now I have to pay off his student loan debt. He still can't find a job."
- "My daughter's husband is a drug addict. She left him with her five kids and now she lives at home with us. She has a college degree but can't work because three of her kids are under 12 years of age."
- "My father lost his job as an executive when the store he worked for closed. He has used up his 401(k) savings. Now he lives with us. He wants to work but can't find a high-paying job."
- "My financial advisor's advice has not made me any money. I am six years from retirement. I am wondering how I will be able to retire."
- "My business partner is ill. Now I have to support him and his family."
- "I owe back taxes. The government is threatening to garnish my wages. The reason I owe back taxes is because I do not earn enough to live on. I can't even

afford to live paycheck to paycheck. I fall further behind every month. On top of that, I can't afford prescriptions for my wife and me."

At the end of the discussion, I ask, "Do you still think education is preparing people for the real world?"

It's a warning that bears repeating: In the Information Age, because change is invisible and money is invisible, without real financial education how parents know what schools have not taught and are not teaching their children?

One of Fuller's reasons for writing *Critical Path* was:

"Because of my driving conviction that all of humanity is in peril of extinction if each one of us does not dare, now and henceforth, always to tell only the truth, and all the truth, and to do so promptly—right now."

Translation: For humanity to survive, each of us needs to start telling the truth. When people start talking about the human liabilities in their lives, they start telling the truth about the inadequacy of their children's and their own education.

Simply put, education is failing to prepare people for a changing world of accelerating acceleration, a world of invisible change and invisible money.

Without real spiritual education, people are paralyzed because fake teachers teach them not to make mistakes and not to ask for help, because asking for help is cheating.

Without real financial education, people are blind because it is easier for the academic elite to steal the wealth of blind people via the money they work for.

Without real spiritual and real financial education, you are right. *You cannot do what I do.*

This is not new information. It's stood the test of time in the Bible: "My people are destroyed from lack of knowledge."

There is good news. In the next chapter, you will learn about entrepreneurs in education, people who are doing what needs to be done... outside the obsolete educational system.

YOUR QUESTIONS... ROBERT'S ANSWERS

Q: Isn't there value in a college education, apart from the academics?

Gary B. – Singapore

A: Sure there is. For many people, college can be the first time they're exposed to a wide variety of points of view. It's a time to test wings and boundaries... a time to experience new things and meet new people who, in many cases, will have different backgrounds, ideas, and opinions. Education takes many forms, and the college experience is one of them. What each person must weigh is the ROI, the return on the investment into a traditional college education and the potential burden of student-loan debt. There is no one-size-fits-all formula and each person must evaluate the pros and cons as well as his or her goals and vision for the future against the expense.

Q: What irks you most about most traditional education?

Adam C. — Czech Republic

A: A few things, actually—and they're all connected. Bottom line is that traditional education does not prepare people, of any age, for the real world. We don't exist or work in silos... we need to cooperate and collaborate. School calls that "cheating." And, in my opinion, the true measure (and test) of intelligence is our ability to be open minded enough to evaluate and appreciate other points of view, other ways at looking at things. In school, there's usually one "right answer." In the real world, the "right answer" is often dependent upon individual circumstances or conditions.

Q: When you say that saying "I can't" or "I can't afford it" shuts down your mind, what do you mean?

Cecilia J. – United Kingdom

A: I mean that statements like those close your mind to possibilities. It's small thinking—when you should be thinking big… or at least *bigger*. If you ask yourself, instead, "How can I afford it?" you are engaging your brain to think of ideas, solutions, and opportunities.

Q: Would it be better to start learning in university with lower cost and then try to move to a better one?

Agim B. – Estonia

A: Each of us needs to decide what's right for us. The value of any particular 'school'—university or otherwise—is often a product of the student.

Q: So what IS real education?

Billy K. – South Africa

A: Real education should empower you to do whatever it is that you want to do. That education comes from real teachers— people who have actually done what you want to do—and you should be an active participant in the process.

Q: In this age of "accelerating acceleration" with information overload and everything moving so fast… how do you know who you can trust?

Alexi C. – Turkey

A: That's the million-dollar question, isn't it? And, as with so many things in life, the answer starts with education. It starts with *you* becoming smarter so you can better evaluate truth from lies, and what's real and true from what's fake.

Q: How can I learn the language of money?

Angela S. – New Zealand

A: Start with expanding your vocabulary related to words about money, finance and the economy. Words have power. Learn a new word every day... and soon you'll find that you hear those words on television and on the radio... and see them in news articles or on the Internet. Take the time to understand what you hear and read—and if you don't understand something find someone who can explain it to you and discuss it with you.

Q: I've always felt that a huge part of education is the responsibility of parents. What's your take on that?

Justin J. – USA

A: Well... since I call my most powerful mentor "rich dad," I guess the answer to that question is pretty obvious. Our parents are our first, and in many cases best, teachers. This is especially true if parents raise children who are naturally curious, eager to explore and experience, willing to ask questions, and open to considering more than a single 'right answer.' Most important, perhaps, is that parents can have a huge impact on how a child views mistakes. Mistakes are how we learn—and there's a lesson in every one of them. Mistakes are opportunities to learn... positive experiences in our learning-curve-of-life.

Chapter Twelve

ENTREPRENEURS IN EDUCATION

CAN YOU SEE THE FUTURE?

I n July 2018, U.S. President Donald Trump issued an executive order proclaiming the reeducation and retraining of American workers. Many big corporations are behind the president's education initiative.

This is an example of fake news. President Trump's executive order sounds great, a great idea, obviously timed to attract more votes from workers.

REAL NEWS: The real news is that the United States already spends over $1 billion a year on reeducation and retraining of its work force.

REAL NEWS: The real new is that reeducation and retraining programs are not working.

Why Reeducation Does Not Work

The idea of retraining and reeducation is a noble idea. The problem is that reeducation programs, as they exist, have not worked. And the reason the programs do not work is because our educational methods do not work.

All one has to do is look at the Higher Levels of Teacher diagram and it becomes apparent that how we teach is obsolete, ineffective, and boring.

As stated earlier, one of the greatest crimes of education is how many young people leave school hating school. How many people struggle financially because they left school hating school? How many people are in jail because they hated school? How many people are stuck in jobs they hate… because they hated school?

Granted, traditional education does a great job for approximately 25 percent of the population. The chaos that it creates for the other 75 percent is the problem. I was on the borderline, often close to dropping out because I hated school. I knew I was not stupid. I had high aptitude scores. I just hated traditional schools, traditional teachers, and especially the boring process of traditional education.

Eight life events saved me from quitting school:

1. Being an apprentice to rich dad and working in a real business.
2. Rich dad teaching via the game of *Monopoly*. He made learning fun.
3. Having great teachers such as my fifth-grade teacher, Harold Ely, a teacher who inspired me to learn, rather than memorize answers.
4. Attending a military academy, rather than a traditional university.
5. Attending seminars regularly rather than returning to traditional schools for advanced degrees.
6. Following the three wise men from the Bible, constantly seeking great teachers, outside the educational system.
7. Having two dads and learning that all coins have three sides.
8. Learning that in real life there is more than one right answer.

President Kennedy and Education

President Trump is not the first president to propose the reeducation of our displaced workers.

As Steven Brill recounts in his book *Tailspin*, in 1962, President John F. Kennedy proposed that the United States expand global trade by lowering tariffs and restrictions on foreign imports. Both Republicans and Democrats were tentatively in favor of trade liberalization at the time during the Cold War, though the Republicans were more protectionist.

Kennedy was aware expanding global trade would wipe out U.S. jobs. That is why, in 1962, he also proposed the formation of TAA, Trade Adjustment Assistance, a federal program to reeducate unemployed workers.

President Kennedy did want not a small group of workers who would lose their jobs to be the price for a national benefit to millions of Americans. Kennedy said:

> *When considerations of national policy make it desirable to avoid higher tariffs, those injured by that [foreign] competition should not be required to bear the full brunt of the impact. Rather, the burden of economic adjustment should be borne in part by the Federal Government.*

TRANSLATION: Lower tariffs will benefit America and Americans. A few will lose their jobs. The burden of reeducation of unemployed workers should be the responsibility of the federal government.

Kennedy's TAA offered displaced workers as much as 65 percent of the individual's average weekly wage for 52 weeks (and up to 65 weeks for workers over age 60), and enrollment in education and training programs "to develop higher and different skills."

The program also provided funds to families if they needed to relocate to find a new job.

Strong Opposition

President Kennedy's program faced strong opposition from Republicans. One of the most vocal opponents was Senator Prescott Bush, father and grandfather of future presidents George H.W. Bush and George W. Bush. In spite of the opposition, Kennedy succeeded in getting TAA passed.

TAA has had mixed reviews. It's been reported that during the first six years after its passage—and although TAA came with a $1 billion price tag—not a single worker had received assistance from the government. For most workers who lost their jobs, TAA proved to be an extension of unemployment insurance, not education or job retraining.

One reason why workers did not use the education and retraining program was due to TAA's educational requirements, the prerequisites before the worker was qualified to receive educational assistance.

Workers had to complete a high school equivalency and enroll full-time in a community college or vocational school before TAA allocated funds for further education and training. This was impractical because most workers needed to replace lost income as soon as possible. They could not afford to go back to school before they received TAA funds for education and training.

EBT vs. Education

Earlier in this book I mentioned that in 1994 the sugar plantations left Hilo, Hawaii, and leaving many once-highly paid workers unemployed. Many sugar plantation workers did not have a high school diploma, because they did not need a high school education to get a high-paying job. Today, rather than receive the education and retraining they need, many live on EBT cards.

Rather than reeducate workers, which would return them to being taxpayers in a capitalist system, they receive welfare in a socialist system. That is why socialism is growing in America.

As Brill further researches in *Tailspin*, in 2001, the Government Accountability Office (GAO) conducted case studies, including one in Martinsville and Henry County, Virginia. The study found that, of the 6,000 jobs lost in less than a decade, fewer than 20 percent of the TAA-eligible workers enrolled in reeducation programs. Of the 20 percent who did enroll, many dropped out because they could not complete remedial classes and occupational training before their income support expired. Another GAO study found three-quarters of workers who did qualify for TAA never used it. Another TAA program study reported that, the few who did complete the program never ended up with jobs "remotely equivalent to the jobs they had lost."

It's Our Education... Stupid

Our education is the problem. It is what we teach, how we teach, and who teaches that is the problem.

Again, I'll refer to the Higher Levels of Teacher diagram.

1. How many times have you been sitting in class only to realize that your body was there—but your brain wasn't?
2. How many times have you sat in class looking at the time, rather than listening to the teacher?
3. How many times have you crammed for a test, rather than being inspired to learn?

Learning from Rich Dad

I love the Higher Levels of Teacher diagram because it illustrates the difference between my rich dad and my poor dad.

I worked for free as an apprentice for my rich dad, doing the real thing. In exchange, rich dad had us play *Monopoly* and narrated lessons as we moved our pieces around the game board. On a regular basis, we would visit his *real* green houses, which eventually became a giant red hotel.

Real education was fun, exciting, and challenging, certainly never boring.

There were so many times that I got in trouble at home because I came home late. I came home late because I did not want to stop learning from rich dad. I always wanted to learn more.

When I came home late, the only words I heard were, "Have you done your homework? If you don't get good grades, you won't get a good job."

Becoming an Entrepreneur in Education

In 1983, after Fuller passed and I read *Grunch of Giants*, I knew I could no longer remain an entrepreneur in the rock and roll business making a lot of money, producing licensed products for rock bands like Duran Duran, Van Halen, Judas Priest, Boy George, Ted Nugent, and The Police.

Something inside of me told me it was time to become an entrepreneur in education. I did not know how I was going to do it—I just knew I could not keep doing what I was doing.

In 1983, I met Kim, someone who was also searching for her life's purpose. In 1984, we held hands and took our leap of faith, leaving beautiful Hawaii and landing in California. It was not long before our money ran out, yet we kept going. After our money ran out, we were homeless for a week, sleeping in an old brown Toyota Celica at beach parks in San Diego, California, before finally living in the basement of a friend who took us in.

It was our test of faith.

David versus Goliath

In 1983, Kim and I realized we were taking on the educational system of *Grunch* and the academic elites. It was David versus Goliath. What kept us going were friends and family who encouraged us to stay the course, many of whom offered financial assistance, which we never accepted. We were on a mission to find out if there really was a God. And we knew if we accepted money, that money would dilute our faith.

Instead we survived on wisdom from people like Bucky Fuller, who went through a similar test of faith for years, never working for money, only doing what he thought God wanted him to do and constantly asking himself, *What can I do? I'm just a little guy?*

It took Kim and me 10 years to achieve financial freedom. In 1994, Kim and I retired, financially free. Kim was 37, and I was 47.

In 1996, Kim and I created the *CASHFLOW* board game. In 1997, *Rich Dad Poor Dad* was released as a self-published book, because every book editor we approached said that I did not know what I was talking about. In 2000, Oprah called, and the rest is history. In 2002, Donald Trump and I met backstage at an event where we spoke to thousands of raving fans in America and Australia. Since then we have written two books together, becoming partners in real financial education.

In 2008, I was interviewed by Wolf Blitzer on CNN and predicted the crash and bankruptcy of Lehman Brothers. Six months later, Lehman Brothers filed for bankruptcy and the Great Recession began. The gap between the rich, middle class, and poor is growing—just as Donald Trump and I predicted and wrote about in our books.

Repeating Fuller's statements from his introduction to *Critical Path:*

TWILIGHT OF THE WORLD'S POWER STRUCTURES
"Humanity is moving ever deeper into crisis—a crisis without precedent."

TRANSLATION: In 1982, Fuller was warning the Information Age is coming. Grunch will lose its power in the Information Age. The crisis will grow worse because Grunch will fight to hold on to its power.

Desperate people do desperate things.

Fuller also stated the Information Age will usher in the Age of Integrity. Grunch will be exposed. The crisis will accelerate due to Grunch doing anything in its power to hold on to power.

You can sense Grunch holding on for dear life, its central banks being challenged by the people's money, such as Bitcoin.

Another way Grunch holds on to its power is via a corrupted education system, a system without a soul and void of real education.

That is why Kim and I became entrepreneurs in education. Our board game *CASHFLOW* is designed to bypass the education system and return real education to the people of the world, via people teaching people.

People Teaching People

Kim and I designed the *CASHFLOW* game, not to give people answers that people should memorize but to inspire people to learn more, by giving players a tiny glimpse into the possibility of a richer life. Each time a person plays the game, they gain another spiritual glimpse into a brighter future for themselves and their families.

My earlier warning to parents bears repeating, I think: in today's invisible world of technology and money, it is almost impossible for teachers, parents, and students to know what is missing from real education. In the Information Age, it is imperative that people take back control of education from the government.

Clinton and China

In 1962 President John Kennedy, concerned about globalization, introduced TAA.

In 1972, President Richard Nixon opened the door to China.

In 1999, President Bill Clinton encouraged the admission of China into the WTO, the World Trade Organization. Clinton promised that opening trade with China would increase U.S. jobs and reduce our trade deficit.

He also said: "This is a hundred-to-nothing deal for America."

In 2001, China was admitted into the WTO.

As you know, Clinton often has a problem with the truth. The deal turned out to be a hundred-to-nothing deal—in favor of China. As Brill notes in *Tailspin*:

> *From 2000 to 2009, the U.S. trade deficit with China nearly tripled, ballooning from $83 billion to $227 billion. ... Over the same period, the U.S. lost 5.6 million manufacturing jobs, including 627,000 in computer and electronic products. ... By 2016, the trade deficit with China was $347 billion.*

The Side Effects of Trade Deficits

The lopsided trade deficit not only has hurt workers who have lost their jobs. The trade deficit hurt mom-and-pop savers, homeowners, and investors.

The trade deficit contributed to the financial collapse in 2008. Brill writes:

> *Because the Chinese were accumulating so much cash and need a safe place to invest it, they dramatically increased demand for U.S. Treasury bonds. That pushed interest rates in the United States down to unprecedented lows, which contributed to easy money being available to finance even the riskiest mortgages and, with them, the mortgage-backed securities and their derivatives.*

In 2008, the stock market and real estate markets nearly collapsed and interest rates plunged further.

In 2018, the crisis is not over; it's only gotten bigger.

As Fuller wrote in 1981, "Humanity is moving ever deeper into crisis—a crisis without precedent."

The good news is entrepreneurs are coming to the rescue.

Entrepreneurs in Education

One notable entrepreneurial business is Khan Academy, a company that makes academic education available to millions of students throughout the world. Students do not need to take out student loans to learn from Khan Academy.

In *Tailspin*, Brill highlights C4Q, which stands for Coalition for Queens, an educational organization started by Jukay Hsu, a U.S. Army Captain, an Iraq War veteran, and an immigrant born in Taiwan and educated at Harvard. As Hsu tells Brill, "Some of the smartest, hardest-working people I've ever met were soldiers who didn't graduate from college." C4Q teaches non-techies to become techies who are able to write computer code.

While there are many schools and educational programs that teach the same subject, C4Q is different in the way it teaches. A few differences are:

1. Founder Jukay Hsu is not a programmer. He has no computer background or experience.
2. Jukay Hsu hires real teachers from industry, rather than fake teachers from academia.
3. C4Q is run like a military academy. The educational process is devoted to intense team work, with teachers and students working cooperatively, rather than competitively.
4. In 2013, his first class of 21 students earned about $18,000 a year. Most were service workers without much education. 52 percent of graduates are female and 60 percent African Americans. 55 percent lacked college degrees.
5. The 88 recruits who started in September 2016 and graduated in June 2017 landed jobs averaging $85,000 a year. They were hired by companies such as Uber, Blue Apron, Pinterest, Google, BuzzFeed, and J.P. Morgan Chase.

6. The graduates agree to pay the organization 12 percent of their earnings for the following two years.

7. It is not like a student loan, which often traps students who do not graduate or get good jobs into a lifetime of horrible debt.

8. The 12 percent inspires charitable donors to become investors sharing in the returns from successful students, making it more than another "hot charity." Adding a capitalistic profit component to the nonprofit C4Q adds a financial component socialism lacks: financial sustainability.

Brill also highlights Year Up, founded in 2000, another private nonprofit offering reeducation and training for broader mix of job categories. This from *Tailspin*:

> *Year Up currently has 20 locations across the United States and has trained over 18,000 students for technology-related jobs such as hardware repair, help desk operations, and communication skills that employers expect for those filling entry-level, middle-skill jobs.*
>
> *Each student signs a contract committing to tough standards of conduct and participation. They receive 200 points at the beginning and lose points for any transgressions, such as being late, or disrespectful, or failing to complete homework on time.*
>
> *Twenty-five percent, typically, lose their 200 points and are removed from the program.*

Much like a military school, brains and grades at Year Up are not enough.

Much like the U.S. Merchant Marine Academy, a student could be removed for "demerits" received for not obeying the Code of Honor and/or not behaving like an officer and a gentleman, even if they had the highest grades.

Although Year Up does not secure its graduates the high-paying jobs students that C4Q secures for its coders, Year Up gets students out of poverty and into the middle class.

Small Potential for Success

Another academic elite like Steven Brill breaks his silence. This time it's a Harvard alum named Shawn Achor, who has become an entrepreneur in education. In his book *Big Potential,* published in 2018, the lecturer writes:

> *Three years ago, as I was researching the hidden connections that underlie success and human potential, I had a breakthrough. I became a father.*
>
> *When my son, Leo, came into the world, he was quite literally helpless. He couldn't even roll over by himself. But, as he grew older, he became more capable. And with each new skill he picked up, like any good positive psychology researcher would, I found myself praising him, saying, "Leo, you did that all by yourself! I'm proud of you." And after a while, Leo began parroting it back to me in a soft but proud voice: "All by myself."*
>
> *That's when I realized: First as children, then as adults in the workplace, we are conditioned to disproportionately value things we do on our own. As a father, I stopped my praise and guidance there, my son might come to view independent achievement as the ultimate test or our mettle. But in reality, it is not. There is a whole other level.*
>
> *The cycle begins at a young age. At school, our kids are trained to study diligently and individually so they can best others on exams. If they seek help on projects from other students, they are chastised for cheating. They are given multiple hours of homework a night, forcing them to trade time with others for more time working in isolation.*

Sabotage—and Win

My wife, Kim, recalls being a student at University of California at Santa Barbara. She said, "Students would sabotage other students' projects just for a better grade." She also said, "A few students would go to the library and actually cut out the pages of books that other students needed to study."

Kim ultimately left UC Santa Barbara before graduating, graduating from the University of Hawaii, simply to get her degree and get out of school.

I left, never wanting to return to higher education and higher degrees.

The Rise of Depression

Achor's *Big Potential* is a big book for our times. A few of the book's main points are:

> *The formula is simple: Be better and smarter and more creative than everyone else, and you will be successful. But this formula is inaccurate. ...*
>
> *Success is not just about how creative or smart or driven you are, but how well you are able to connect with, contribute to, and benefit from the ecosystem of people around you. It isn't just how highly rated your college or workplace is, but how well you fit in there. It isn't just about how many points you score, but how well you complement the skills of the team. ...*
>
> *By clinging to the old formula for success we are leaving enormous amounts of potential untapped. I saw this firsthand during my twelve years at Harvard as I watched students crash upon the shoals of hyper-competition, then get stranded on the banks of self-doubt and stress. ... A staggering 80 percent of Harvard students report going through depression at some point in their college life.*

Leaving Harvard and becoming an entrepreneur in education, Achor began sharing his findings on the power of cooperation to schools and businesses all over the world.

> *Now that I have done this work all over the world, I know [depression] is not a problem reserved for Ivy League students. The average age of being diagnosed with depression in 1978 was 29. In 2009, the average age was 14 and a half.*

Depression and Violence

Could the rise in students murdering students—in schools, with guns—be due to depression, loneliness, and isolation?

Why was U.S. Congressman Steve Scalise shot, while practicing baseball, just because he was a Republican? Why was Congresswoman Gabby Giffords shot, while greeting constituents, just because she was a Democrat?

Why is gun violence in major cities on the rise?

Why are people less civil and more disrespectful toward each other?

Why is bullying in school a serious and growing problem?

Do terrorism and violence begin in school?

Virtuous Cycle

Achor offers solutions. One is called the Virtuous Cycle, which he defines as such:

> *"A positive feedback loop whereby making others better leads to more resources, energy, and experiences that make* you *better, fueling the cycle again. Thus, making others better takes* your success *to the next level. Thus:*
>
> *SMALL POTENTIAL is the limited success you can achieve alone.*

BIG POTENTIAL is the success you can achieve only in a Virtuous Cycle with others.

Schools promote small potential by competing rather than cooperating.

Achor teaches how to unlearn what is taught in school, learning how to cooperate and tap into your bigger potential by first helping others become more successful.

Rich Dad's Virtuous Cycle

Rich dad had his own virtuous cycle, one Saturday each month. That is how he and his group got smarter and richer, learning from each other. They were real teachers, working together, helping each other solving real problems—without going back to school.

One of the most popular new Rich Dad books is *More Important Than Money*. The book includes chapters by each of the Rich Dad advisors, real teachers, doing the real thing, in real life. The book is about how we all support each other getting smarter, richer, and more successful— without going back to school, where cooperating and helping fellow students is considered cheating.

A Picture Is Worth a Thousand Words

These two pictures tell the story about the difference between civilian flight school and military flight school.

CIVILIAN FLIGHT SCHOOL
GOAL = FLY SOLO: Small Potential

MILITARY FLIGHT SCHOOL
GOAL = FLY AS A TEAM: Big Potential

Intense teamwork requires intense spiritual education.

THEY CALL THIS CHEATING

What does it take to become a military pilot?

Intense spiritual education requires dedication to a mission, the highest degree of respect for yourself and for everyone on your team, and precise mental, emotional, physical, and spiritual discipline, while training to be the best of the best.

This intense spiritual teamwork is instilled in every student pilot from the first day of flight school.

This intense spiritual teamwork is carried into every mission, in every pilot, even if they do not become one of the elite Blue Angels, the best-of-the-best pilots in the world.

Intense spiritual teamwork is the reason entrepreneurs in education are making a difference while traditional education programs, like TAA, cost billions and are failing.

In the next chapter, you will learn who your best teacher can be.

YOUR QUESTIONS... ROBERT'S ANSWERS

Q: You call them "elites"... Who are they, specifically?

Alex P. - Germany

A: Elites are generally higher-income, college-educated people. Most elites are not rich. Many are managers, executives, and professionals—people who make more money than the working class. There are differences between *elites* and *snobs*. The world has many snobs, many of whom are neither elite or rich.

Q: Where are these "elites" found and how many of them are there?

Pippa M. - Romania

A: Elites tend to gather in neighborhoods, organizations, and clubs. But so do the rich, the poor, and the working classes. They gather around shared values, and interests and are often unified by education and economic status.

Q: Are all "elites" bad?

Paul G. - Ireland

A: No. Not at all. "Elite" does not mean bad. Most of them do great work and contribute greatly to society. Elite is more of a socio-economic-educational classification... juxtaposed against the working class.

Minorities join the "elite" via higher education. Many minority families, including my family, stress higher education for that very reason. Four generations ago, my ancestors came to Hawaii as laborers. Going to college was their ticket off the plantations, out of the working class, and into the ranks of the educated elite.

As you know, I did not want to be a highly educated elite government employee like my poor dad. I wanted to be rich. So I became an entrepreneur like my rich dad.

Q: Sometimes it's hard to tell the difference between what's real and what isn't. How do we know if *you* are fake or real?

James V. - South Africa

A: You don't. Only my bankers and accountants know if I am real or fake. In today's world of fake social media, I can be anything. I've been called a "fake" many times, by many people. I'll let my numbers, my financial statement, speak for me.

Q: What's your response to those who say that gold is obsolete?

Peter C. - USA

A: I say, "Ask that same question in 20 years. Then you will have your real answer." Until then, "In gold I trust."

Q: Do you think that the introduction of the Internet, iPhone and other technologies will eventually expose the elites and what they have done to the rest of us?

Elaine K. - United Kingdom

A: According to Roger McNamee, author of *Zucked*, artificial intelligence will only make fake news and disinformation, more potent, more real, and more destructive to the lives of the unsuspecting.

Simply said, AI (artificial intelligence) will make our lives much better—and much worse.

The Information Age is just beginning. We have not seen anything yet.

Chapter Thirteen

A STUDENT OF GOD

CHOOSE YOUR TEACHERS WELL

"**M**ayday! Mayday! Mayday!"

"Yankee Tango 96!"

"Engine failure!"

"We're going in!"

Our gunship had been circling in an oval racetrack pattern, about a mile away from the carrier at 1,500 feet… when our engine quit. We had been circling waiting for the larger troop transport helicopters to launch. Our tiny, single-engine aircraft was heavy… very, very heavy with a crew of five, six machine guns, canisters of ammunition, and two rocket pods that held 18 rockets.

When I am asked, "How does a gunship fly without an engine?" my answer is "like a rock."

Due to years and years of practicing emergency procedures, including crashing, every day we flew, the moment the engine failed, I reflexively pushed the aircraft's nose toward the ocean… although everything in me was screaming, *Pull back! Pull back! Pull back! Add power! Add power! Add power!* If I had pulled back on a control called the cyclic (the stick) and added power, pulling up on the collective (the gas), we would have all died.

Helicopters do not glide like planes. When the engine on a helicopter quits, there is no glide time, no time to "think about" what to do. There are no parachutes for helicopter crews. When the engine quits, we go down. That is the reason why on every flight, we simulate an engine failure by turning off the power. I assure you, practicing an engine failure is frightening, although we know we can turn the engine back on.

On every practiced engine failure, we roll the power off, pushing the nose forward, and go face to face with the eyes of death.

Helicopter pilots repeat to ourselves the mantra:

> *Pilots who pull up (to avoid death)... die.*
> *Pilots who push forward (to face death... live.*

As the Higher Levels of Teacher diagram explains, for years we "simulated" engine failure after engine failure. On this day, we graduated to "do the real thing."

As soon the engine quit, the crew, two gunners, and a crew chief also began following their training, jettisoning the machine guns, rockets, and throwing ammo cans out the door. We were well-rehearsed. We were now doing the real thing.

There was no time for panic. The fall from the sky went into a slow-motion silence. A calm came over all of us, as the noise and chaos going on outside the aircraft faded from our consciousness.

Going Exterior

Suddenly, as I sat, flying a dead aircraft, I entered another dimension of life. Later, I wound learn this dimension is called "going exterior," or some spiritual practices call "becoming the observer."

For an "eternity" there was a break in the reality we call "time." There seemed to be no past, no future. Only the present. Only the "Now." I was now "observing" myself and the crew from another dimension of life. I could "see" the back of my own helmet, the back of my co-pilot's helmet, the crew behind the pilots, systematically running through the to-dos on their emergency checklist. I could also see the aircraft carrier and the other ships in the flotilla in the distance, and the vast ocean below. For an "eternity" I was exterior to that moment in time. I was outside of "time." Rather than fear, I felt a sense of peace, compassion, and love for myself and my crew as the aircraft silently auto-rotated toward the ocean and our possible deaths.

All in all, it was surreal… not of this world.

The final phase of the crash was textbook, as they say. There was no panic, no fear, just a calm sense of being in the present, outside of time. Just before aircraft impacted the water, I finally pulled back, causing the craft to "glide" silently, just above the water. As airspeed bled off, the nose pulled, now pointing into the sky, the blades grabbed the air, the silence disturbed by loud *whup, whup, whup…* after stalling, I then rocked the nose forward, to level, and just before the aircraft hit the water, the collective (the power control that guides the aircraft up or down) was finally pulled, and the centrifugal forces stored in the blades come to life, holding the aircraft to "hover" for one last time and allowing the gunship to settle gently into the ocean.

As soon as the aircraft touched the water, the aircraft tipped to the right, the blade hit the water, tearing the engine and transmission off, cutting through the cockpit, as the aircraft began to sink into the ocean, almost as fast as we fell toward the ocean.

All five of us were rescued four hours later by a Navy motor launch. Swimming in shark-infested waters for four hours was more terrifying than the two-minute fall from the sky.

During the post-crash debrief and investigation, I said nothing about going "exterior" to the investigators or my crew. The experience was outside my reality at that time and had no way to sensibly talk about an experience I had never previously experienced, so I said nothing because I did not know how to talk about it.

My Search for Teachers

As stated earlier, I returned from Vietnam to be stationed in Hawaii in January 1973 for the final years on my military contract. My flying days were coming to an end and I, like the three wise men, went in search of my next teachers.

To keep my poor dad happy, I enrolled in traditional education. I enrolled in the MBA program at the University of Hawaii. I did not care for the MBA program or the teachers and dropped out after six months.

At the suggestion of my rich dad, I enrolled in a three-day real estate investment seminar. I wanted to learn to use debt, or no money down, to make money. I loved the seminar and the teacher.

Ninety days after leaving that three-day course, analyzing 100 properties, I purchased my first income property for nothing down, using 100 percent debt, putting $25 a month in my pocket, tax-free, an infinite return, and a life-transforming experience.

SATORI: In Buddhism, a satori experience is a flash of enlightenment. Creating $25 out of nothing, even if it was only $25, was my satori experience. Although only $25, it was still an infinite return. I had money without using any of my own money. I had made $25 a month out of pure financial education. In that satori moment, I realized I would never have to spend my life working for money, chasing a paycheck, clinging to job security, living below my means, saving money, and investing in the stock market in hopes of a secure retirement, as most people will spend their lives doing.

I called my real estate instructor to thank him. Almost, every year since, I have attended one or two investment seminars a year seeking higher financial enlightenment, not job security.

Also, at the suggestion of my rich dad, I began job interviews with companies that offered sales training programs. Rich dad said, "The number one skill of an entrepreneur is the ability to sell." He also said, "Sales equal income. The reason most people struggle financially is because they can't sell."

One business that advertised professional sales training as a benefit was New York Life, so I called and asked for a job interview. I showed up in downtown Honolulu in my Marine Corps uniform, which was risky in many ways and on many levels.

The executive in charge of hiring was a great guy. He sung praises on how great New York Life's sales training program was, as well as how much money I could make. As the interview wound down, he asked me questions I had never been asked before. It seemed he was searching for my spiritual aspirations more than my money and professional dreams. Realizing I had no idea what he was talking about, he reached into his desk and handed me a ticket to a "free" guest seminar.

Having the evening of this free seminar open, I showed up at the Hilton Hotel's Coral Ballroom in Waikiki, this time not in my military uniform yet obviously in the military due to my Marine haircut. Immediately, I was pleasantly surprised at the lines of happy, smiling people greeting me along the way to the ballroom. No one was spitting or glaring at me. Even the women were nice to me, which was a real surprise, since back then, women tended to avoid men in uniform. Immediately, I suspected they were phonies or members of some strange hippie or religious cult.

There were about 300 guests at the seminar. There was no alcohol being served, and I needed a drink. I sat farthest from the front and nearest the back door. Finally, all these happy smiling people began to clap as a stunningly beautiful woman named

Marcia Martin, dressed in white, took the stage, welcoming us before introducing the speaker. Werner Erhard, was just as spectacular, trim, fit, handsome, also dressed in white and an even more eloquent speaker. There was no rah-rah, or motivational phoniness. Although clear and eloquent, I had no idea what either of them was talking about.

It was not long before I was ready to run. I knew it was some Kool-Aid-drinking cult, yet for some reason I decided to stay at least until the first break. Even at the break I still had no idea what they were talking about. I heard a lot about "getting it" although I had no idea what I was supposed to get.

At the break, the full-court press was on. These happy smiling people were walking around putting the hard sell on the guests. I saw the executive from New York Life and avoided him. The other smiling guys were easy to stiff arm. But I could not say no to the beautiful, happy women.

A girlfriend of a fellow pilot was there. Her name was Linda and she was one of the smiling beautiful women, so I felt more at ease to ask her more direct questions. "How much do you get paid to sell for this guy Erhard?" was my first question. Her answer was, "We do this for free."

"Why do you do this?" was my next question. When she could not answer that question, at least to the satisfaction of my logical mind, I was gone. I was ready to leave.

As I turned to leave the guest seminar, my fellow pilot's girlfriend came up to me and asked, "So are you going to sign up for the EST seminar?"

"Hell, no," I said. "I don't need this, whatever it is."

She asked again, and again I said, "I do not need this stuff."

Fed up with me, she finally said, "Of all the people in this room, you need this training the most. You know I love your fellow pilot, Jim. He wants to marry me. But I can't marry him. He won't even do what you did tonight: show up and listen to something new, a different type of education. He needs this two-week program as much as you do. You Marines have the biggest bullshit macho act running your lives. You guys are all acts—great guys, but total acts, total machines, total robots. I just wish one of you had the guts to take a look behind your super macho, Marine pilot acts, and find out who you really are."

At one level she was pissing me off. On another level I finally kind of understood what the guy at New York Life, Erhard, and my fellow pilot's girlfriend were talking about. I was finally "getting it."

Giving in, I put my $35 deposit down for the next two-weekend EST, or Erhard Seminar Training, and left without returning to the guest seminar.

About a month later, I was walking into another hotel ballroom in Waikiki for a two-weekend EST training. EST had great teachers. I thought the Marines were tough; these guys were as tough, if not tougher. The opening statement from instructor Landon Carter, a Harvard graduate, was, "Your lives do not work." I had to agree. My life looked good from the outside but on the inside, I knew my life was a mess. No one could go to the bathroom or for any break for over 11 hours. Three hundred of us sat there through process after process, reexamining our lives that were not working.

At the end of two weekends, I had a breakthrough. I popped into a different dimension, and better understood where I went on the day of my crash, the day I went exterior, met the observer, the day I radioed "Mayday! Mayday! Mayday!"—the day I called for help.

Our Mind Is Our Problem

The reason I could not talk about my Mayday day was because of my mind. My mind was the problem.

The reason I could not understand what the recruiter at New York Life was talking about was my mind. My mind was my problem. My mind was in the way of the message.

The reason I could not understand Martin or Erhard was because my mind was in the way. The reason Jim and I could not understand Linda was because his mind and my mind were in the way.

Only when she insulted my ego, calling us both super-macho acts, was there a brief crack in the armor of my mind, and I heard what she was desperately saying.

It took two long and painful weekends for the EST trainers to get my mind out of the way, put a crack into my macho act, and let the sunshine in.

When I returned to my squadron the Monday after the seminar, my fellow pilots thought I had joined a religious cult, drank the Kool-Aid, become a pot-smoking hippie, or come out of the closet—none of which was true. I was simply happier and more at peace with who I really am, behind my macho-Marine pilot act. I was even happier with my act. The difference was, I knew it was an act, not the real me.

Seminar Junky

After the EST experience, I became what is known as a seminar junky. Whenever there was a new, "New Age" seminar in town, I was there. The stranger, the weirder, the more out there, the better. I simply wanted to get outside my limiting mind and ego, and test my reality. When movie star Shirley MacLaine came to town to give a talk on past lives, I was in the audience, keeping an open mind, doing my best to expand my awareness of life.

My Marine pilot friends knew I had tumbled off the deep end. I had dropped out of the MBA program and was buying real estate with no money using 100 percent debt for "infinite" returns. I was less macho, and most importantly, I was happier with me. I was also dating beautiful, happy women I happened to meet at these seminars. Anytime a fellow Marine called me a "new-age hippie" or used other slurs and insults, I would simply smile, introduce them to my happy beautiful date, and ask them how their "luck" was picking up women at the Officers Club.

Our Mind Is Our Enemy

For centuries, humans have prided themselves with the education of the human mind. We still do, which is why so many people worship at the altar of education, and why so many parents say to their child, "You must go to school." Or as adults, we often say, "I'm going back to school," hoping to find some sort of financial salvation from the challenges of life.

Humans realize it is the development of our minds that separates us from the animals. And granted, the human mind has done some miraculous things, such as rockets to the moon, life-saving medicines, wonderful art, and an extremely high standard of life.

Split-Screen Mind

The problem is the human mind is a dualistic, often ego-driven mind. Our mind is like a split-screen TV. It sees the world through the prism of right and wrong, good and bad, up and down, in and out, pretty and ugly. That is why all humans have a good side and dark side.

Many wonderful and magical human experiences are derivatives of our split-screen mind. So are wars, arguments, fights, divorces, crimes, unhappiness, addictions, depression, murders and suicides— all derivatives of the same dualistic mind.

Our educational system educates our split-screen minds. If we did not have smart people and stupid people, schools would go broke.

Religions would go broke without saints and sinners. Why do religions promote holy wars and crusades against other religions?

All sports are played for split-screen TV minds, with winning teams and losing teams. If there were no winning teams and losing teams, the multibillion-dollar sports industry would go broke.

Without an enemy, real or imagined, the multitrillion-dollar global military industrial complex would go broke.

Why are so many students walking into a classroom and murdering their own classmates with guns?

Why is advertising about making our outsides more beautiful while youth depression grows?

Why is social media so antisocial?

Without Republicans and Democrats, liberals and conservatives, we would have governments that functioned.

The question is, how do we turn off our split-screen dualistic, ego-driven minds, before we destroy ourselves?

Evolution or Extinction

Technology is going through evolution after evolution. Just look at what has happened since the turn of the century. A few years ago, the iPhone did not exist. Today iPhones are everywhere.

Our minds are in the process of developing space tourism and driverless cars and trucks.

The United States spends billions on weapons, yet a hacker with a laptop can do more internal systems damage than all our military weapons.

When I was a kid, no one locked their doors. Today, locks on doors will not keep predators, thieves, or perverts out. They enter invisibly from all over the world.

Today we have billionaire Millennials born in the 1980s. At the same time, in many parts of the world as well as in the United States, youth poverty is rising.

The human mind is flawed.

Evolution

The problem is that technology is evolving—but humans are not. Humans have not changed much in the last 500–1,000 years.

Throughout history, humans have always used the latest technology against other humans. Today, much of social media is antisocial bullying. This is the problem with having split-screen, dualistic, ego-driven right and wrong, up and down, good and bad minds that never shut up. We have all seen people walking around talking to themselves. In reality, we are no different. We are always talking to ourselves, commenting, criticizing, labeling, and kibitzing about anything and everything. How many times have you been talking to someone and their body was there but they were not? Their mind was talking to themselves. How many times have you been that person?

For humans to evolve, the next education level will require us to turn our minds off, shut up, and tune into God.

Again, I am not talking about a religious God. I support religious freedom. We all know religions have a lot to answer for and many religious zealots thrive in the Garden of Good and Evil.

If humans do not learn how to turn off their split-screen, right and wrong, dualistic mental TVs, we will use our mind-created technology to destroy ourselves. If we do not learn how to turn our minds off, humanity is finished.

We Are All Angels

During one of the New Age seminars I attended, the presenter told this story.

Not too long ago, all of us were happy little angels, floating around heaven.

One day, GOD (the General Overall Director) announced, "I need a few volunteers to go to down and create Heaven on Earth."

Immediately, all the little angels raised their hands, saying, "Pick me, I'll go. I want to save the world."

After selecting the new recruits, they were prepared for the birth process, parents, and country assigned, and wished "Good luck."

Before saying goodbye to God and the rest of the angels, one of the new human beings asked, "What can be so hard about this? Doesn't every human being on earth want what we have, Heaven on Earth?

"Yes, they do," smiled God. "Remember, they are all angels too."

"So why will our job be so hard? Why will it be so hard to create heaven on earth?

"Because I've given all human beings a mind."

"What is wrong with having a mind?"

"When you have a mind, your mind takes over and you forget about Heaven. The first thing your parents will do is start educating your mind to their way of thinking, send you to church to learn about the right God and the wrong God, and then send you to school, teaching your mind there are smart people and stupid people."

"So, our job when we get to Earth is to remember to get past our mind, remember we are all angels, and create Heaven on Earth?"

"That's right," God said, smiling. "The word most used by humans is the word 'I.' 'I' comes from the ego and the mind. 'I' stands for illusion. 'I' creates separation, not unity. The moment a child learns the word 'I,' all connection to Heaven is lost."

The angels listened to God's warning about the word 'I.' Finally an angel asked, "And what happens if we fail to remember we are all angels, and fail to create Heaven on Earth?"

"You will keep dying and being born again and again until you finally remember you really are… a little angel."

The little angels looked at each other and then God.

"This will be my last direct communication with you," said God. "In a moment, Heaven will be erased and you will receive your own mind."

"But how do we talk to you?" asked one of the angels.

"When you get to Earth, you will be taught to pray. When you pray, you are talking, I am not."

"How will you talk to us?"

"You will never hear my voice again," smiled God. "I will communicate with you through stillness."

"Do you mean silence?"

"No," said God. "Stillness is that peace beyond silence. You sense stillness when you see a lake early in the morning, before the wind creates waves. Stillness is the peace you feel when you gaze at the heavens."

"How will we know it is you talking to us?"

"When your mind is silent and your being is still, you will know I am with you. As long as your mind is talking, you will never hear me. Your mind is very arrogant. Your mind will actually believe it can understand me and is smarter than I am. Your mind is extremely arrogant and knows nothing."

"What will we know?" asked an angel.

"You will know I am with you when you are at one with a beautiful sunset, one with the stars, one with a tree, a flower, a bubbling stream. When you are at one with what is outside of you, you will sense I am with you. When your mind is silent and your being still, and your inner soul connects as one with the flower or stream or human being in front of you, I am with you in the present, in the now."

"When we are at one, we will be with you?" asked one of the angels.

"Yes. As soon as you receive your mind, you will become two; you will be separated from all of my creatures and creations. Your mind will label, criticize, judge, and pretend it is God."

"How do we connect with you?"

"Through stillness connecting to other of my creations. And you can also meditate. When you connect your inner beauty to the beauty outside of you in stillness and in meditation, I will be with you."

"When we pray, we to talk to you. For you to talk to us, we must practice shutting our minds off, being still, meditate, and you will talk to us?"

"Yes. But you will not hear a thing I say."

"What will happen if we practice stillness, meditation, being in the now?" asked one of the angels.

"You will be with me more and more. One day, you will see a flower and from your soul, not your mind, you will say, 'Oh my God.' That will be me talking to you through the flower. One day you will sense the innocence of a child and in your soul, you gasp, 'Oh my God.' In that moment, I will be me talking to you through that child. Every time your soul says, 'Oh my God,' I am with you."

"And that will be you talking to us?" asked the angel.

God just nodded. "Now go. You will not remember any of this, but when you feel the peace and wonder of 'Oh my God' in your soul more and more every day, you are with me because you are remembering you are a little angel, working with me to create Heaven on Earth."

"And someday, we may live every moment in an 'Oh my God,' blissful moment?"

God just nodded.

"But we do not have to be little angels on Earth, do we?" asked another angel.

"That is right," smiled God. "That is why you will be given a split-screen, ego-driven mind. As a human being, you will always have the freedom to choose which of the two screens your being wants to be. Always remember, everything on earth is duality. You will have two eyes and two hands. You will think in right and wrong, up and down. Your human challenge will be to get back to being 'one with life,' connected to everything, not split in two."

It was time to go. To each little angel, God then handed beautifully wrapped presents, "Here is your mind. Each mind is unique which means you will all be humans, but very different beings. Learning to be one with other, connected in spirit, loving each other in spite of your differences, will be your challenge."

As all the angel accepted their beautifully wrapped presents, God said, "Now go." The moment each angel accepted the beautifully wrapped gift of a mind, their memory of Heaven was erased.

The day in 1972 I cried out, "Mayday! Mayday! Mayday!" was not just for me but for a band of brothers, my crew of five. Even in war, we are all doing our best to create Heaven here on Earth. War and peace are opposite sides of the same coin.

Church Lady

My mom was church lady. Every time I watched Dana Carvey play his Church Lady character on *Saturday Night Live*, I'd burst out laughing. My mom was not as obnoxious as the church lady played by Carvey, but my mom had girlfriends who were just as "churchy."

My dad was not church dad. His church was coffee at home with the Sunday paper.

Mom insisted all four kids go to Sunday School and to church. Finally, my younger brother revolted and refused to go. I followed. My two sisters liked church. One sister became a Buddhist nun, one of the few Western women ordained by His Holiness the Dalai Lama.

I reached a peace agreement with my mom. I had to go to church till I was 12, but I could choose my church. I did not have to go to my mom's church. I simply did not like the pastor. He was not about love and peace. He was all hell, sin, and damnation.

For about two years, I went with my classmates to their churches around town. I learned a lot by going to religious services of different religious. The church I liked best was Pentecostal or the church of the "Holy Rollers," as my mom's church-lady friends called this denomination. My mom was bit embarrassed her son was a Holy Roller, yet while singing, clapping, and shaking my tambourine, I did feel the presence of God.

On my 12th birthday, I stopped going to church and went surfing.

No Atheists in Foxholes

The night before every mission in Vietnam, I would go alone to the bow of the aircraft carrier and sit in silence. For about an hour, I would sit in peace, listening to the rush of the carrier's massive bow cutting through the waves. It was peaceful, sitting in silent solitude as the ship surged up and down in harmony with the ocean swells. I was meditating, turning into the spirit of God. For the last few minutes, I would pray. I did not ask to live or to kill. I simply prayed I would fly with courage… not for me, but for my crew. If we were to die, so be it, as long as we flew with courage. The word "courage" is derived from the Old French word *corage*, or "heart." We flew with love, at one with each other.

There is an old saying that goes, "There are no atheists in fox holes." As I sat alone on the bow, before every mission I remembered my mom's wish that I attend church. I now knew why going to church was important to her.

One day, we picked up an emergency medical evacuation. A young Marine had stepped on a landmine and we were flying him to a field hospital. A leg was gone. He was hemorrhaging, crying out for his mother as life left his body. He stopped calling for his mom just before we reached the hospital. All of us were crying as the medics removed his lifeless body from our aircraft.

I went for a walk, finding a private spot to say thank you to my mom. She had died two years earlier at the age of 48 while I was still in flight school in Florida. Every night before a mission, I included her in my thoughts and prayers as I sat on the bow of the aircraft carrier. I flew with her spirit in my heart the next morning.

About a month later, while parked in a remote field, I found young boys planting satchel charges in our aircraft. My mind immediately labeled them Viet Cong. They were no longer little boys. They were now the enemy. Immediately, I grabbed one of the boys, put my pistol to his head, and demanded the other boys get away from the aircraft. The boy I was holding kicked me, bit me, and was attempting to get away. I pulled my hammer back and was preparing to kill him.

Suddenly, I heard my mom pleading with me, saying, "Please, please, do not kill him. I did not give you life for you to take another mother's child."

Pausing, realizing I had better listen to my mom before I did something that would scar my soul, I put the hammer of my pistol down. Still holding onto the boy with one hand, I picked up a soccer ball in the other, and signaled the other boys to play soccer with me. It took a while, but soon we were one again, all little boys playing soccer rather than killing each other.

Flying back to the carrier than evening, I realized my career as a Marine was over.

Secret to My Success

I am often asked, "What is the secret to your success?" "How did you write the number one personal finance book in history?" "How did you get on the Oprah Winfrey Show?" "How did you get to write two books with Donald Trump, now the president of the United States?" "How did you survive the ups and downs of your life, the giant mistakes, the failures, the betrayals of friends and partners, the millions in losses and millions in gains?"

There really is no logical answer. My only answer to you, the reader of this book, is the secret to my success had nothing to do with my formal education or what I learned in school. The secret to my success came from my search for spiritual teachers, teachers like my mom, my friend's girlfriend Linda who got me to drop my ego, new age seminars, and spiritual books written by spiritual masters living and dead who taught me to be silent, be still, and become a student of god, the general overall director.

The New Ancient Age

During the 1950s and 1960s, ancient Eastern and Asian wisdom washed up on America's shores. Hippies traveling world, often seeking drugs, came home with ancient teachings such as Transcendental Meditation (TM) and Transactional Analysis (TA). The Beatles went to India to study with their guru and soon the effects of Eastern music were heard in their music.

True to Western culture, ancient Eastern practices such as meditation have been modernized, often stepped up in speed and effectiveness, repackaged and made more acceptable to Western minds. Westerners do not have the time or patience to meditate for 16 hours a day for 20 years in search of enlightenment. Westerners want it faster and better. That is where EST, Shirley MacLaine,

Timothy Leary and LSD, and new age seminars come from, including Tony Robbins teaching millions to walk on fire.

Today there is "mindfulness" and EST has morphed into Landmark.

The good news is, more and more people are asking for help. Today, Michael Phelps, the most decorated Olympic athlete in history, is the spokesperson for online therapy. Prince Harry acknowledged he needed help as he is still grieving the loss of his mother, Princess Diana.

Asking for help is the first step in healing the pain all humans feel.

Dividing Is Easy—Uniting Is Hard

Since uniting is difficult and dividing is easy, my key team members practice the same spiritual practices I practice. The purpose is to make us a tighter, stronger, more productive team.

We all follow the process described in *The Miracle Morning*, by Hal Elrod:

1. Mediate following Holosync meditations, which combines ancient Eastern meditation with Western processes developed by Ilya Prigogine, who won a Nobel Prize for chemistry in 1977, and Georgi Lazanov's research into "superlearning," developing faster ways for humans to learn, including meditation.

2. Twice a year we get together for a three-day book study. One book study is a business book and the second book study is a spiritual book. Examples of the spiritual books we have studied are:
    Rules for a Knight, by Ethan Hawke
    Awareness, by Father Anthony de Mello
    The Untethered Soul, by Michael Singer
    The Power of Now, by Eckhart Tolle

I thank these writers for contributing insights to the parable of the little angels.

Studying together twice a year and following the same daily spiritual practices keeps us united in a world that is always dividing, which includes our school system.

The Story of Judas

While in junior high school, a friend's father came to class to show us a coin he claimed was one of the 30 silver coins paid to Judas to betray Jesus. The coin and the story of Judas's betrayal fascinated me.

In 1972, I was sent to the island of Okinawa to "stage" before being sent into Vietnam to join an operational combat squadron.

Our commanding officer (CO) on the island of Okinawa was my favorite commanding officer of all time. He was a "mustang," which means he started out as an enlisted Marine, a rifleman during World War II.

During the Korean War, he became an officer and flew the A-1 Skyraider, a propeller-driven bomber. The A-1 was nicknamed "the Flying Dumptruck," because it could carry a lot of ordnance and stay on station a very long time.

For the Vietnam War, our CO was promoted to major and his job was to train new pilots like me, fine-tuning us before sending us into the real war.

One day during our morning pilots meeting, our Commanding Officer said, "One of you is a Judas."

And much like the story of Christ and the disciples at the Last Supper, the eight pilots started asking, "Is it me?" "Am I the Judas?"

Our CO stood in silence for about five minutes, watching each of us squirm, questioning ourselves at the possibility of being the Judas.

Finally, one of the lieutenants raise his hand and asked the Major, "What makes you so certain one of us is a Judas?"

Our CO smiled, pleased that one of us had finally questioned him, asking him what made him so sure one of us was a Judas. After grinning for about another minute, the major said: "Because there is a Judas in all of us."

The eight new pilots sat there for a moment, letting his answer sink in.

Slowly our CO said, "When you get to your operational squadron, do not expect anyone to welcome you or be nice to you. No one will trust you because they do not know you. They do not want to get close to you because new gunship pilots are often dead within 30 days. They do not know who will be flying your plane: a Marine pilot or a Judas. They will not know if you can be trusted until after you have been tested under fire. Until you have been tested, you will be the FNG, the f****** new guy, a potential Judas who will betray himself and his fellow Marines.

After my crew and I were rescued from the ocean, I was promoted from FNG to pilot.

The Power of Spirituality

Today, the most important thing I do is follow the process in *Miracle Morning*. Meditating and studying spiritual masters is the magic in my life, because I am in better control of the Judas in me.

Ray Dalio, founder of Bridgewater Associates and one of the richest and most successful hedge funds in the world today, told *Maxim's* Justin Rohrlich this about meditation:

> *Dalio, like any hedge fund manager worth his salt, won't divulge the secrets of his investment strategy. However, he has called Transcendental Meditation, which he began to explore as a college student after hearing the Beatles had become practitioners, "the single most important reason for whatever success I've had. ...*

Dalio has donated millions of dollars to the David Lynch Foundation, which champions the meditation technique (Martin Scorsese and Jerry Seinfeld are also devotees), and he'll pay the tuition for any Bridgewater staffer who wants to study it.

I will leave you with my thoughts on meditation, spiritual education, and Judas.

Judas is a fake teacher. People who allow the Judas in them to stab others in the back—or stab themselves in the back—are playing God and are no longer a student of God.

The true purpose of meditation and spiritual education is to remind the Judas in us… "that we are all little angels."

STILL SEEKING WISE MEN AND WOMEN
Rich Dad Radio Show

In Sunday School, I learned one of life's great secrets: The Three Wise Men were wise because they went in search of a great teacher. When I was nine years old, I went in search of the teacher that became my rich dad. My search for great teachers continues to this day.

Today, most people are cautious about the food they put in their body. How many people are as cautious about the *information* they put in their brain? Just as there are people and businesses selling junk food, there are people and businesses selling junk information.

When it comes to money, how many people choose their teachers wisely? When it comes to money, how many people read books or attend seminars, in search of wise men and women? Many people would like to, they say, but they "just don't have the time." Rich Dad Radio was created for these people.

There are three parts of my work that I love. They are:

1. I get to work and learn from my partners and advisors in my businesses. Every day is real-life education... not theory or text-book learning.

2. I am invited to be a speaker at seminars and conferences all over the world. I only attend seminars and conferences that have interesting speakers... people I can learn from.

3. I get to interview real teachers, real wise men and women on the Rich Dad Radio Show. I invite great teachers that I meet at other seminars to join me on Rich Dad Radio.

In other words, I spend most of my time working and learning... from wise men and wise women.

I invite you to join Kim and me, each week, for our Rich Dad Radio Show. Every week, for one hour, we discuss topics and issues with some of the leading minds and thought leaders in the world today. In just an hour, you will learn more than you learn in a week at work. Rich Dad Radio is a global podcast that gives you the opportunity to listen to and learn from real teachers.

All Rich Dad Radio programs are archived, which means you can listen to the programs on your schedule. If one of our podcasts is important to your friends, family, or co-workers, you can listen to the program together and discuss what you learned. I think you'll find that your learning and comprehension will skyrocket. In one hour, your financial genius will come alive.

Keeping Pace in a Fast-Moving World

As you know, the world of money is changing. Fast. Even if the world economy is slowing... the world of money is speeding up. Bucky Fuller predicted that humanity would be entering the age of "accelerating acceleration." Unfortunately, due to an obsolete education system, millions of people are struggling financially... and falling further and further behind.

Here are a few of the interviews you'll find on Rich Dad Radio—interviews with very wise people from inside the real world of money. For those who to want to catch up, get ahead, and stay ahead in today's changing world of money, I recommend dropping in on the following interviews...

G. Edward Griffin

G. Edward Griffin opened the eyes of the world to the inner workings of the mysterious and most powerful bank in the world—The Federal Reserve. Ed is a researcher. He digs for the real truth. I take advantage of every opportunity to listen to Ed Griffin.

Richard Duncan

Richard Duncan was an economist with the International Monetary Fund and the World Bank. He is an insider with insights from the perspective of the world's largest banks. Today Richard lives in Thailand and is an advisor to wealthy individuals and private investment funds.

Anytime I want to know what is going on in the macro-world of money, I call Richard.

Richard offers a subscription service Macro-Watch. The best thing about Macro-Watch are the charts Richard generates, turning numbers into easy-to-understand graphs, so you can "get the picture" of what is going on in the world.

Nomi Prins

Nomi Prins is a Wall Street Insider... deep inside.
She has been a managing director at Goldman
Sachs and Bear Sterns. After the 2008 crash,
Nomi traveled the world, learning first-hand
what was *really* going on, after the crash.
She has put her findings in her book *Collusion:
How Central Bankers Rigged the World.*

Bert Dohmen

If your wealth is in the stock market, you'll
want to consider subscribing to *The Wellington
Letter.* Bert's ability to predict and explain the
ups and downs and twists and turns of the stock market borders on
pure genius. He has gotten people in and out of markets early—
and explains why. Bert has the uncanny ability to see what really is
going on inside the markets.

Although I am not invested in the stock market, I look forward to
receiving *The Wellington Letter.* Bert takes the time to educate and
inform, using his 40-plus years of experience, to explain why things
are happening in the global markets. He is a real teacher, a friend,
and a regular guest on Rich Dad Radio.

James Rickards

Jim is an attorney and investment banker. He is
an insider from the hedge fund industry and was
with LTCM, Long Term Capital Management,
a giant hedge fund, founded by Nobel Prize-
winning economists. LTCM nearly collapsed
the world economy, when the Russian ruble
collapsed in 1998.

The collapse of LTCM gave Jim insights into the fragility of the world economy, an experience he took with him when he became a consultant to the U.S. Defense Department and the CIA, the Central Intelligence Agency. Jim's books, his presentations and his interviews on Rich Dad Radio are electrifying.

The following are examples of who else you'll find on archived Rich Dad Radio Shows:

- Donald Trump: "The Donald" announced he was thinking about running for President on a RD Radio show.
- David Stockman: David was Ronald Reagan's Director of the Office of Management and Budget.
- Ken Langone: Founder of Home Depot
- Mohamed El-Erian: Former CEO of bond giant PIMCO

Rich Dad Radio is offered for free from The Rich Dad Company. We do not advise. We do not sell anything. We only educate… via real teachers. You can learn more about Rich Dad Radio at RichDad.com

YOUR QUESTIONS... ROBERT'S ANSWERS

Q: Do the team members who surround you now have similar personalities to the team you served with in Vietnam?

Alejandro B. – Columbia

A: Yes and no. The biggest difference between Marines and civilians in business is Marines go through an extreme unifying experience. Most civilians know these experiences as boot camp, Navy Seal training, or jump school. When I flew with my crew, we were all Marines before we flew together.

Having this shared extreme bonding experience made us stronger as a team. We come from the same "culture," "family," or "tribe."

When we climbed into our helicopter, we all have different jobs and different training. For example, two of us trained to be pilots, two trained to be weapons specialists, and one was an aircraft mechanic. Although we had different jobs, we were first and foremost all trained to be Marines.

In the civilian world, people come together from different experiences, cultures, and tribes. They do not share an extreme unifying experience.

When I joined Xerox, after the Academy and the Marine Corps, Xerox spent a lot of time and money attempting to get the employees to "bond" to develop a "team spirit," a "corporate culture." Xerox sponsored team-building exercises, corporate retreats, and awards dinners, hoping to develop the "band of brothers" culture that the military develops.

While I found these corporate team-building exercises interesting and useful, they never got close to the extreme culture the military develops. On a scale of 1 to 10, Xerox bonding was a 1 and the Marine Corps bonding was a 100.

And there is one thing that corporate team building can never develop. When my crew and I climbed into our aircraft, there was an unspoken code. That unspoken code was not service to God, country, or the Marines. The unspoken code was that we were willing to give our lives for each other, for our "band of brothers." (There were no women flying in combat at the time.)

One day, my crew chief received word from home that he was the father of a new baby boy. That same day, we were flying into combat. As the pilot, my job was to make sure my crew was ready to fight and die if necessary.

I vividly recall asking my crew chief, "Is it OK with you if your son grows up without a father?" Without hesitation, the crew chief, nodded, then smiled and said, "Yes, sir." The good news is that that crew chief returned home six months later to meet his first child.

The Marines mottos are:

"*Semper fidelis*" which means "always faithful."

"*Death before dishonor*" which needs no explanation.

Simply said, Marines are willing to give our own life so our fellow Marines could live. I have never found that "level of spirit" in the civilian world.

Q: Regarding your "going exterior" experience, would you say that this closely resembles Einstein's theory of relativity in that time can be different for the observer depending on the situation?

Brian R. – USA

A: I do not know. You would have to ask Einstein that question.

Personally, being exterior is not that complex. It is simply being aware of the thoughts coming out of your mind. For example, I was in a clothing store yesterday and I could hear my mind, chattering away, saying "You would really look good in that jacket. People will really think you are cool when you wear that jacket to the club."

Did I buy a jacket that I did not need? I did. That is a real example of my mind, my ego—not my spirit—running my life.

My real point for mentioning this phenomenon of "going exterior" is to point out that the purpose of our schools is to develop our mind... not our spirit. The Academy and the Marines developed my spirit, not my mind. That is why the words *mission, honor, code, discipline,* and *respect* are the core words of the military.

Other words I hear from most people is: "What's in it for me?" Those are the core words of a greedy person.

The key to real health, wealth, and happiness is *not* letting our mind and our ego run our lives.

The mind wants to know "How much money can I make?" The spirit wants to know "How many people can I serve?" You may have "to go exterior" when you ask yourself the latter question.

Q: How do you differentiate a "good" seminar from one run by a bunch of scam artists trying to rip you off?

Mark K. – USA

A: I do my best to avoid the words good and bad.

The more I get out of my mind and live in my heart, I can see the "good in the bad" and the "bad in the good."

In December of 2018, I took some heat when I said publicly, "I hope the stock market crashes."

A real investor is able to see the good and the bad in a crash.

A fake investor lives in a fantasy world, and actually believes (or believes he believes) a stock market crash is bad.

In the real world, the best time to buy any investment is right after a crash. In the fake world of investing, markets only go up. Markets never crash. That is delusional.

Rich dad taught his son and me:

"Good and bad are two sides of the same coin."

F. Scott Fitzgerald said:

"The test of a first-rate intelligence is the ability to hold two opposed ideas in mind at the same time and still retain the ability to function."

In my classes, I say:

"If we want more peace and prosperity in our lives, we need to train our brains to see both sides of the same coin."

Q: Do you think that the introduction of the internet, the iPhone, and other technologies will eventually expose the elites and what they have done to the rest of us?

Joao B. - Brazil

A: That's a very interesting question. My answer is yes and no.

Fuller predicted humanity was entering the Age of Integrity. New technologies will make it easier to "see" what humans have not been able to see, exposing the flaws in Grunch.

The problem is the Age of Integrity will lead to more chaos and disruption, as people and organizations attempt to survive when they are exposed or wiped out, as technologies continue to wipe out the ignorant, corrupt, lazy, and inefficient.

Whenever I get comfortable and complacent, I simply remind myself of the Kodak Company. One day, Kodak film ruled the world. In a flash, digital photography put a giant company out of business.

That means, none of us is safe and secure in a world of accelerating acceleration of technology.

As Andy Grove of Intel wrote: "Only the paranoid survive."

This is why I recommend spiritual education. Your mind is paranoid. Your spirit is much more powerful than your mind.

PART
THREE

FAKE ASSETS

My banker always said:
"Your house is an asset."

But whose asset is it... really?

– RTK

INTRODUCTION

PART THREE

Why are the poor and middle class getting poorer?

Because they invest in fake assets
that they think are real assets.

– RTK

Introduction to Part Three
FAKE ASSETS

"The rich do not work for money."

"Savers are losers."

"Your house is not an asset."

These are statements from *Rich Dad Poor Dad*, first published in 1997.

These statements were so controversial back in 1997 that every book publisher we approached turned the book down. A few of them stated, "You do not know what you are talking about."

That was more than two decades ago.

In 2018, many highly educated elites continue to say that I do not know what I am talking about. Statements like "your house is not an asset" and "savers are losers" violate every cell in their highly educated elite brains. They want to believe their house is an asset and that saving money is the smart thing to do.

The problem is: a house is a fake asset. So are our savings—our money and our retirement savings.

In Part Three of this book, you will learn that most people are investing in fake assets or counting on fake assets to provide a paycheck for life once their working days are over.

In Part Three: Fake Assets, you will find out that most people are investing in real liabilities, not real assets.

The good news is that in Part Three, you will find out *why* most people invest in fake assets… and how you can invest in real assets.

Chapter Fourteen

WHY RETIRE YOUNG?

THE NEXT BIG CRISIS

I n June 1974, I signed my discharge papers and drove off the Marine Air Station in Hawaii. Returning my last salute from the Marine Guard, I drove to my new home in Waikiki a free man. I had been in the military since August 1965, the month and year I entered the U.S. Merchant Marine Academy at Kings Point, New York.

My new home was a 1-bedroom, 1-bath condo in the Ilikai Hotel, a luxury hotel on Waikiki Beach. I chose the Ilikai because it had condominiums that could be placed in the hotel rental pool, i.e. turn my home liability into an income-producing asset. The main selling point was I had full use of all the hotel amenities—pool, gym, restaurants, nightclubs, and room service. The price was right: only $32,000 for a tiny 600-square-foot hotel condo. As a 27-year-old single male, 600 square feet in the heart of the nightlife of Waikiki was all I needed.

I started working at the Xerox Corporation in downtown Honolulu the following Monday. I did not take any time off because I now had a mortgage to pay.

Retire in 20 Years

My poor dad did not want me to leave the Marine Corps. He wanted me to stay in the Marine Corps for 20 years and retire.

On both my mom and my dad's sides of the family, retirement benefits seemed to be more important than the actual job. On my mother's side, two of her brothers had careers with the fire department of the State of Hawaii County. They retired with government pensions and benefits after 20 years of service. My mom's two brothers did not have to work after the age of 40 with a State of Hawaii retirement. They fished and played golf for the rest of their lives. Once a year, they traveled to Las Vegas on their annual pilgrimage to the mainland. They enjoyed a great retirement.

On my dad's side of the family, it was a similar story. A few relatives actually had two (and one, even *three*) government retirement pensions, plus Social Security and Medicare benefits. The uncle with three retirement pensions—who first retired from the Army after 20 years, then retired from a federal government job after five years, was working on a third retirement paycheck from the state of Hawaii—was the envy of my dad and the reason why he wanted me to stay in the Marine Corps for 20 years.

The 401(k) Plan

In 1971, President Richard Nixon ended convertibility between the U.S. dollar and gold. It marked the start of a massive transfer of workers' wealth to the academic and financial elite. It was those same elites whom Steven Brill wrote about in *Tailspin*.

Earlier in this book, I quote Brill's account on how the academic elite from our nation's top schools began creating exotic financial products such as CDOs and MBSs, financial derivatives that add very little value to the economy and rip off the working class, yet make the academic and financial elite extremely rich.

1974, the year I left the Marine Corps, was also the year the Employee Retirement Income Security Act, which protected employees' company pensions, went into effect. Four years later, 401(k), another financially engineered retirement program, got its beginnings.

There was a problem with this. Suddenly non-investors, men and women without any financial education, were expected to become investors. That was the start of a massive financial rip-off by "too big to fail" banks, the U.S. government, and Wall Street.

The years 1971 and 1974 will go down in history as turning points. Fifty maybe 100 years from now, scholars will look back at 1971 and 1974 as the years the academic and financial elites of America perpetrated a massive cash heist, stealing the wealth of millions of Baby Boomers who innocently participated in trillion-dollar, government-sanctioned cash heists... known as retirement plans.

By the way, 1972 was the year Nixon opened the door to China.

The Looming Retirement Disaster

Today, the world faces many growing disasters, disasters such as the poisoning of the environment, massive global debt, and cyberterrorism.

A disaster in the making that few are paying attention to today is the same disaster my poor dad faced in the 1970s: entering his retirement years—without a retirement paycheck.

Pensions Going Bust

Consider these reports:

APRIL 16, 2018

INVESTOR'S BUSINESS DAILY

Pension Crisis: As the media relentlessly focus on the federal government's burgeoning debt, a new report says that states face their own ticking debt bomb: the exploding liabilities for lavish state and local public-employee pensions. Reform won't be easy, but there is no choice.

JUNE 22, 2018

SIMON BLACK, SOVEREIGN MAN

The city of San Diego has a $6.25 billion shortfall on obligations promised to current and retired employees.

The State of New Jersey has $90 billion in unfunded pension liabilities.

And of course, Social Security and Medicare have unfunded liabilities totaling tens of trillions of dollars.

The situation isn't any different in Europe.

Spain's Social Security Reserve Fund has been heavily invested in Spanish government bonds for several years—**bonds that had an average yield of NEGATIVE 0.19 percent.**

You read that correctly.

Unsurprisingly, Spain's pension fund is almost fully depleted.

The United Kingdom has trillions of pounds worth of unfunded public pensions.

Even conservative Switzerland has a public pension that's only 69 percent funded—a seemingly fantastic number by today's dismal standards.

Last year, the Swiss government proposed a plan to save its pensions, asking to increase the retirement age for women by one year (from 64 to 65, the same as men), and increase VAT by 0.3 percent.

But the plan was rejected by Swiss voters in a national referendum—the third time in 20 years that pension reform failed to pass.

And that's really the key issue here: pension plans are almost universally toast.

Most of the time, politicians just ignore the problem and try to kick the can down the road to the next administration.

But occasionally they try to do something to help.

Yet whenever they do… voters reject the plan. Or the union sues. Or something else happens that prevents much-needed reforms from passing.

This merely accelerates the inevitable: these pensions are going bust.

MARCH 4, 2018

MARTIN ARMSTRONG, ARMSTRONG ECONOMICS

The largest public pension fund in the United States is the California Public Employees Retirement System (CalPERS) for civil servants. California is in a state of very serious insolvency. We strongly advise our clients to get out before it is too late. I have been warning that CalPERS was on the verge of insolvency. I have warned that they were secretly lobbying Congress to seize all 401(k) private pensions and hand it to them to be managed. Mingling private money with the public would enable them to hold off insolvency a bit longer. Of course, CalPERS cannot manage the money they do have so why should anyone expect them to score a different performance with private money? Indeed, they would just rob private citizens to pay the pensions of state employees and politicians.

CalPERS has been making investments to be politically correct with the environment rather than looking at projects that are economically based. Then, CalPERS has been desperate to **cover this and other facts up** to deny the public any transparency. Then, because stocks they thought were overpriced last year, they **moved to bonds** buying right into the Bond Bubble. Clearly, California's economy **peaked right on target** and ever since there has been a steady migration of residents out of the state.

JULY 30, 2018

SARAH KRAUSE, *THE WALL STREET JOURNAL*

Moody's Investors Service estimates state and local pensions have unfunded liabilities of about $4 trillion, roughly equal to the economy of Germany, the world's fourth-largest economy.

OCTOBER 11, 2018, AFP

"Trillions in U.S. net worth vulnerable to recession: IMF"

The biggest source of risk comes from state and local government retirement pensions, which can lose money when Wall Street sinks—meaning the shortfall has to come from local government budgets.

Towns and states then have to cut spending elsewhere creating a drag on the economy.

Nationwide, such pension funds are already underfunded by about 8 percent of GDP.

Read on… for more startling and sobering facts.

ZIMBABWE

In 2000, Zimbabwe's money became the laughing stock of the world when President Robert Mugabe began printing trillions and quadrillions in fake money to pay government employee pensions and war debts.

Many wealthy Western nations are following Zimbabwe's financial policy of print, print, print.

NICARAGUA

In 2018, Nicaragua is on the verge of revolution because the government cannot pay for the government employee's retirement.

RICH CITIES

Today, in 2018, millions of families are living on the streets of many great cities such as New York, San Francisco, Seattle, and Honolulu.

ITALY

On October 13, 2018, *The Economist* reported that "Italy, in particular, is a ticking time bomb. ... It would not take much to set off a new crisis, which would be extremely difficult to control. Panic in Italy might radiate out across financial markets, putting a chill on investment and growth worldwide."

THE WALL STREET JOURNAL, JULY 19, 2018

RICH STATES

The three states with best-funded employee pensions:

1. South Dakota 100 percent funded
2. Wisconsin 99.9 percent funded
3. Washington 98.7 percent funded

POOR STATES

And the three states with the worst-funded programs:

48. Connecticut 51.9 percent funded
49. Kentucky 48.9 percent funded
50. Illinois 47.1 percent funded

"Ohio workers' pension fund woes are symbolic of national problem"

MARK MILLER, REUTERS, JULY 27, 2018

Roberta Dell has worked for 46 years making lollipops, and she loves her job. But she worries that retirement may not be as sweet as the Dum Dum lollipops she bags.

Dell works for the Spangler Candy Company in Bryan, Ohio—a family-owned business that employs 550 workers and makes the venerable candy. Spangler was organized by the International Brotherhood of Teamsters labor union in 1950, and it became part of the Central States multiemployer pension plan in 1972.

But the outlook for her pension is highly uncertain. The Central States Pension Fund has said it is on a path to insolvency within 10 years. The fund, which covers more than 400,000 retirees and active workers, has become a symbol for all that has gone wrong with multiemployer pension plans—traditional defined benefit plans jointly funded by groups of employers. These are typically small companies in industries like construction, trucking, mining, and food retailing that would not typically sponsor a pension plan of their own.

"I always thought the pensions would be there for me when it came time to retire," Dell said in an interview. "I thought of it as my savings plan."

Dell, who is the Teamster chief steward at Spangler, testified earlier this month at a hearing of special U.S. congressional committee in Columbus, Ohio that examined possible solutions for workers like her.

More than 10 million retirees are covered by 1,400 multiemployer pension plans. But roughly 200 plans are severely underfunded—the result of stock market crashes in

2001, and 2008–2009, and industrial decline that led to no consolidation and declining employment.

The problems threaten not only the pensions of individual workers, but also cause the multiemployer insurance program of the Pension Benefit Guarantee Corporation to become insolvent within a decade. The PBGC is the U.S. government agency that acts as a backstop to troubled pension plans by insuring the pensions of millions of American workers.

NOTE: Very few American workers have heard of the PBGC. They will when the PBGC goes broke and their pension is downsized.

… Dell is 65 and widowed—her husband also worked at Spangler before his death in 2015. She expects to work a few more years before retiring and expects her pension to pay about $1,200 a month. Social Security will provide another $1,400. But as things stand now, pension benefit cuts loom in 2025.

Poor Dad's Dilemma

In 2018, millions of employees will be in the same situation my poor dad faced in 1974: his retirement years without a retirement check. Millions of Baby Boomers may have their dreams of a happy retirement wiped out if or when the next giant crash wipes out their retirement savings and the PBGC.

Investing in Fake Assets

This is what happens when people invest in fake assets or trust their retirement savings to fake fund managers who invest in fake assets such as stocks, bonds, mutual funds, ETFs, insurance, and cash.

The GAP

The chart below tells the story of America's decline into poverty.

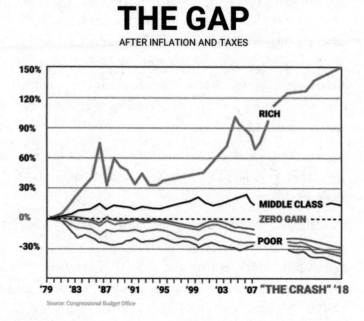

THE GAP

AFTER INFLATION AND TAXES

Source: Congressional Budget Office

A 2018 study by the Schwartz Center for Economic Policy Analysis at the New School has concluded that 40 percent of the American middle class will slide into poverty as they enter their retirement.

Tomorrow's poor have jobs today... but no retirement for tomorrow.

Retire Young

In 1974, I made a vow I would retire young. Not because I wanted to retire, but because I wanted to *challenge myself* to retire young. If I failed to retire young, I still had years to keep working on my goal of retiring young. I did not want to be 65 years old and find out that my retirement had been wiped out in a market crash or that I did not have enough money to carry me through retirement.

As I've stated in previous chapters, I have failed many times in my life. It took me till age 47 to find my personal formula and be able to retire without a job or pension. My purpose for being willing to fail and learn was that failing and learning from my mistakes was how I'd learn to be an entrepreneur and, eventually, a person who would never need a job, a steady paycheck, or a pension.

It took me 20 years to retire. If I had stayed in the Marine Corps, "doing my 20" as my poor dad wanted me to, I would not have been smarter or richer after 20 years in the military.

Retire Rich

Another important reason for being willing to fail and learn was because I wanted to retire young—and then retire rich. Back in the 1970s, a great retirement was about $500 a month. Today, $500 a month in retirement income is living in poverty.

In 1974, my goal was $120,000 a year in passive income. Then I could "retire young."

In 1994, Kim and I reached that goal. Kim was 37 and I was 47. Again, it took me 20 years. It took Kim only 10.

Once we achieved $120,000 a year, our next goal was $1.2 million a year. Once $1.2 million was achieved, our next goal was $12 million per year.

It was our personal challenge. First to retire young... then to retire rich. The math is not difficult. First it was $10,000 a month, then $100,000 a month, then $1 million a month.

If I had stayed in the Marine Corps for 20 years, I might be making $5,000 a month.

Back in 1990, I remember a woman saying to Kim and me, "You only earn $120,000 a year?" What she did not understand was that we had $120,000 a year coming into our household—without working. Her husband, an attorney, earned about $500,000 a year, but he could not stop working.

Today, Kim and I earn more in two weeks, without working, than her husband earns in a year working as an attorney.

Giving Back

Kim and I have a goal of donating $100 million a year or more to charity when we retire. Our plan is to make money and then give it back.

Once Kim and I found our own retirement formula, we retired young. And then we become rich.

The key first was to invest in what we loved. We did not invest in what some financial planner wanted us to invest in.

You might think all of this begs the question *How much is enough?* Our goals and our plan to be financially free and wealthy have nothing to do with "enough." I went beyond enough a long time ago.

Why do I need to make so much money? I don't. Making money on the B and I side of the quadrant is only a game to me. Some people spend their lives chasing a little white ball around a golf course, hoping to shoot below par. Some people spend their lives singing, hoping to be discovered or become a movie star or sports superstar. That is their game.

The important question is this: are you passionate about your game?

That's kind of a loaded question. People who are passionate do what they want to do. Passion is often selfish. On the flip side, passion is better than doing what you hate. And new studies show that 70 percent of all Americans hate what they do… up from 62 percent just a few years earlier.

I'm often asked if getting richer is my life's purpose. No. Many people work with a purpose—putting food on the table, getting their kids through school, or doing work they feel is meaningful.

In 1983, while studying with Dr. R. Buckminster Fuller, he said, "I do what God wants done." So, I asked myself, *What does God want done?* It's a question I encourage others to ask themselves.

In 1983, I was in the rock and roll business. I was having fun. I was cool, hanging out with some of the greatest bands of the time like the Police and Van Halen. But I could not honestly say that producing products for rock bands was what God wanted done, even though I was making a lot of money.

So I'll ask the question: What do you think God wants done?

Although I can't say I really know, I suspect God does not want people to live in poverty. So, I began teaching what my rich dad taught me about money, and it seems to have God's support.

So I keep on teaching. And—yes—make a lot of money. I would be a fake teacher if I was teaching people to be rich and I myself was poor.

Now, let me ask you a few questions.

What do you think God wants done... that you want to do?

Are you willing to do what God wants done?

If you could cure cancer, would you?

If you could eradicate world hunger, would you?

If you could solve global warming, would you?

Or do you only want to make enough money for you?

In 1974, I already had two high-paying professions, one as a ship's officer sailing tankers for Standard Oil and the other flying for the airlines. Both were careers as a high-paid employee in the E quadrant. I wanted to find out if I could make it in the B and I quadrants.

Going through Hell

As Winston Churchill said, "When you're going through hell... keep going."

Transitioning into the B and I quadrants was a tough journey. As stated in the last chapter, if not for my spiritual education and spiritual teachers, I would not have made it.

Going through hell made Kim and me smarter and stronger, better able to do what god wants done.

Rich dad said, "There are many doors to financial heaven. There are even more doors to financial hell."

As you know, most entrepreneurs go through hell before achieving success in the B and I quadrants. Examples include Steve Jobs' departure from Apple, his own company. And Bill Gates was sued for Microsoft being a monopoly. Mark Zuckerberg was sued by the Winklevoss twins, who claimed Facebook was their idea. Even Jeff Bezos had a few setbacks in founding Amazon.

Rich dad warned, "Many people take the door to financial hell and never come back."

As you know, many people sell their souls hoping to get rich. Many people have ripped off millions of people. Many are still in power at the highest levels of banking, especially Goldman Sachs, the Federal Reserve Bank, and the U.S. Treasury.

A few of the more famous culprits are Bill Clinton, Robert Rubin, Larry Summers, Alan Greenspan, Jack Lew, Tim Geithner, Hank Paulson, Ben Bernanke, Warren Buffett, and Phil Gramm. They claim to have saved the economy. In fact, they saved the rich. Bad karma.

If there is another financial catastrophe, millions of innocent hard-working people will be sent to financial hell by these leaders without souls.

This is why I am critical of an educational system that teaches students nothing about financial education, punishes students for making mistakes, and views cooperation as cheating.

Our education system… is a system without a soul. Everyone uses money. Every day. Why not teach money in school?

Learning to Become an Entrepreneur

In 1974, I started working at Xerox to learn how to sell. I was not a natural salesman. I struggled. I hated knocking on doors, facing rejection after rejection. After the Xerox office closed, I would sit in my office writing sales proposals for potential new customers. If I did not sell, I did not eat or pay my mortgage. If I did not learn to sell, I would never be an entrepreneur in the B and I quadrants. I failed for two years before becoming number one in sales for Xerox in the Honolulu office.

Between 1974 and 1976, I took a certified financial planner (CFP) course. It was a great course. It was tough. It was grueling, and I learned a lot about professional financial planning.

There is a significant difference between a CFP and today's 30-Day Wonder financial planners who get their license in a few weeks. It takes about two years for a massage therapist to get his or her license.

Most of today's 30-Day Wonder financial planners know little to nothing about investing. They study only to pass a Series 7 license.

The difference between a 30-Day Wonder and a CFP is much like the difference between a bookkeeper and a CPA.

After a 30-Day Wonder receives their license, they hit the streets looking for clients. Most are looking for a person who is unhappy with their current financial planner. The new planner then convinces the unhappy customer to switch the "assets" in his 401(k) or IRA over to him, and he will make the magic happen. Most of the time, the magic does not happen. How can there be much magic? All financial planners are selling basically the same products: stocks, bonds, mutual funds, ETFs, savings, and insurance.

The Name of the Game

Magic does not happen because the name of the game financial planning companies play is *not* "Make our clients rich." The game financial planning companies play is "assets under management," or AUM. When you watch financial programs such as CNBC or read ads in financial magazines such as *Money* magazine, you will see advertised, The Big Magic Fund, $100 billion, Assets Under Management. To the average person $100 billion AUM sounds impressive, yet it means little to the average investor. The primary job of the 30-Day Wonder, a.k.a. financial planner, is to increase their company's AUM, not make their client's future more secure. More on AUM later.

The primary reason I took the CFP course was not to become a certified financial planner. My primary reason for taking the CFP course was to find out how to retire as young as possible. I learned a lot. Here's what I learned:

1. There are two basic types of financial planners. For fee working by the hour, and for commission selling the client assets.
2. Most only know about paper assets, stocks, bonds, mutual funds, ETFs, savings, and insurance. Financial planners know little about being entrepreneurs, real estate investors, or gold or oil investors, and most importantly, most do not know how to use debt and taxes to gain wealth.
3. Most 30-Day Wonders and CFPs are not professional investors. Most are employees or self-employed working for a paycheck, for fees, bonuses, and commissions.
4. Studying for my CFP, I did not learn how to retire young or retire rich.
5. I did learn a lot about insurance, which was what most CFPs focused on selling because the commissions are lucrative.

Rich Dad's Plan

Rich dad taught his son and me that there are four basic asset classes. They are:

1. Business
2. Real Estate
3. Paper Assets (stocks, bonds, mutual funds, ETFs, and savings)
4. Commodities (gold, silver, oil, food, water)

Most financial planners and CFPs sold only paper assets and insurance for commissions.

Invest in What You Love

Most people are taught, "Do what you love." Rich dad taught his son and me, "Invest in what you love."

After completing the CFP course, I knew what I was going to invest in.

1. I knew my love was to learn to become an entrepreneur, starting and building businesses in the B quadrant, not the S quadrant. Becoming an entrepreneur in the B quadrant, 500 employees or more, was my challenge.
2. I already knew I loved real estate. After making $25 monthly with none of my own money I was hooked, and I paid no taxes, legally. I was hooked on infinite returns, the art of making money without money.
3. I was not interested in paper assets, especially after taking the CFP course. I knew paper assets were fake assets. I also knew paper assets were best for the average person, Es and Ss without a real financial education.
4. I already loved commodities. I loved gold, having purchased my first real gold coin in Hong Kong in 1973. I was also interested in oil because I was trained to be a tanker officer at the academy.

Again, paper assets are best for the average investor, a person without much financial education.

Liquid Assets

The primary reason paper assets are best for the average investor is because paper assets are "liquid" which means you can buy and sell quickly. If you make a mistake, you can sell almost immediately.

The same is true for gold and silver coins. They are almost as liquid as paper assets.

The weakness with paper assets is the same as their benefit. They are liquid. When there is a crash, a panic, mass selling can wipe out an average investor's portfolio in minutes.

Today, with high-frequency trading (HTF), paper assets can be bought and sold, 10,000 in a second.

The average investor, investing for the long term, could be wiped out over lunch.

Dark Pools

Early in this book, I stated most of the world of money is now invisible because today, modern money is cyber, not paper. The same is true with paper assets. "Dark pools" are where giant institutional investors, such as banks, hedge funds, and large professional investors such as Warren Buffett meet to buy and sell in secret. Today, it is estimated 40 percent of all paper asset trades are done in dark pools. Mom-and-pop average investors have no idea what is going on.

When the next crash comes, Mom and Pop may lose their retirement savings in a flash.

When Alan Greenspan was questioned about the 2008 crash, he said something like, "Well, no one saw it coming." Was his statement real or fake?

Greenspan is a professional economist in the I quadrant. "I" also stands for "insider." Greenspan is an insider. Today, I am an "insider" on my investments. Mom-and-pop investors, following their financial planner's advice, are "outsiders."

In early 2008, six months before Lehman went bankrupt, I was on CNN telling Wolf Blitzer that the markets were going down. If *I* saw it coming, Greenspan had to know. Insiders in the I quadrant knew what was going down.

Predicting the Crash

If you would like to see the CNN video of me predicting the bankruptcy of Lehman and the 2008 crash, go to https://vimeo.com/183740821

Q: How did you see the crash coming?

A: Because I am an insider, an investor from the "I" quadrant. Years before the crash, I was on television and radio warning of the coming real estate crash.

Q: What did you know that others did not know?

A: I saw trends. Between 2005 to 2008, our apartment buildings were losing tenants. Many tenants, most who could barely afford the $500 a month rent, were leaving our apartments and going out to buy $300,000 to $500,000 homes.

Q: How did they afford these homes?

A: They were receiving NINJA loans, *No Income, No Job* loans. They were receiving subprime loans, because they were subprime borrowers.

Q: How do you know Warren Buffett knew?

A: Because Buffett's company Berkshire Hathaway owned a stake in Moody's, the company that was rating these subprime loans, as "prime." Once they were rated as "prime," they were sold as mortgage-backed securities and collateralized debt obligations (derivatives) to pension funds, government funds, hedge funds, private equity funds, and other big investors all over the world.

Gasoline is a derivative of oil. Jet-fuel is a derivative of gasoline. The further the derivative is removed from the original, in this case, oil, the more volatile the derivative becomes.

In 2008, these "derivatives" exploded, when subprime borrowers could not pay and the whole world nearly collapsed.

Millions lost their jobs, homes, and pensions but not one of the "big boys and girls" was prosecuted. Only one small neighborhood bank in New York's Chinatown, a bank owned by Chinese-Americans, was brought to trial and later found innocent.

PBS did a documentary on this bank. The title of the documentary is *Abacus, Small Enough to Jail*. The government picked on a tiny bank rather than the real criminals.

As almost everyone knows, the "too big to fail" banks, such as Goldman Sachs, Wells Fargo, and Citibank caused the crash, made billions, and no one was prosecuted. The bankers who made billions from these fake assets were also paid billions in bonuses after the crash. To me, this is criminal.

So, if I knew subprime loans were criminal and a crash was coming, I suspect Buffett knew. I suspect he knew Moody's rating of subprime loans as prime was fraudulent.

After all, it is Buffett who called derivatives "financial weapons of mass destruction."

That is a benefit of being an "inside investor" in the I quadrant with real financial education.

When the markets did crash, in 2008, Kim and I made millions.

That is why I do not invest in paper assets such as stocks, bonds, mutual funds, ETFs, and savings. I do not like being an outsider. Also, all paper assets are a form of derivatives. They are not real assets. They are fake assets.

Yet, paper assets are best for the "average" investor without financial education because paper assets are liquid. Paper is easy to get into and easy to get out of.

Business and Real Estate

The problem with a business and real estate is they are illiquid. If you make a mistake, you become the skipper of the *Titanic*. I know. As an entrepreneur, I have been captain of Titanics a number of times.

I have never lost money in real estate, which is why I recommend taking real estate courses before investing in real estate, then start small, follow the Higher Levels of Teacher, and practice, practice, practice.

Remember, business and real estate are illiquid. That means you must be a lot smarter than the average investor, because when you are an entrepreneur in business or real estate, you are an insider.

My Formula

When I am asked about my formula, I have two answers.

Answer #1: I say my financial education began with my rich dad playing *Monopoly* with his son and me. Today, Kim and I play *Monopoly* in real life. Kim and I like real assets, not derivatives of assets. Kim and I like being insiders, not outsiders.

Answer #2: Kim and I follow the McDonald's formula for great wealth. In *Rich Dad Poor Dad*, I quoted Ray Kroc, founder of McDonald's, addressing an MBA class at the University of Texas. During the class, Ray Kroc asked, "What business is McDonalds in?" One student offered the obvious: "Hamburgers."

Ray's reply was, "No, McDonald's business is real estate."

I follow the McDonald's formula. My businesses are in the business of real estate.

The McDonald's formula looks like this:

Real Estate

More on this formula later.

The Power of Words

When I am asked, what is the secret to becoming rich, I say, "There are many 'secrets.' One of the secrets is the power of words. If a person wants to become rich, they must learn to control the words they think and speak. Most people think and speak words that make them poor and keep them poor."

In Sunday school I learned: "And the Word became flesh and dwelt among us." (John 1:14)

My rich dad taught me:

Poor people say, "I can't afford it."
Rich people ask, "How can I afford it?"

Poor people say, "I'm not interested in money."
Rich people say, "If you are not interested in money, money is not interested in you."

Poor people say, "I'll never be rich."

Rich people say, "I must be rich."

Lesson: People who think and speak the words of poor people should use a financial planner and invest in paper assets.

For people who think and speak the words of a poor person, stocks, bonds, mutual funds, ETFs, savings and insurance are enough, *possibly* better than doing nothing.

Assets vs. Liabilities

Rich dad's definition of assets:

"Assets put money in your pocket."

Rich dad's definition of liabilities:

"Liabilities take money from your pockets."

Remember: Nouns plus verbs. To tell if something is a real asset or real liability, requires a noun, plus a verb. For example, the word "asset" is a noun. The word "flow" is a verb. You cannot tell an asset from a liability with the verb. For example, a house could be either an asset or liability, depending upon which direction the cash flows.

During the 2008 crash, millions of Es, employees, lost their jobs and soon their homes, finding out their houses were a real liability, not an asset.

Fake Assets Are Real Liabilities

Billions of people invest in fake assets.

A 401(k) is a fake asset because cash keeps flowing out of your pocket... for years. An Individual Retirement Account, or IRA, is a fake asset because takes money out of your pocket... for years.

A government pension is a fake asset because it is taking money out of your pocket... for years.

A mutual fund is a fake asset. So are stocks, bonds, ETFs, and savings. They are all derivatives. Mutual funds are loaded with fees, fees that make the rich richer. And you poorer.

Insiders know, mutual fund investors put up 100 percent of the money, take 100 percent of the risk, yet gain less than 20 percent of the profits.

Again, mutual funds and ETFs, which are derivatives (and fake assets), are best for the average investor, passive investors without real financial education.

The problem is, if there is another crash, Mom and Pop's money may disappear, just as it did in 2008.

Remember:

Assets put money in your pocket.

Liabilities take money from your pocket.

In the next chapter you will find out where all the money disappears to when markets crash.

YOUR QUESTIONS... ROBERT'S ANSWERS

Q: You mention doing "what God wanted done." What were the signs you received from God that made you think that you were doing the right thing(s)?

Bruno T. – France

A: I am not claiming that God talked to me. Nor am I so presumptuous to believe, "God chose me to do this job." Besides, only an extremely arrogant and/or delusional person would believe they know what God is thinking. I sincerely doubt a human's mind is capable of operating at the same level of the mind of God... if there is a God.

Bucky Fuller made me aware that I was doing what most people dream of doing—doing what I love... to make money.

I was doing what I loved. I was an entrepreneur. I owned my own company. I was the boss and I was working with the biggest rock bands in the world. I got backstage passes. I loved it. My ego loved it. It was fun. I lived in the most exclusive condo on Waikiki Beach, had factories in Korea and Taiwan, and offices across the United States. I drove a Harley-Davidson and a Mercedes convertible and I dated beautiful women. I was cooler than cool.

Yet deep down I knew my rock and roll products were not doing much for the world. God did not have to tell me my products were not making the world a better place to live. I knew that. My rock products were what Fuller called "obnoxico." Obnoxious products produced by an obnoxious company.

As Fuller suggested I opened my eyes and asked myself what I thought God wanted me to do. Fuller, a futurist, was constantly looking at the evolution of evolution. He asked himself "What did God want for humanity, for the planet, for the future?"

Fuller believed humans were God's *multimillion-year experiment*, to see if humans could "get it." Fuller believed God wanted to know if humans would use our minds to create *heaven on earth* or *hell on earth.*

He also believed that humans were in "the final examination." He believed that if humans did not "get it," we (the human race) would use our minds to kill ourselves and our tiny planet. Fuller said after we and our planet were "extinct," God would allow planet Earth to heal, life would appear again, and God would put a new bunch of primates on Earth, and another multimillion-year experiment would begin.

Fuller's view on life was measured in millions of years. Humans' view of life is measured in decades. That is why his predictions on the future have been so accurate. He looked at the future from God's mind, not humans' minds.

It was after spending a week with him that I began to ask myself, "What did God want done?" not "What do I want to do?"

Since I hated poverty, and I doubted God wanted people to be poor, I saw financial education as a possible answer to the problem of poverty. I began to teach what my rich dad had taught me. It was a leap of faith.

Bucky went through a similar process. He would eventually ask himself: "What can I do? I'm just a little guy."

After asking himself that question, he stopped working for money and began asking himself what God wanted done… and what could he do.

I do not know if God wants *prosperity* rather than *poverty,* but that is why and how The Rich Dad Company was formed. We believe in teaching people to fish, rather than giving them fish.

Q: Do you see a possibility of another world war breaking out if things continue the way they're going?

Melinda G. – Australia

A: Yes. We are already in that war. It is a war on many fronts and many levels. Today's wars are known as a currency wars, trade wars, terrorism, technology wars, military wars, and social media wars.

In the words of Alexis de Tocqueville:

> "All who seek to destroy liberty in a democratic nation should know that war offers them the surest and shortest route to success."

I am afraid the America I was born in is gone, as is the American Dream.

I am afraid we are already in another world war, this time a war of greed, ignorance, hate, and mobs incited via social media.

I am afraid we are at the tipping point of the world Ayn Rand wrote about in her classic *Atlas Shrugged,* a world run by Socialists and Fascist bureaucrats, aka the Illuminati, while the real Capitalists, the real producers of wealth, go into hiding.

In many ways, I am already in hiding.

Q: Do you think that U.S. dollar devaluation and hyperinflation will finally expose these elites and end this dominance over the other 99 percent?

William J. – Sweden

A: No. There will always be people who want to dominate, oppress, and take away the freedom of others.

It is this arrogant, oppressive, greedy and domineering character of human nature that Fuller described when he talked about humans "not getting it," and why humans are in the "final examination."

When Fuller talked and wrote about humans "getting it" he was describing human evolution, evolving from you and me working only for ourselves to you and me working for a world that worked for everyone... not just a world that works for those who have education and money.

To quote Alexis de Tocqueville again:

"The greatness of America lies not in being more enlightened than any other nation, but rather in her ability to repair her faults."

America lost her greatness when the Fed ripped off the world by printing trillions of dollars in 1998, 2008, and today. America lost her moral compass when America printed money in the name of protecting the rich, destroying the middle class, and creating an underclass of educated, working poor.

Our educational system is an accomplice in this process of the rich and educated ripping off the rest of humanity, destroying our environment, all in the name of making fake money.

Chapter Fifteen

WHO TOOK MY MONEY?

HOW RETIREMENT, PENSIONS, AND FAKE ASSETS ARE CAUSING THE POOR AND THE MIDDLE CLASS TO GROW POORER

S ince 2008, the four biggest Central Banks have printed over $9 trillion to save the world economy.

Where did all that money go? *Who got the money?*

Did you?

And why are so many pensions going broke?

Threats to the World Economy

Today as I write in late 2018, there are four serious threats to the world economy. They are:

1. **Rising interest rates**

    After 2008, the central banks of the world lowered interest rates to the lowest levels in recent history. The Central Banks needed people to borrow money.

    Cheap debt blew the world into massive assets bubbles. Stocks, bonds, real estate, and businesses became hot air balloons.

    Rising interest rates will bring these hot air balloons down.

2. **China**

China is in trouble. China may have the worst debt-to-GDP ratio of all major countries. China borrowed and loaned out more money than any other country. If China crashes the world crashes.

Countries like Australia and Brazil that export raw materials to China suffer when China struggles.

3. **A strong U.S. dollar**

When President Trump lowered tax rates, especially for B-quadrant businesses, the United States became a tax haven. Billions poured into the U.S. economy, causing the U.S. dollar to grow stronger.

A strong dollar is not good for workers because U.S. products become more expensive, and jobs are lost if demand for U.S. products drops.

A strong U.S. dollar is not good for emerging countries that borrowed in U.S. dollars. A strong U.S. dollar means their currency becomes weaker. This makes it harder for these smaller countries and companies to pay off their debt in U.S. dollars.

4. **Pensions**

As stated in an earlier chapter, worker pensions all over the world are going bust.

In the United States, Social Security and Medicare are on life support, just as millions of Baby Boomers retire and need to rely on these social programs.

Here's a fact you may be familiar with: The number one cause of bankruptcy in America is medical expenses.

In 2030, the year Baby Boomers become "super seniors," (85+) the global pension systems may collapse—just when Baby Boomers need the money most.

Repeating quotes on the growing pension crisis from the previous chapter:

IMF warns:

> "The biggest source of risk comes from state and local government retirement pensions."

Simon Black warns:

> "Spain's pension fund is almost fully depleted."

> "The United Kingdom has trillions of pounds worth of unfunded public pensions."

> "Even conservative Switzerland has a public pension that's only 69 percent funded—a seemingly fantastic number by today's dismal standards."

Martin Armstrong warns:

> "The largest public pension fund in the United States is the California Public Employees Retirement System (CalPERS) for civil servants. California is in a state of very serious insolvency. We strongly advise our clients to get out before it is too late."

Reuters warns:

> "The Pension Benefit Guarantee Corporation to become insolvent within a decade. The PBGC is the U.S. government agency that acts as a backstop to troubled pension plans by insuring the pensions of millions of American workers."

If millions of workers contributed trillions of dollars into these pension funds, why are these funds going broke? Who got all that money?

A better question might be: Why are the rich getting richer?

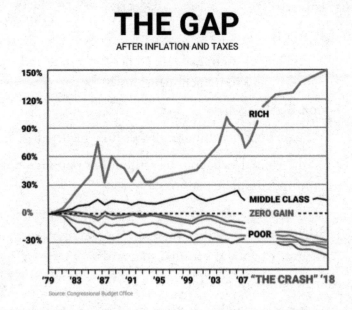

THE GAP
AFTER INFLATION AND TAXES

A: A picture is worth a thousand words. This chart shows the pension money went from the poor and middle class to the rich.

Q: Wait a minute. Are you saying our pension money flowed from the poor and middle class to the rich?

A: I am. Without real financial education, the poor and middle class are lost in space. They have no idea how their money and wealth are being stolen by the rich via the money they work for, their taxes, their homes, their savings, and their retirements accounts.

The Cash Heist

In 1983, I read Bucky Fuller's book *Grunch of Giants*. Grunch, you may recall, stands for Gross Universal Cash Heist. In 1983, I became a student for the first time in my life, wanting to find out how Grunch stole our wealth.

I found out Grunch steals out wealth via our governments, our educational systems, our money, religions, banks, and Wall Street.

The following are five ways Grunch steals our wealth via our money, savings, and investments.

Five Reasons Why the Poor and Middle Class Lose
REASON #1: Gamblers Run the Casino

During the 1950s and 1960s, only gamblers invested in the stock market. It was considered unethical for a financial advisor to recommend stocks to their clients.

The fear of the 1929 stock market crash and decades-long depression that followed, remained fresh on the WWII generation's minds. During the 1950s and 1960s, smart investors purchased government bonds or saved money.

In the 1950s to 1960s, my poor dad and my rich dad were savers. Saving money was safer than the stock market because after the 1944 Bretton Woods Agreement, the U.S. dollar was backed by gold. The U.S. dollar became the reserve currency of the world, or "good as gold."

In 1971, the Nixon put the final nail in the coffin of the gold standard.

The dollar and all government money became debt. Gamblers took over the government casino. Debtors became winners and savers became losers.

The educational systems of the world never mention this crucial turn of events in world history.

Poor dad continued to save. He did not change. He was counting on his savings government pension to save him.

Rich dad did change. He had to change because, as an entrepreneur, he did not have a government paycheck or pension to fall back on.

Sometime in 1973, rich dad changed his tune entirely. In 1973, after realizing what the government was up to, rich dad came up with his lesson #1, which is: "The rich do not work for money."

In 1973, rich dad realized money was toxic, designed to steal the wealth of anyone who worked for money, saved money, or invested money in government sponsored investments such as 401(k)s, IRAs, stocks, mutual funds, and ETFs.

In 1973, rich dad advised his son and me to learn to use debt to acquire assets. That is why I took my first real estate course. I also took stocks and bond courses, as well as my certified financial planner courses.

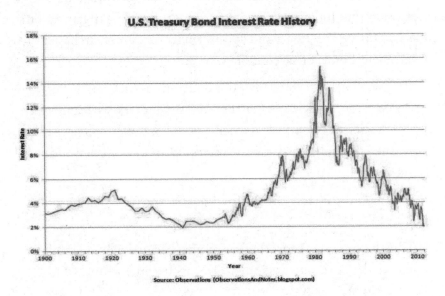

As you can see by this chart, savers did well up until around 1990.

After 1990, interest rates began to decline. Poor and middle class savers became losers.

After 1990, the gamblers, led by the Fed, Big Banks, and U.S. Treasury, began printing more and more money, to save themselves and their rich friends.

WHY SAVERS ARE LOSERS

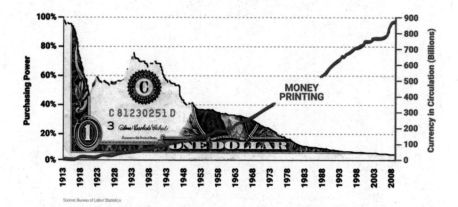

Source: Bureau of Labor Statistics

Printing money made the working poor and middle class poorer because fake money creates inflation and inflation makes life more expensive.

REPEATING RICH DAD'S LESSON #1:
"The rich do not work for money."

REPEATING POOR DAD'S LESSON:
"Go to school, get a job and work for money,
save money, and get out of debt."

I did not listen to my poor dad.

A Brief History of a Heist

After 1971 gamblers became winners. Notice the accelerated rise in illustrated in 125-year history of Dow Jones Industrial Average, the stock market, after 1971.

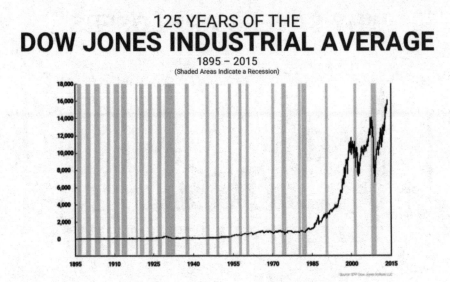

125 YEARS OF THE
DOW JONES INDUSTRIAL AVERAGE
1895 – 2015
(Shaded Areas Indicate a Recession)

In the 1970s, business schools started to bad-mouth gold, calling it by John Maynard Keynes' phrase, a "barbaric relic." Today, most MBA graduates and corporate executives know only fake money and fake assets. They do not know much about God's money, gold and silver.

In the 1970s poor and middle class kids were admitted to Ivy League schools, schools for the rich. In his book *Tailspin,* Steven Brill writes about how poor and middle class kids like him were admitted to the Ivy League schools and began rubbing shoulders with multigenerational really rich kids, rich kids whose parents owned businesses and real estate, like the Kennedys, the Bush family, and Trump's family.

Poor and middle-class students of our finest schools such as Barack Obama and Bill and Hillary Clinton realized they had to catch up to their rich classmates. Notice all three are attorneys. As Brill, also an attorney from Yale, writes, attorneys from poor and middle-class backgrounds began inventing fake assets, financially engineered derivatives that made them richer, but ripped off the poor and middle class.

In 1972, President Nixon opened the door to China. The working poor became poorer, as wages stagnated and/or jobs were lost.

In 1974, ERISA, the Employee Retirement Income Security Act, was passed. ERISA was pushed through by the lobbyists, Big Banks, the Fed, Wall Street, and thousands of other special interest groups, the military, teachers' unions, and NGOs ("the swamp," as President Trump calls them) that want government tax dollars. Four years later, we saw the origins of the 401(k).

ERISA, 401(k)s, and IRAs are products of "the swamp."

ERISA paved the way for the 401(k), IRAs, and employee pension plans. ERISA opened the doors to the big casino known as the stock and bond markets to millions of poor and middle-class workers without any financial education.

As leaders printed money, ripping off most workers, a few middle-class investors, such as my rich dad, caught on to the heist and did well as the stock, bond, and real estate markets were blown into bubbles.

By 1978, millions of amateurs were forced into the giant casinos of banks and Wall Street, owned by the rich.

Rich dad called these giant casinos the "house of cards."

This "house of cards" became even more unstable in 1999 when the 1933 Glass-Steagall Act, which separated commercial and investment banking activities, was repealed.

President Bill Clinton and his band of elite bandits, led by Treasury Secretary Robert Rubin, former co-chair of Goldman Sachs and Chairman Emeritus of Council on Foreign Relations, put the nail in the coffin of the working poor and middle class.

Q: How did the Glass-Steagall Act put the nail in the coffin of the working poor and middle class?

A: Glass-Steagall allowed bankers to take Mom and Pop's savings and invest their savings in the great casino.

When the casino lost Mom and Pop's money, the Fed and U.S. Treasury bailed out the casino, saving the rich at the expense of Mom and Pop's future.

The rich bet Mom and Pop's money, the rich lose Mom and Pop's money, Mom and Pop pay for the loss of their money via taxes, and the bailout money pays the bonuses of the rich who bet and lost Mom and Pop's money.

The House of Cards Collapses

Even with all this abuse of Mom and Pop, things were OK. After all, who cares if only a few million people are stepped on.

Then the house of cards begins to wobble.

In 1998, the foundations of global paper casino began to crumble and giant crashes began.

After the 2008 crash, the global central banks and U.S. government printed an estimated $9 trillion, to save themselves and their friends.

As I write in 2018, the world is in another giant bubble economy. Stock, bond, and real estate prices have made millions of gamblers very rich.

Between 1971 to 2018, gamblers were the winners.

Between 1971 and 2018, the poor and middle-class workers who worked hard to earn fake money, saved fake money, and invested it in fake assets run by fake fund managers educated in our finest business schools became today's biggest losers.

Three Giant Bubbles
GIANT BUBBLE #1:

1998: Thailand bust

1999: Long-Term Capital Management bust

2000: Dot.com bust

GIANT BUBBLE #2:

2008: Real estate derivatives bust

GIANT BUBBLE #3:

Bubble Top Year 2018?

In 2018 as interest rates rose, stock and real estate markets fell.

According to CNBC, "super-rich" Asians lost over $100 billion in the first six months of 2018 in the Asian bear markets.

It's been reported that between October 1 and 14, 2018 an estimated $6 trillion evaporated from global capital markets.

Is the end near?

Were the crashes of 2018 a sign that the rich have left the casino?

Ten years after 2008, are Mom and Pop about to lose again?

Triple Tops

When I was in high school, I spent most of my time surfing or gazing out the classroom window, watching for ocean swells.

Every surfer knows, giant waves come in sets. Generally, sets of three. That means, when if you miss the first two waves, turn and head out to sea. The giant third wave is coming.

I vividly remember the biggest wave I ever rode. It was winter, the time when the giant waves hit the shores of Hawaii. I should not have been in the water. I should have been standing on the beach with the crowd, gathering to watch the show. The waves were bigger than my surfing ability, yet ego got me into the water and kept me in the water.

On this day, I heard a surfer much further out from me shout, "Outside!" That meant I was too far inside, right in the break zone.

Immediately, I turned my board and paddled frantically, hoping to get "outside."

The first of the waves was like a mountain. I barely got over the top, only to see the second mountain heading toward the shore. As I cleared the top of the first wave, I saw the "outside" surfers still paddling. I knew the giant third wave was coming. I knew I had to catch the second wave or get wiped out by the third wave.

I was a little late on my takeoff on the second wave. I estimate it was a 12- to 15-foot swell. It probably crested to 18 feet as I stood and "took the drop." My legs wanted to quit as I raced ahead of the wave crashing behind me, but somehow I kept my balance, rode as far as I could, got to the beach, picked up my board and ran as fast as I could up the beach, to get out of the way of the third wave that was just beginning to crash.

The sight of fellow surfers, going up the face of the giant third wave, not making it, watching the swell crest, then break, and seeing their boards flying through the air is burned in my memory.

When people ask me how I learned to time markets, I simply say, "I grew up surfing."

The chart below shows the biggest financial waves in history.

WHY THE RICH DAD COMPANY WAS FORMED

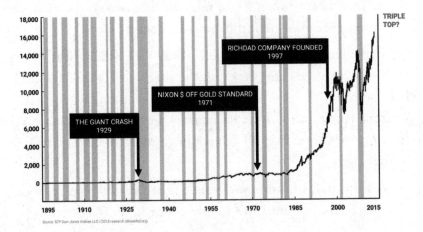

Notice the three peaks. In trader talk, this chart pattern is known as a "triple top."

The first top was 1998. The second top was in 2008. When will we see the third top?

Historically, the third peak signals the long-term exhaustion point. Often a plunge follows after the third peak.

I suspect that, between 2019 and 2025, many amateur gamblers who are rich today may become tomorrow's biggest losers.

Q: When will the giant crash occur?

A: I grew up on the Big Island of Hawaii, the island where the volcano is erupting today. Before every eruption there were "foreshocks," which are small earthquakes that warn the residents an eruption or giant earthquake is coming. After the eruption or giant earthquake, there are aftershocks.

Today as I write, the number of foreshocks is increasing. As I write, most Americans are happy because unemployment is low, jobs are plentiful, and wages are rising.

Q: What are some of the foreshocks?

A: Rising national debt and entitlements, flash crashes in the bond market and stock market, major environmental disasters that will cause insurance rates to rise, cyber-hacking, a global war on terrorism without end, and government leaders who fight and call each other names, rather than solve our national and global problems.

... and Nero Fiddled

There is an old saying that goes, "Nero fiddled while Rome burned."

The chart below shows America burning while our leaders raise money for their next election campaign.

THE GAP
AFTER INFLATION AND TAXES

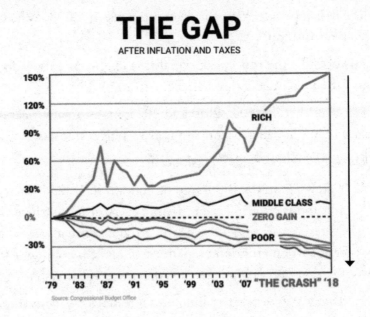

Source: Congressional Budget Office

Is the Golden Age of gamblers coming to an end?

As the saying goes: "Gambling: the sure way to get nothing for something."

As Matthew 20:16 states: "The last will be first… and the first will be last."

This book is dedicated to those who may be last today, and who want to be first tomorrow.

Here are the four additional reasons how retirement, pensions, and fake assets cause the poor and middle class to become poorer.

REASON #2: Inflation

> "Blessed are the young for they shall
> inherit the national debt."
>
> —*Herbert Hoover*

> "If there were no government-guaranteed student
> loans, college tuition would be much lower."
>
> —*Gary Johnson*

Concern for the Coming Generations

Baby Boomers in the United States had an easy life. We grew up during biggest economic boom in world history.

Their children and grandchildren—Gen X, the Millennial generation born after 1982, and the Gen Z internet-generation born after 1995—have a very hard road ahead. Not only are many Millennials unemployed or underemployed, but many start their adult lives burdened by onerous student loan debt. They also inherit a massive national debt, a financial disaster left behind by their parents, grandparents, and great-grandparents.

History Will Haunt the Future Generations

If the future generations do not change a corrupted system, what will their children and grandchildren inherit?

> "By a continuing process of inflation, government
> can confiscate, secretly and unobserved, an
> important part of the wealth of their citizens."
> —*John Maynard Keynes (1883–1946)*

> "The way to crush the bourgeoisie (middle class) is
> to grind them between the millstones of
> taxation and inflation."
> —*Vladimir Lenin (1870–1924)*

> "Inflation destroys savings, impedes planning,
> and discourages investment. That means less
> productivity and a lower standard of living."
> —*Kevin Brady (1955–)*

Q: Why does the government want inflation?

A: To pay the national debt with cheaper dollars.

Q: What happens if the government fails to create inflation?

A: The opposite side of the same coin is deflation. If there is excessive deflation, the U.S. and world economies may slide into the next Great Depression.

Q: Are you saying the government wants us to work for inflated dollars that are worth less and less? '

A: Yes.

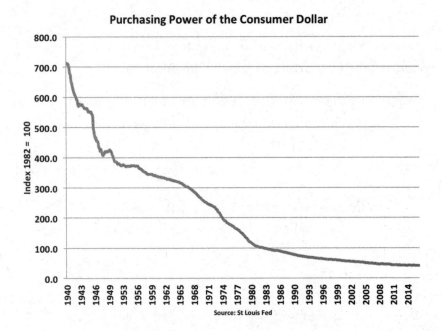

Purchasing Power of the Consumer Dollar

Source: St Louis Fed

This diagram shows how inflation in the United States has eroded the purchasing power of the dollar.

Q: How does the government create inflation?

A: There are many ways. One way is via printing money. Printing money makes money less valuable. As long as the government and banks are printing money, savers are losers. Debtors are winners.

Remember: The banking system is based on printing money. It is known as the fractional reserve system. That means, for every dollar a saver saves, the bank is allowed to lend out a "fraction" of that money. If the fractional reserve is 10 percent a bank may lend out $9 to debtors for every $10 of savers' money. When the $9 goes to the debtor's bank, the debtor's bank may lend out $8.10. The sad truth is, there is only $1 of real money in savings. That is why if savers panic, banks may not be able to give the savers back their money.

Bail Ins

We have all heard of bail-outs. In the future they may be bail-ins, which means the money you have in the bank is converted into "bank stock." You become an investor in the bank.

That is why it may be smart to get a fire-rated home safe and keep gold, silver, cash, and important documents out of banks.

Fake Safes

Some people have "fake safes." If the person is robbed, the owner may show the robber their fake safe, and let the robber have their fake valuables, such as fake jewelry and fake Rolex watches. Their real safe is best out of the home, in a storage locker or behind a "fake wall."

Better yet, if you have a lot to protect, you may want to keep your valuables in another country... but do it legally. Many people secretly hide money and wealth overseas but do it *illegally* and it can be confiscated. There are attorneys who specialize in this type of legal offshore banking.

If you do anything I write about, please do it legally.

The Definition of Money

In Part One of this book, I wrote about the criteria
in order for "money to be money":

1. **Money is a store of value**: After 1971, all government money became toxic and could not be trusted to be a store of value. By definition, all government money is no longer money because it no longer holds value.

2. **Money is a unit of account**: The U.S. dollar is a globally accepted unit of account, for now.

3. **Money is a medium of exchange**: Again, the U.S. dollar is a globally accepted medium of exchange, for now.

Q: So, one reason why the poor and middle class grow poorer is because they trust government money such as the U.S. dollar?

A: Yes. After 1971, all government money became toxic, stealing the wealth of those who work for money and save money.

REASON #3: Real Assets Make the Rich Richer

Amazon founder Jeff Bezos is a billionaire. Do you think he became a billionaire because he receives a billion-dollar paycheck?

The median income of an Amazon employee is $28,446 in 2017.

Jeff Bezos earns more than $28,466 in 12 seconds. Jeff Bezos' annual paycheck is only $1.7 million.

Although Bezos' salary of $1.7 million a year may (technically) be low, there's a reason he's called the richest man in the world. His net worth is skyrocketing, mostly due to the fact that he owns about 80 million shares of Amazon stock.

This same chart explains why Jeff Bezos is so rich.

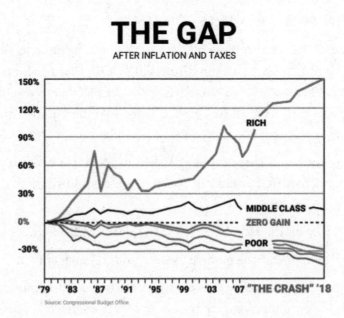

THE GAP
AFTER INFLATION AND TAXES

Every month, a portion of the billions of dollars from millions of workers' 401(k)s and retirement plans flow from their paychecks into shares of Amazon stock.

Jeff gets richer although his salary may stay the same.

Lesson: "Cash" and "flow" are the two most important words in the world of money. Every month, retirement cash flows from the Moms and Pops of the world into the pockets of the Jeff Bezoses of the world.

REASON #4: Crashes Make the Rich Richer

When the market crashes—and it always does—the poor and middle class are wiped out.

When markets crash, the rich simply borrow money and buy back workers' shares at bargain basement prices.

REASON #5: Rubber Chicken Dinners

When I was just starting out in search of my formula to riches, I would go to "rubber chicken dinners" (RCDs), that reminded me of political fundraisers. At these RCDs, potential clients would sit (people like me), have an RCD, then listen to a presentation by a money management company or financial planner.

At a number of these rubber chicken dinners, I nearly threw up the rubber chicken. I could not *believe* people could swallow the rubber chicken BS.

Q: How do the rich get richer if pension funds are going broke?

A: The name of the game is "assets under management.'"

Even if Mom and Pop's investments are not making money, the rich make money via fees and more fees from assets under management.

> *Forbes*, May 27, 2013
>
> **"The Heavy Toll of Investment Fees"**
>
> "The thought of giving up 40 percent per year in investment return to pay for portfolio management and advice would cause most people to walk away. Yet, this is the price many people pay when they hire an investment adviser to manage a mutual fund portfolio or exchange-traded fund (ETF) portfolio."

> NerdWallet, May 11, 2016
>
> **"How a 1 percent Fee Could Cost Millennials $590,000 in Retirement Savings"**
>
> "NerdWallet's analysis found that from ages 45 to 65, the loss to fees increases from 12 percent to over 25 percent.
>
> "'Everyone talks about the benefits of **compounding interest,** but few mention the **danger of compounding fees**,' says Kyle Ramsay, NerdWallet's head of investing and retirement." (Emphasis added.)

The Cost of a Rubber Chicken Dinner

I have gone to many rubber chicken dinners. At these dinners, I listen to financial experts tell me how their magic formula will make me rich.

At one of these rubber chicken dinners, I broke out my calculator, read the glossy brochure's fine print, and computed the total amount in fees I would pay if I started investing at the age of 35.

The numbers were stunning. If I started investing just $750 a month into a 401(k), I would be paying over $2.5 million in fees and hidden fees if the account returned 8 percent a year. You can buy a lot of rubber chicken dinners for $2.5 million.

I had my accountant verify my numbers and all he said was, "It was a good thing you walked away."

What disturbed me were the number of people who did not walk away. Most were waiting in line to sign up for a personal financial analysis.

Why were they waiting in line? Because most were not happy with the returns of their current financial advisor.

As I stated earlier, the name of the game is "assets under management" not "return on investment for the client."

The hot shot from New York's new magic formula was not that magical. As best as I could ascertain, the expert's magic formula was not much more than following the S&P 500, something anyone with a fifth-grade education could do.

The same hot shot claimed his fees were only 1 percent. Yet when I studied the fine print, the fees were much, much higher. This did not stop desperate people from throwing hundreds of thousands of dollars—possibly millions—at him.

Q: What were the people desperate for?

A: Most average investors seek return on investment (ROI), yield, or capital gains. They simply want their money to "grow," not shrink.

Fewer than 5 percent of fund managers beat the market. Yet fund managers always win even if you lose.

Rather than watch the stock market go up and down, I think it's smarter to watch the percentage in fees fund managers are charging.

And there are all kinds of fees:

- **Brokerage account fee:** This could be an annual fee to maintain a brokerage account, a subscription for premium research to help with trading strategy, and/or a fee to access trading platforms.
- **Trade commission:** Charged by a broker when you buy or sell certain investments, such as stocks.
- **Mutual fund transaction fee:** Charged by a broker to buy and/or sell some mutual funds.
- **Expense ratio:** An annual fee charged by all mutual funds, index funds, and exchange-traded funds as a percentage of your investment in the fund.
- **Sales load:** A sales charge or commission on some mutual funds, paid to the broker or salesperson who sold the fund.
- **Management or advisory fee:** Typically, a percentage of assets under management, paid by an investor to a financial advisor.
- **401(k) fee:** An administrative fee to maintain the plan, often passed on to the plan participants by the employer.

A Real Certified Financial Planner

Long-time friend John MacGregor has been certified financial planner for over 25 years. John wrote a book called *The Top 10 Reasons the Rich Go Broke*. His book is about real horror stories of rich people following a financial planner's advice and losing everything. John's book is a must-read for anyone who has their retirement in managed funds.

John tells a funny story of going to one of these rubber chicken dinners and noticing the financial expert looked familiar. John suddenly realized the "expert" was not a fund manager, but a Hollywood actor, who has appeared in many TV commercials. At this dinner, the actor was only playing a fund manager.

John said he got sick watching almost everyone in the room lining up to give this actor their money.

Return on Fees

I realize people need money. That is why brokerage firms charge money for fees, commissions, advice, and for management.

I do not begrudge anyone their right to fees or commissions.

My point is, investors need to be aware of the words "on average," because averages are lies: ROI and ROF, "return on fees."

Analyze Your Fees

If you have a retirement account or are investing in government-endorsed plans such as a 401(k) or IRA filled with mutual funds, ETFs, and money market accounts, first look into the fees, not the returns. If you are not good in math or reading the fine print, hire someone like an accountant or attorney to read and analyze the fine print for you. It may be worth millions over the long term—much, much more than the fee your accountant or attorney charges you.

The fees you pay your accountant or attorney to read the fine print may be worth more than a college education.

I pay a lot of money in fees.

Why? Because my ROF is fantastic.

I pay thousands of dollars in fees to my partner and Rich Dad advisor Ken McElroy's real estate investment company.

Why? Because Ken's ROI is infinite. Ken does not charge a fee until investors have all their money back. After the investors' money is returned, then Ken shares in the ROI, which for Kim and me is in the millions. An infinite return is the antithesis of "fake."

More on this in an upcoming chapter.

A Case for Higher Commissions

When Kim and I moved to Phoenix over 20 years ago, we wanted to know who was the number one commercial real estate broker in Phoenix.

It did not take us long to find out who it was. Kim and I met with Craig, liked him and his philosophy on investing, and made him an offer we make all great real estate brokers. We would pay him more than the 6 percent most real estate agents charge. We agreed to pay him 10 percent plus 10 percent ROI of the investment for being a partner.

Let me explain why Kim and I do this.

Kim and I noticed that many investors ask the broker to work for less. For example, the buyer and seller's brokers come to the table. Just before buyer and seller's agents come to an agreement, quite often the buyer or seller will ask the brokers to "shave their commission," which means work for less. For example, they might ask the broker to work for 3 percent rather than 6 percent.

Why people do that, I do not know. They must think shaving a broker's commission is smart.

Kim and I do not do that. If our broker is the best in town, we want that person to be a partner.

Look at the CASHFLOW Quadrant.

On the left side: the poor and the middle class. On the right side are the rich.

Most people see the world from the E and S side. Most people treat real estate brokers as S-quadrant people, "brokers."

Being from the B and I side of the quadrant myself, I want partners in the B or I quadrants as well if the person is the best. Kenny is our partner in the B and I quadrants. Craig is our partner in the I quadrant.

One day, a friend asked me how I find such great investments. My reply was, "I treat agents as partners, not as real estate brokers."

Our partners have made us millionaires, many times over. We have made millions while most investors attempt to pay their brokers less.

Worst Advice Ever

A few years ago, a friend suggested Kim and I switch accounting firms. Always open to learning more, Kim and I agreed to meet with a name-brand national accounting firm.

We agreed to allow them to analyze our financial statements.

A few weeks later, a follow-up meeting was scheduled.

Kim and I sat in the room as the head accountant announced, "Our financial planning expert has flown in from Washington, DC to advise you on your portfolio."

The expert, dressed like an East Coast preppy with tortoise-rimmed glasses, sat down and said, "I have reviewed your portfolio. You are overweight in real estate. I suggest you sell all your real estate and put the money into stocks, bonds, and mutual funds."

Kim and I burst out laughing. We thought he was kidding. Could he not see most of our income came from cash flow from our properties?

He was not laughing. He was serious.

Later, I asked Tom Wheelwright, a CPA and our personal accountant, "Did he not see we make millions, tax-free, from our real estate?

Tom nodded his head. "Yes, he did."

"So why did he recommend we sell all our real estate?"

Tom said, "He does not receive a commission from your real estate."

"What does he earn money from?" Kim and I asked.

"Assets under management."

The Power of Words

As a kid, we use to say, "Sticks and stones may break my bones, but words will never hurt."

Nothing could be further from the truth. Words are powerful—very, very powerful. We have all had our feelings hurt by words. We have all felt wonderful because of words. We have all been inspired and discouraged by words. And, we have all been deceived, lied to, and misled by words.

One reason I left the MBA program was because of words. Many professors did not use the words used in the real world of business. Most used words based on theory, not reality.

It was my accounting teacher who sealed the deal. When he was using fake definitions for the words "assets" and "liabilities," I left.

The following are definitions of assets and liabilities taught in schools.

> **Asset** (*n*): a resource with economic value that an individual, corporation, or country owns or controls.

I do not know about you, but that definition was vague and ambiguous, not clear or useful.

> **Liability** (*n*): a company's legal financial debts or obligations that arise during the course of business operations.

This is why so many people and accountants call a person's house, car, and refrigerator "assets."

Ambiguous definitions allow accountants and people to "lie to themselves."

That is why so many people say "my house is an asset" when it is really a liability.

That is why, when someone says "my net worth is…" I tune out. Net worth is often worthless—"worth less"—because net worth is based on lies, hopes, dreams, and hallucinations. A person can count their car in net worth, their furniture, clothing, house, even artwork at exaggerated values. That is why rich dad repeatedly said, "Networth is worth less."

RICH DAD LESSON: Rich dad often said, "A person with a big house and nice cars is often poorer than a person with nothing. A person with a big house and nice car may look rich and have a high net worth, but they may be less than 30-days away from bankruptcy if they lose their job."

And that is why rich dad often said, "Your banker wants to see your financial statement, not your report card from school. Your financial statement reflects your financial IQ, how smart you are with your money."

Rich dad wanted exact numbers. Numbers he could measure and verify. That is why rich dad taught his son and me that the two most important words in business are "cash" and "flow."

Rich Dad's Teachers

As stated earlier, rich dad learned business from real teachers. Being only 13 years old when he took over his father's business, his teachers were his bankers, accountants, attorneys, bookkeepers, and others.

Since he was only 13 years old, his teachers had to KISS, Keep It Super Simple.

That is why rich dad taught his son and me when we were about 10 years old: "Assets and liabilities are nouns. You need a verb to know if the noun is an asset or a liability. For example, a house is a noun. You do not know if it is an asset or liability until you add the verb 'flow'."

If a house is a rental property and putting money in your pocket, the house is an asset.

If the house is your home and taking money from your pocket, then it is a liability.

And that is why rich dad's son and I learned:

1. Assets put money (cash flow) into your pocket.
2. Liabilities take money (cash flow) out of your pocket.

Your Greatest Liability

From the moment you are born, your retirement is your greatest liability... the day when you stop working or unable to work.

If you are fortunate to live a long life, life grows more and more expensive.

That is why Social Security and Medicare are bankrupt today, just as Baby Boomers are retiring.

Squirrels instinctively know to store nuts for the winter. Humans do not. If a human being is unable to store enough financial support to keep them alive after their working days are over, the winter of their lives and the lives of their families may be like the lives of squirrels who run out of nuts during winter.

A friend of mine was no longer able to care for his mom at home. He found a nursing home that would provide the 24-hour medical attention she required. The home is costing him $9,000 a month. She has been there for six years and is expected to live longer.

They did not expect her to live this long. His mother's nursing home cost more per month than he earns. He and his wife are living on income and retirement savings.

Who will care for you when you can no longer earn a living?

You Cannot Catch Fish in Clean Water

Earlier in this book I stated, "After 1971, money became invisible."

Without a real financial education, most people cannot see money.

Most people swim blind in dirty water. Without a real financial education, most people do not know the difference between assets and liabilities.

This makes it very easy for the ultra-rich who control the central banks, governments, Wall Street, "too big to fail" banks, and our elite schools, to become very rich… catching little fish swimming blind in dirty water.

Once the fish are trapped, swimming in giant nets of fake money, the ultra-rich sell the little fish fake assets such as savings accounts, stocks, bonds, mutual funds, and ETFs.

For Mom and Pop, their retirement years are their greatest liability if they live a long life.

The ultra-rich know this.

They sell fake *assets* to Mom and Pop, because fake assets are real assets for the ultra-rich. Just watch the cash flowing.

Follow the Money

To understand the difference between real assets and fake assets, just look again at all the charts and follow the money.

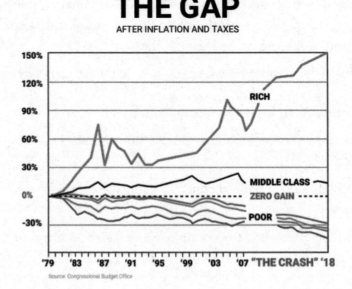

THE GAP
AFTER INFLATION AND TAXES

Source: Congressional Budget Office

WHY SAVERS ARE LOSERS

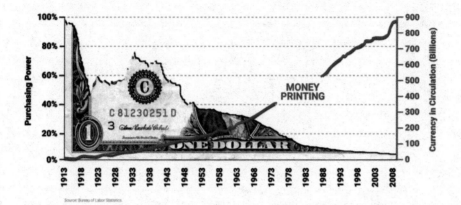

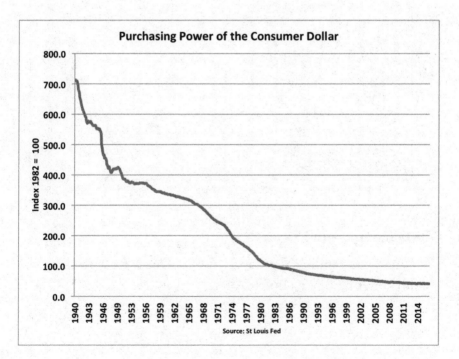

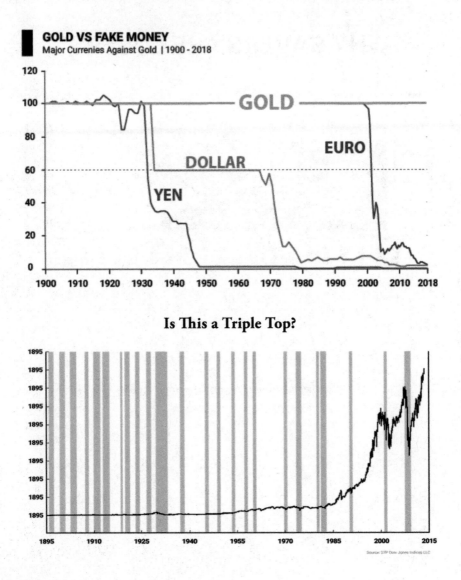

GOLD VS FAKE MONEY
Major Currenies Against Gold | 1900 - 2018

Is This a Triple Top?

Source: STP Dow Jones Indices LLC

The Quadrant—and Taxes

When you combine the CASHFLOW Quadrant with taxes, the muddy water becomes a little clearer.

TAX PERCENTAGES PAID PER QUADRANT

Those who work for money pay the highest percentage in taxes.

Those who invest workers' money make the most money and pay the lowest percentages in taxes.

The Worst Financial Advice

This is why the advice to "go to school, get a job, work hard, save money, buy a house, get out of debt, and invest in a well-diversified portfolio of stocks, bonds, mutual funds, and ETFs" could be the primary reason for the lines on chart below:

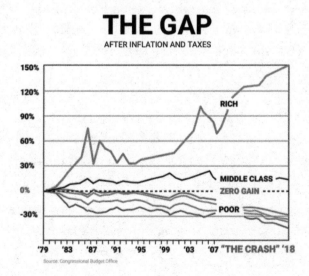

THE GAP
AFTER INFLATION AND TAXES

Without real financial education in our schools, the end of the poor and middle class is near.

I'll pose some questions:

What will happen if the gap grows wider?

Is the world heading for a two-class world: a peaceful world of the rich and the poor?

Or, could the world be heading for another French or Bolshevik revolution, a war between the rich and the poor...the *have-nots* taking from the *haves?*

Can this gap between rich and poor be narrowed?

Could a little financial education change the future of the world?

Yes, the gap can be narrowed with a little real financial education. But you have to seek that education for you and your family.

Our education system is controlled by the very people who want to keep the water dirty.

Q: Who controls our education?

A: In 1903, the ultra-rich like John D. Rockefeller played a role in creating the General Education Board. Today, the rich continue to control what subjects are taught in our schools. That is why there is no real financial education in our schools.

In Conclusion

Rich dad often said, "When your banker tells you your house is an asset, he is not lying. He's just not telling you the truth. What he does not tell you is that your house is the bank's asset, not yours."

The same could be said for your savings, stocks, bonds, mutual funds, ETFs, and retirement plan. They are all fake assets because the cash flows to the ultra-rich via compounding fees and expenses.

All you have to do is follow the money, and you will see who the cash is flowing to.

As legendary investor John Bogle, founder of Vanguard Funds, said, "[Investors] put up 100 percent of the cash, took 100 percent of the risk, and got 33 percent of the return."

And if the mutual fund crashes, the investor loses 100 percent. If the mutual fund makes money, investors receive 20 percent of the reward, the owners of the mutual fund receive 80 percent.

Remember, the name of the game is not, "Take care of the investor's money." The name of the game is "assets under management."

Even if Mom and Pop lose everything, and even if the fund crashes, burns, and dies, the owners of the fund always win, due to fees, fees, and more fees.

All It Takes Is Clean Water

Warren Buffett said it best: "If you've been in the [poker] game 30 minutes and you don't know who the patsy is, you're the patsy."

All it takes is clean water to see:
1. Who the cash is flowing from
2. Who the cash is flowing to

Then you will be able to see real assets and real liabilities. Most importantly, you will know who the real patsy is.

If you want to learn how to see cash flowing, take real accounting classes from real accountants, read *Tax-Free Wealth* by Rich Dad advisor Tom Wheelwright (a *real* accountant), and have fun playing the *CASHFLOW* game.

People Teaching People

Kim and I created *CASHFLOW* in 1996 so people could teach people how to see cash flowing. Today, there are thousands of CASHFLOW Clubs all over the world.

Once you can see cash flowing, you will be better able to see fake money, fake teachers (especially fake financial advisors and brokers), and fake assets.

Most importantly, once you can see cash flowing, you will no longer be a fish swimming in dirty water.

In the next chapter, you will see what the rich see, and why the rich get richer.

YOUR QUESTIONS... ROBERT'S ANSWERS

Q: It seems that most people are distracted from these important issues (by television, sports, fake news, etc.) So could the next crash be the final wake-up call as to what's really going on?

Ellie B. – Romania

A: Let's hope so. In financial literacy terms, the world has been in a *secular bull market for approximately 70 years.* That means the markets and economy have been going up since the 1944 Bretton Woods Conference, the year the United States took control of the world economy, and the year the dollar became the reserve currency of the world.

I suspect that *70-year secular bull market* is about to come to an end, because America used its financial authority to make the rich richer, at the expense of the poor and middle class of the world. This is the Grunch that Fuller wrote about.

We may be entering a *secular bear market...* possibly the collapse of the U.S. dollar and a new global depression. As rich dad would say about economic change, "The toilet will flush."

This is bad news for most people. It can also be great news for those who are aware and prepared for a brave new world of money.

Q: Many people believe in giving people fish—free education, free food, free healthcare. Which answer is right?

Michael S. – Scotland

A: Both answers are right. The right answer depends upon the person seeking their answer. A more important question is, "What do you think God wants done?"

Q: Do you think the next crash will result in a new totalitarian government in the United States resembling Nazi Germany of the 1930s and 1940s?

Lydia J. - Lithuania

A: Yes. The word is fascism, a form of government run by bureaucrats. There is a big difference between businesspeople and bureaucrats. Bureaucrats are fascists who make rules and expect everyone to live by their rules. There are bureaucrats in every walk of life.

Don't get me wrong. Rules are important. We need rules. For example, it is best we all drive on the same side of the road and obey speed limits.

The problem is that bureaucrats want everyone to live in a world governed by their rules. The problem is most bureaucrats, like most academics, do not live in the real world of money. Most bureaucrats tend to be socialists and communists, not capitalists.

Ayn Rand wrote about this world in her book *Atlas Shrugged*. That book is about a world where the economy is broken, a world where nothing works because bureaucrats now run the world. In response, the last remaining capitalist go into hiding, refusing to be exploited by non-producing bureaucratic parasites.

Chapter Sixteen

FISHING IN
CLEAN WATER

FAKE NEWS... AND TRANSPARENCY

H ere are some headlines that should get you thinking...
and drive home a few points about what is real and what
isn't...

Jared Kushner Paid No Federal Income Tax for Years, Documents Suggest

New York Times

October 13, 2018

"Over the past decade, Jared Kushner's family company has spent billions of dollars buying real estate. His personal stock investments have soared. His net worth has quintupled to almost $324 million.

"And yet, for several years running, Mr. Kushner—President Trump's son-in-law and a senior White House advisor—appears to have paid almost no federal income taxes, according to confidential financial documents reviewed by *The New York Times*."

Fake News... or Stupid Journalists?

In Warren Buffett's words:

> "The smarter the journalists are, the better off society is. For to a degree, people read the press to inform themselves— and the better the teacher, the better the student body."

> **Q:** Are these *New York Times* writers smart journalists, stupid journalists, or promoters of a fake news story?

> **A:** We may never know. If you just read the headlines, it sounds like Jared Kushner, husband of President Trump's daughter Ivanka, sounds like another crook, much like his father-in-law, "The Donald."

Without much financial education, millions of people, especially academic elites like my poor dad say, "The rich are crooks."

Here are some questions you might want to think about: Is Buffett correct? Do we need smart journalists for a smarter society? Do people read the press to inform themselves?

If Buffett is correct—and I believe he is—what are fake news, anti-social social-media, journalists (bloggers included) without real financial education doing for our society? How many journalists are like my poor dad, academically bright, well educated, financially naïve individuals who deep down believe the rich are crooks?

The answers? We may never know.

The New York Times article continues (emphasis added):

> "[Kushner's] low tax bills are the result of a common tax-minimizing maneuver that, year after year, generated millions of dollars in losses for Mr. Kushner, according to the documents. But the losses were only on paper—Mr. Kushner and his company did not appear to actually lose any money. *The losses were driven by depreciation, a tax benefit that lets real estate investors deduct a portion of the cost of their buildings from their taxable income every year.*

"In 2015, for example, Mr. Kushner took home $1.7 million in salary and investment gains. But those earnings were swamped by $8.3 million of losses, largely because of 'significant depreciation' that Mr. Kushner and his company took on their real estate, according to the documents reviewed by *The Times*."

More questions to ponder:

Are the journalists saying or implying that, "Jared Kushner is a crook"? (For the record, they're not. The article clearly states, "Nothing in the documents suggests Mr. Kushner or his company broke the law.")

How can Mr. Kushner take home $1.7 million in income and his earnings be swamped by $8.3 million in losses?

If he lost $8.3 million, why isn't Jared Kushner bankrupt?

Is *depreciation* some mysterious tax loophole used by the nefarious crooked rich? Or is *depreciation* a legal government tax incentive that can be used by everyone, including the journalists?

Depreciation is a legal government tax incentive that can be used by everyone: you, me, and even the journalists.

Q: Did Jared take home $1.7 million in income and pay nothing in taxes because he lost $8.3 million via depreciation.

A: Yes.

Q: Is that legal?

A: Yes.

Q: Do the journalists want people to believe Jared, his family, and the Trumps are crooks?

A: Only you can answer that question.

The New York Times article continues:

> "Nothing in the documents suggests Mr. Kushner or his company broke the law. A spokesman for Mr. Kushner's lawyer said that Mr. Kushner 'paid all taxes due.'

> "In theory, the depreciation provision is supposed to shield real estate developers from having their investments whittled away by wear and tear on their buildings.

> "In practice, though, the allowance often represents a lucrative giveaway to developers like Mr. Trump and Mr. Kushner."

Q: Why do the journalists use incendiary words such as "lucrative giveaway to developers like Mr. Trump and Mr. Kushner"?

A: This an example of "yellow journalism."

Q: What is yellow journalism?

A: Yellow journalism and the yellow press, according to Wikipedia, are American terms for journalism and associated newspapers that present little or no legitimate well-researched news while instead using eye-catching headlines for increased sales. Techniques may include exaggerations of news events, scandal-mongering, or sensationalism.

Q: Why don't the journalists teach the tax lessons Tom Wheelwright your personal advisor teaches? Tom teaches that the tax-code has only a few pages on *how to pay taxes*. Most of the thousands of pages of tax code are dedicated to *how not to pay taxes legally*. And this is true in most Western countries."

A: In his book *Tax-Free Wealth* and in his classes, Tom teaches people like you and me that a capitalist government needs partners.

- In a capitalist government, a democracy wants citizens like you and me to be partners, investing in projects the government needs done.
- A communist government is centralized and most capital projects are run by government bureaucrats. In China, for instance, most of the rich are friends of bureaucrats, or "princelings," children of bureaucrats.
- In the United States, "a free-market economy" means that ordinary people and citizen entrepreneurs are encouraged to participate in projects the government wants and needs done via tax incentives.

Tax Incentives for Housing

For example, the government needs entrepreneurs to provide housing. This is why "depreciation" is a tax incentive for real estate investors.

Tax Incentives for Jobs

The government also wants people to provide jobs. That is why entrepreneurs in the B quadrant with over 500 employees pay less in taxes.

In 2018, Amazon was shopping for a new city to relocate their new headquarters. Many cities would have loved to have thousands of highly paid employees, which is why so many cities offered tax incentives to Amazon.

Elon Musk's Tesla Motors received over $1 billion in tax incentives to build his battery factory in Nevada.

Tax Incentives for High-Paid Employees

Amazon and Tesla have thousands of well-paid employees. Generally speaking, the more an employee is paid, the more tax revenue is generated. Highly paid employees attract hundreds of small businesses. Small business owners pay higher taxes. That is why local governments offer tax incentives to companies like

Amazon and Tesla to move their businesses to cities and states across the United States.

Big business attracts small business, which means more jobs, and more jobs mean more housing, more schools, more government service employees, and more taxes to city and state governments.

Tax Incentives for Energy

Civilization cannot grow without energy. If energy became scarce or more expensive, civilization would crumble.

Hence the government also wants entrepreneurs to provide energy, so there are tax incentives for oil and gas exploration.

Today, the United States is less dependent upon foreign oil.

Tax Incentives for Food

And the government wants you and me to produce food, so there are tax incentives for people to produce food.

If people are hungry, riots follow.

Incentives—not Loopholes

These incentives are not loopholes or "mistakes" that unscrupulous crooks sneak through, as these journalists want readers to believe. These incentives are intentional, legal, and available for everyone, including the journalists.

Again, tax and tax incentives are the engine of capitalism.

Who Pays Taxes

Again, looking at the CASHFLOW Quadrant, you get the picture about who pays taxes.

TAX PERCENTAGES PAID PER QUADRANT

The rich like the Trumps and Kushners prepare their kids for the B and I quadrants.

The journalists probably did well in school and learned the skills and mindset for the E or S quadrant. They are either "yellow journalists" or simply swimming blind in dirty water, financially naïve to what is going on in the B and I quadrants.

The New York Times article continues (emphasis added):

> "The law assumes that buildings' values decline every year when, in reality, they often gain value. Its enormous flexibility allows real estate investors to determine their own tax bills."

Q: The tax law allows real estate investors to determine their own tax bills? Even pay nothing in taxes?

A: Yes. And professional real estate investors can take depreciation deductions that homeowners cannot.

Q: Why doesn't everyone do this?

A: Tax is not a subject taught in high school.

Q: Did you learn about taxes in high school?

A: No. I began learning about money, debt, and taxes working for rich dad when I was nine years old.

Q: Did that give you a financial head start in life?

A: It did. That is why Kim and I created the *CASHFLOW* game in 1996 and wrote *Rich Dad Poor Dad* and founded the Rich Dad Company in 1997. We wanted everyone to have the same financial head start my rich dad gave me… education I passed on to Kim.

In 1996, we submitted our *CASHFLOW* game to Harvard for clinical evaluation. The game was rejected outright and returned. The game box was not even opened.

That was a good thing. It was a slap on the face. A wake-up call.

When Harvard rejected our game, poo-pooing the idea that people learn via "simulations," having fun, and making mistakes, Kim and I realized we were marketing to people like my poor dad, academics with jobs.

Failure is the other side of the success. Failing to have Harvard evaluate our game was a good thing. We knew who our customer was. We knew it was not universities, schools, or school teachers.

People Teaching People

Kim and I were now certain who our customer was.

In 1997, I wrote *Rich Dad Poor Dad.* The book was originally written as a brochure, a simple book, a real-life story to explain the importance of financial statements and accounting, and to sell the *CASHFLOW* game to people who wanted to learn… rather than close-minded professors who know all the answers.

The same year we founded The Rich Dad Company. Our mission is, "To elevate the financial well-being of humanity."

To fulfill our mission, we knew we had to bypass an obsolete, expensive, slow, boring, arrogant, out-of-touch-with-reality educational system. Our business plan was simple: Teach what schools do not teach… the subject of money. A subject—a life skill—everyone in the world uses.

The Rich Dad Company focused on building financial education products designed to educate via *people teaching people.*

You need to go to school to be a doctor or lawyer, a tradesman, or a highly paid employee. But you do not need to go to school to become a rich entrepreneur or investor.

As the cover of *Rich Dad Poor Dad* states, "What the rich teach their kids about money that the poor and middle class do not."

What Jared Kushner Knows

This next segment of *The New York Times* article explains what the rich teach their kids, what kids like Jared Kushner know, that the poor and middle class do not.

> "Mr. Kushner's losses, stemming in large part from the depreciation deduction, appeared to wipe out his taxable income in most years covered by the documents.

> "He is reporting the losses even though he bought his properties with borrowed funds. In many cases, Mr. Kushner kicked in less than 1 percent of the purchase price, according to the documents. Even that small amount generally was paid for with loans."

> **Q:** Jared Kushner borrowed the 1 percent he applied to the purchase price of billions of dollars in real estate? Does that mean he purchased billions with nothing?

> **A:** Yes. It is known as an "infinite return"… aka "money for nothing." The same lesson I was taught in 1973 in my first real estate seminar.

Q: So, you don't need money to become rich?

A: Correct. But you do need real financial education and real experience.

The moment I understood infinite returns, I never again had to say: "I can't afford it. I don't have any money."

You don't need money to become rich once you understand the power or infinite returns.

Infinite Returns on Information

FREE VIDEO: Tom Wheelwright and I did a 45-minute presentation at the 2018 New Orleans Investment Conference. The title of our presentation was, "Infinite ROI: Return on Information" You can watch it here: http://reg-backoffice.s3.amazonaws.com/videos/kiyosaki-noic18/Kiosaki.mov

Watching this video, you will better understand how and why Jared Kushner can buy millions of dollars of real estate without money and pay no taxes. Kim and I use the same formula.

The New York Times article continues (emphasis added):

"The result: Mr. Kushner is getting tax-reducing losses for spending someone else's money, which is permitted under the tax code. Depreciation deductions are available in other industries, but they generally don't get to take losses related to spending with borrowed money. ...

"As far as the Internal Revenue Service is concerned, the Kushners have been losing money for years. ...

"Unlike typical wage earners, the owners of such companies can report losses for tax purposes. When a firm like Kushner Companies reports expenses in excess of its income, the result is a "net operating loss." That loss can wipe out any taxes that the company's owner otherwise *would owe. Depending on the size of the loss, it can even be used to get refunds for taxes paid in prior years or eliminate tax bills in future years."*

Q: So debt and taxes make the rich richer?

A: Yes, but doing so, requires a sound financial education, lots or practice, and a team of very, very, smart advisors like Tom Wheelwright. Always remember:

"There are many doors to financial heaven. And even more doors to financial hell."

The *New York Times* article continues:

"'If I had to live my life over again, I would have been in the real estate business,' said Jonathan Blattmachr, a well-known trusts and estates lawyer, now a principal at Pioneer Wealth Partners, who reviewed the Kushner documents. 'It's fantastic. You get tax deductions for things you don't pay for.'"

Q: Even a very smart trust and estate lawyer does not know how the rich use debt and taxes to get richer and richer?

A: Correct. Very few people do. I encourage you to watch the free video of Tom and me, and you will learn what very few people know. [See Sidebar on page 378 of this chapter.]

The *New York Times* article continues:

"Last year's tax legislation eliminated that benefit for all industries but one: real estate."

Q: Is that why you sold all your paper assets, stocks, bonds, mutual funds, and ETFs in 2016?

A: What do you think?

Swimming in Clean Water

In another article, *The New York Times* reported that Jared Kushner and Ivanka Trump earned $82 million in passive income in 2017. Probably tax-free.

It is *information* that makes the rich richer... not money. Information that is not taught in schools.

Pictures are often better than words. Pictured below is what is taught in schools.

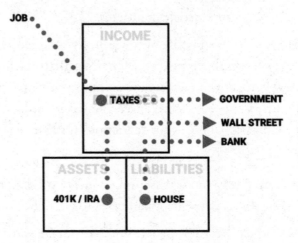

POOR & MIDDLE CLASS

This is what students are taught in schools. Notice where the cash flows from and to.

This is what dirty water looks like. This is what happens when you say to a child, go to school, get a job, buy a house, get out of debt, invest for the long term. This mantra muddies the water... to dirty water.

Is the water getting clearer?

McDONALD'S FORMULA

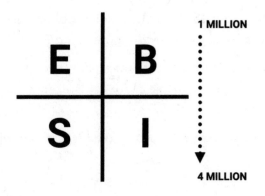

In *Rich Dad Poor Dad*, I wrote about Ray Kroc, founder of McDonald's, asking an MBA class at the University of Texas this question, "What business is McDonald's in?"

A student replied, "Hamburgers."

Kroc's response, "No, McDonald's is in the business of real estate."

In the movie *The Founder*, the idea that McDonald's is in the real estate business is made very clear.

Rich Dad Is in the Real Estate Business

The Rich Dad Company is also in the business of real estate. As this diagram shows, if The Rich Dad Company earns $1 million, we borrow $4 million. We step up our passive income and we are now able to depreciate $5 million in passive losses.

Like Jared Kushner, our passive losses from real estate, offsets our income from our businesses and we pay little to nothing in taxes... legally.

Q: The tax law encourages you to borrow and invest and get richer?

A: Yes. If Kim and I do not borrow and invest in real estate, we pay taxes.

Remember, after 1971, the U.S. dollar became debt. If people stop borrowing money, money disappears and the economy crashes.

That is why credit card companies offer incentives for cardholders to acquire and use credit cards… and, essentially, borrow money.

That is why student loan debt is the biggest asset of the U.S. government.

Debt is money.

People who recommend "living debt-free" are actually hurting the economy. Rather than living debt-free, take real estate courses and learn how to *use* debt and taxes to get richer.

Swimming in Clean Water

This is what clean water looks like. This diagram of cash flowing is how the rich fish in clean water.

With real financial education the rich know:

1. How to use taxes to acquire assets.
2. How to use debt to acquire assets.
3. How to reinvest gains without paying taxes.
4. Why it makes sense to save gold and silver, not fake money.

WHY THE RICH GET RICHER

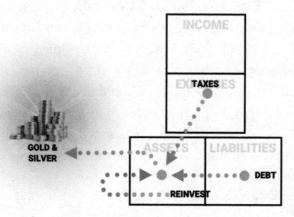

"You Can't Do That Here"

No matter where Tom Wheelwright and I go, every time we show the diagram above, someone will raise his or her hand and say, "You can't do that here."

We have presented this concept and diagram in the United Kingdom, Japan, Russia, Australia, New Zealand, Canada, China, and across the United States.

At the end of every presentation (and explanation of the diagram) someone will say: "You can't do that here."

Q: What do you say to the person saying, "You can't do that here"?

A: Tom and I reply, "Do you have McDonald's here?"

Without financial education, most people cannot see million-dollar opportunities swimming right in front of their eyes.

The New York Times article continues (emphasis added):

> "[Jared Kushner's] low tax bills are the result of a common tax-minimizing maneuver that, year after year, generated millions of dollars in losses for Mr. Kushner, according to the documents. But the losses were only on paper—Mr. Kushner and his company did not appear to actually lose any money. *The losses were driven by depreciation*, a tax benefit that lets real estate investors deduct a portion of the cost of their buildings from their taxable income every year."

More Than Depreciation

TAX FREE INCOME

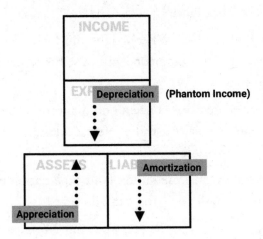

The New York Times journalists focused only on the tax advantages of depreciation. Real financial education must include the tax advantages of depreciation, amortization, and appreciation.

1. DEPRECIATION
    Depreciation is a passive loss awarded to professional real estate investors.

Depreciation is for "wear and tear" on your property and components, such as carpets, lighting, and other essentials required to run a real estate investment business.

2. AMORTIZATION

    Amortization is the reduction of the loan over time.

    Amortization, the reduction of the debt on the property, is paid for by the tenant.

    Amortization gains can be tax-free. One way to get money out of a property is via refinancing, increasing debt, as long as the tenant makes the payments.

    The money borrowed in the refinance is tax-free because it is debt.

    When Mom and Pop refinance their house, that money is also tax-free because it is debt.

    The problem is, Mom and Pop are the tenants making the monthly payments.

    Millions went broke just before 2008 using their home as an ATM, refinancing the appreciation in their home to pay off debt.

    When the market crashed, their appreciation evaporated, and millions owed more on their home than their home was worth.

    Values on millions of homes have not yet returned to pre-2008 prices.

    In my neighborhood, homes that sold for $4 million in 2008 are selling from $2 to $3.5 million in 2018.

    After 2008, many private equity funds and hedge funds bought thousands of foreclosed homes at rock bottom prices.

In 2018, as home prices rise, these funds are selling those same houses, keeping housing prices suppressed.

3. APPRECIATION

Appreciation is the dream of every homeowner.

Millions still believe, "Housing prices always go up."

Real estate flippers dream of capital appreciation.

The problem with flipping a house is a tax known as capital gains.

That is why I prefer to borrow out my appreciation, because there are no taxes on debt.

In the video on infinite returns, there is an example of refinancing a property explaining how the rich use debt to earn millions and not pay taxes.

Jared Kushner and Donald Trump follow the same formula.

Here's a warning: Debt is a loaded gun. A loaded gun can protect you and a loaded gun can kill you.

In the coming crash or collapse, debt (especially corporate debt) will kill the financial future of millions of employees. The collapse will damage employees, even if they are debt-free, because the businesses they work for are loaded with debt and will not be able to pay off their corporate debt.

If millions of employees lose their jobs, millions will not be able to afford the home they live in or the car they drive, because a home and a car are not real assets.

Here's a reminder from history: In 1929, the Dow Jones Industrial Average hit an all-time high of 381. It took 25 years, until 1954, for the stock market to once again reach 381.

Repeating Words from a Rich Man

Warren Buffett's sound words are worth repeating:

> "The smarter the journalists are, the better off society is. For to a degree, people read the press to inform themselves— and the better the teacher, the better the student body."

Warren Buffett operates on infinite returns. He does not use his own money. That is why he is rich.

Return on Information

Again, if you want to learn more about the power of infinite returns, please watch the video with Tom and me at the 2018 New Orleans Investment Conference.

If you really want to learn more, watch the same video with friends, family, and business associates and discuss.

The discussion and learning should be lively, heated, and intense.

People will say, "The rich are crooks."

People who hate President Trump will hate him even more because Tom explains how President Trump gave permanent tax breaks for the rich and took away tax breaks from people who work for money,

Kim and I choose not to be political. Arguing is a waste of time and energy. We simply choose to be rich legally, morally, and ethically.

Most average investors think ROI stands for "return on investment" of money. For the rich, ROI stands for "return on information"... information not found in schools, most books, newspapers, or financial publications.

If you want to swim in clean water, you will need clean information.

In the following chapters, you will learn how to prepare for the coming collapse of a corrupted monetary system and prepare for the future of money.

YOUR QUESTIONS... ROBERT'S ANSWERS

Q: How do we make it clearer to the masses of people that those who are academically smart—but who may know very little or nothing about investing or finance or personal finance—yet write articles about those subjects and are considered experts on finance?

Ella M. – Spain

A: I do not understand the question. Are asking how many academic elite financial experts do not know what they are talking about?

My answer is, ask yourself, why is the writer writing the article? Is the article written to:

1. Sell you something?
2. Educate you?
3. Warn you?
4. Make them money?
5. Make them sound intelligent?

Q: What is the most effective way to reveal to millions of people that tax code is written to provide incentives for investors to do what the government wants investors to do to lower or eliminate taxes? Seems like a daunting task considering all the distractions. Can it be done?

Robert C. – Iceland

A: Doubtful. If everyone knew how and why the rich can earn more and pay less in taxes there might be a revolution because—unfortunately—few people have had access to real financial education to teach them how to pay less in taxes.

Remember, our educational system is designed to teach people to be Es and Ss, not Bs and Is.

Q: The B-quadrant businesses have many ways (and incentives) to reduce their tax liabilities and pay—in some cases—little to nothing in taxes; high-income earners in the S quadrant do not. This is never talked about in the media when we hear about Congress passing tax law. Why not?

Julia H. – USA

A: I doubt Grunch wants the media or the educational system to know about taxes.

I am glad you want to know and learn more about taxes. Wanting to learn is the first step to learning. I do not recommend teaching people who do not want to learn. As the old saying goes: "Don't teach pigs to sing. It wastes your time and annoys the pig."

Chapter Seventeen

THE END OF THE U.S. DOLLAR?

BOOMS, BUSTS, CRASHES...
COLLAPSE?

ames Rickards, in his book *The Road to Ruin,* introduces the reader to his book's theme with Kurt Vonnegut's passage from his 1963 book *Cat's Cradle.*

> *Nice, nice, very nice;*
> *Nice, nice, very nice;*
> *Nice, nice, very nice—*
> *So many different people*
> *In the same device.*

Q: Is Rickards saying we are all being rounded up like cattle, herded into a corral, readied for milking or slaughter?

A: Yes. I think so.

Q: Is that device money?

A: Yes. As well as any financial instrument or derivative of money.

Q: Isn't everything connected to money? Does he mean the world economy, civilization, and life itself are trapped?

A: Yes. It does.

Rickards is a real teacher. He is exceptionally bright, educated in the finest schools, an academic elite, attorney, business insider, and monetary scholar. He was corporate council at Long-Term Capital Management (LTCM), which ended up as one of the biggest financial catastrophes in modern times. The demise of LTCM was Jim's "wake-up call" that led him to research the causes of LTCM's failure and take a deeper look into the murky world of money, power, and who really runs the world.

His findings and insights led him to be an advisor to the Department of Defense on future "currency wars"—hence the title of his book by that name—then to work with the Director of National Intelligence, as well as the people and the powers behind the central banking system running the world economy.

Rickards is a real teacher because he is an "insider's insider." I read *Currency Wars* when it was published in 2011. Being an outsider who wants to be able to see in "dirty water," reading *Currency Wars* was like putting on a dive mask and peering into murky world few people see. His subsequent books were even more illuminating.

If you have any question about gold being God's money, Rickard's 2016 book *The New Case for Gold*, is a must-read.

If you want to see where the U.S. and the world are headed, *The Road to Ruin* will shine a spotlight on the road ahead.

I am honored to be working on projects with Rickards, providing financial education and financial products for the brave new world of money that lies ahead.

The Last Snowflake

Rickards uses the metaphor of an avalanche to describe the coming crash and possible collapse of the dollar. For years, snow accumulates on the mountain peaks above a village. Rather than detonate small charges, causing small avalanches that would ruin the ski season, the powers that be keep building barricades to attract more skiers as more and more snow accumulates, and the threat of the "big one," a catastrophic avalanche grows every year.

Then one day, a tiny snowflake lands on a mountain peak and the village is buried under tons of snow.

This avalanche metaphor has been going on since 1971, the year President Richard Nixon took the U.S. dollar off the gold standard. After each market crash, rather than fix the problem, our leaders print more fake money—and the mountain of debt grows taller and deeper, and the problem grows more ominous every year.

Rather than snow, the world village is about to be buried under an avalanche of debt, fake investments, and fake money.

All we need is that last snowflake.

The End of the Dollar

In 1944, 44 nations gathered at Bretton Woods Conference to agree upon the new rules of the post-WWII international monetary system.

Prior to WWII, the British pound sterling was the top dog in the world of money. Fighting WWII caused England to ship its gold to the United States to pay for the war.

As WWII was coming to an end, the United States held much of the world's gold.

Since the United States had the gold, it promised to back its dollar with gold, and the U.S. dollar became the "reserve currency" of the world. In 1944, the U.S. dollar was as good as gold. Literally. The dollar was trusted and respected. That soon ended.

Between 1950 and 1960, Germany, Japan, England, and the rest of Europe recovered and began exporting products to the United States. Gold-backed dollars left the United States and Nixon and his buddies panicked.

In 1971, Nixon broke the promise made at Bretton Woods, and the United States began exporting fake money in exchange for real products such as Volkswagens and Toyotas.

The world gladly accepted these fake dollars as long as the world had confidence in the leaders of the United States. That confidence was severely tested after 2008.

Is that confidence nearly gone? Is the end near? Is the mountain of debt too high? Will more fake money keep the avalanche from coming down the mountain? Is the last snowflake on its way?

Three Types of Money

Earlier in this book I wrote that there are three kinds of modern money. They are:

1. **God's money:** gold and silver
2. **Government money:** the dollar, peso, yuan, yen, Euro.
3. **People's money:** Bitcoin, Ethereum, and blockchain-based cyber-currencies

---

The Difference between Communism and Capitalism

Communism: Communism is based on centralized government.
Capitalism: Capitalism is based upon centralized banks.

Central banks do not like gold because central banks cannot print gold.

Central banks do not like Bitcoin and blockchain because people's money does not need central banks.

Central banks print government money.

Government money has no integrity.

God's money and people's money have more integrity than central bank money. Why is that?

Q: How much longer will fake government money exist?

A: Not much longer, in my opinion. The U.S. dollar used to be backed by gold and silver. When I was in high school, government money had "silver certificate" across the top. Today, U.S. government has boldly printed on all fake dollars: "In God We Trust."

If you believe God is a co-signer on the national debt, keep believing in government money.

The Next Money

Jim Rickards states that government money may soon morph into SDRs, or special drawing rights, another form of fake money—this time issued by the International Monetary Fund (IMF).

The SDRs will not last. SDRs are more fake money. Will SDRs mark the end, the global collapse of government money? I expect that there are many people pondering that question.

The Real Issue

The real issue of government money is the word: confidence.

As long as people have confidence in our governments and central banks, fake government money such as the dollar, yen, yuan, pesos, and Euro are safe.

The last snowflake is confidence.

The moment confidence is gone, government money is toast, the dollar collapses, and the avalanche comes tumbling down the mountain, decimating everything in its path.

Rich dad's favorite definition of money was:

"Money is an idea,
  backed by confidence,
  representing work truly done,
  and is exchangeable."

Take each line and you will understand why government money is toast.

1. Money is only an idea. Money does not exist.
2. For money to exist, confidence in the leaders of our government and our banks must exist.
3. Real money represents work truly done. Printing fake money requires no real work.
4. Real money produces real value. Fake money is the thief of value. That is why fake money is not a store of value.
5. Printing fake money rips off real people and devalues the real work of real people.
6. Printing fake money makes money manipulators richer.
7. When real people wake up and confidence is gone, fake government money will no longer be exchangeable, and the avalanche of debt will come crashing down the mountain.
8. Financial education is self-defense against the greedy poor and the greedy rich.

As John Maynard Keynes stated decades ago:

"Capitalism is the astounding belief that the most wickedest of men will do the most wickedest of things for the greatest good of everyone."

Here are some quotes on stupidity from Doug Casey, another real teacher:

"Stupidity [is] an unwitting tendency to self-destruction."

"The lesser of two evils is still evil."

"The opposite of gratitude is entitlement."

French author Alexandre Dumas on stupidity:

"Human genius has its limits while human stupidity does not."

American inventor and statesman Benjamin Franklin on ignorance:

> "He was so learned that he could name a horse in nine languages; so ignorant that he bought a cow to ride on."

Quote from then-Fed Board of Governors member Ben Bernanke:

> "The U.S. government has a technology, called a printing press… that allows it to produce as many U.S. dollars as it wishes at essentially no cost."

"No cost"? Really? Wasn't Bernanke a professor at Stanford and Princeton? Shouldn't he know better?

Is Bernanke aware that printing fake money cost millions of people their jobs, homes, savings, and a secure financial future? What do you think?

How to Get Out of the Device

Repeating a passage from Kurt Vonnegut's *Cat's Cradle*:

> *Nice, nice, very nice;*
> *Nice, nice, very nice;*
> *Nice, nice, very nice—*
> *So many different people*
> *In the same device.*

This begs the question: How do I get *out* of the same device?

Many believe that the answer is to get back on the gold standard. That is what I did in 1972.

To review… in 1972, I was already on my own silver standard.

In 1964, after noticing a copper tinge on the edge of fake U.S. silver coins, I began turning in paper money for rolls of silver coins, sorting out real silver coins, and returning fake silver coins to the bank.

In 2018, a real, pre-1965 U.S. silver dime is worth about $2.

I still have bags of real silver dimes, quarters, and half-dollars.

In 1972, after flying behind enemy lines in search of gold, I smelled a rat. I suspected we were being lied to about the Vietnam War and about money.

In 1972, I purchased my first gold coin, a South African Krugerrand, in Hong Kong for approximately $50.

I was now a criminal. In 1972, Americans were not allowed to own gold.

I still have that coin, stored safely and legally, not in a bank but in a country outside the United States.

Today, that $50 Krugerrand is worth about $1,200.

In 1973, I took my first real estate course. I learned about infinite returns. I no longer needed fake money. I had found a real teacher. That year, I dropped out of my MBA program.

Since 1973, I have been on my own gold and silver standard. Additionally:

1. I am out of traditional education.
2. I take seminars and read books in search of real teachers.
3. I invest in real assets where the government wants me to be a partner. By investing in real assets the government wants me to invest in, I pay little to zero taxes, legally.
4. The Fed prints money. I print my own money.
5. I stay out of the grip of the booms, busts, and crashes of "too big to fail" banks, and Wall Street investment banks.
6. I use debt to achieve infinite returns and pay zero taxes.

I follow the McDonald's formula for global wealth… when most people are saying, "You can't do that here."

Q: Aren't you worried about debt?

A: Absolutely.

Q: How do you deal with debt?

A: I study and pay attention to the global economy. I study with real teachers. I offset debt with gold and silver. Gold and silver are a "hedge," my insurance policy protecting me from the stupidity of the government and my own.

Pictures Are Better Than Words

Repeating from an earlier chapter, the pictures below explain my formula for a return to the gold and silver standard.

McDONALD'S FORMULA

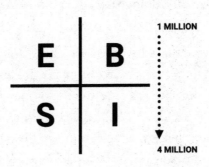

WHY THE RICH GET RICHER

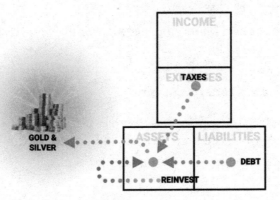

I save gold and silver, not government money. The diagrams on the previous page tell the story of how I stay out of the device.

Q: Do I have to follow your formula?

A: Of course not. In fact, please do not follow my formula. There are better and easier formulas. I followed this formula because I wanted a challenge and I wanted to acquire a lot of assets. You can acquire a lot of assets if you partner with the government, do not need money, and do not pay taxes legally.

Q: Are you a partner with the government when you use debt?

A: Yes. The government wants people to borrow and go into debt. That is why there are no taxes on debt. If people do not borrow, money is not created.

Airline credit cards offer cardholders bonus miles and upgrades for using their cards. In doing that, the airlines are partnering with the government to create more money.

If I invest with dollars I worked for, those dollars are after-tax dollars. It takes a long time to save after-tax dollars I had to work for. I prefer to invest with tax-free dollars, money I did not work for, which is why I use debt. I help the government create money and the government helps me create money. Please take real estate investment courses before you try this at home.

As rich dad often said, "In the hands of an idiot… debt turns into disaster."

We have enough idiots running the world. Please do not be one of them.

The Best Gold-Standard Formula

The best formula for staying out of "the device" is to do as Jim Rickards suggests: keep your day job and 401(k), buy gold and silver coins, and keep them in a safe outside the banks.

Rickards also recommends keeping some cash outside the banks. Kim and I do both: we keep some money outside the banks and some outside the country.

Q: But gold is so expensive. What do I do if I do not have much money?

A: Start with silver. That is what I did. Anyone can buy a real silver coin for about $20. In fact, silver may be a better investment than gold.

Q: Why would silver be better than gold?

A: Silver is an industrial precious metal. That means it is being consumed and as such disappearing every day, and so stockpiles of silver are dwindling.

Do Not Wait

I'm sure you've heard this saying: *There's no time like the present.* I agree. Start investing today.

Q: I have a lot of money in stocks and in savings. Why not wait for the price of gold and silver to go up, then start buying?

A: Because real gold and silver are not fake money or paper assets. Today, the rich are hoarding gold and silver.

Q: Why is the fact that gold and silver are being hoarded important?

A: Because there is only so much "floating gold." Floating gold is real gold available for people like you and me. Rich countries and rich people are acquiring "floating gold" and putting real gold into deep, cold storage.

The United States and China have been manipulating the price of gold, keeping the price of gold as low as possible so that China can acquire gold.

Once China has enough gold, the United States and China will let the price of gold rise.

Why would the United States help China? Because China owns trillions in U.S. bonds. When the United States prints fake money, the value of those bonds go down.

If China starts dumping U.S. bonds, the U.S. economy will collapse.

It is in the best interest for the United States to work with China, keeping the price of gold low, so China can buy cheap gold to offset China's U.S. bond losses.

In 2016, the IMF named the yuan a type of reserve currency for IMF projects.

Now that China has enough gold, the United States and China are willing to let inflation and the price of gold to rise.

Inflation will destroy the U.S. dollar. China will make up its losses in U.S. bonds with the rise in the price of gold.

Q: Once the avalanche starts and the world realizes "floating gold" is gone, will the price of gold rise rapidly?

A: As Jim Rickards says, you and I won't be able to buy real gold at any price.

Q: How high will the price of gold reach?

A: Rickards did the math, comparing number of fake dollars in circulation and how high the price of gold would have to be to back all those fake dollars with real gold. In 2017, that number was $10,000 an ounce, if you could buy it.

Q: Wouldn't the rich sell their gold if the price went that high?

A: No. The really rich do not need to sell because the really rich do not need the money. Remember the article on Jared Kushner. The real rich use debt as money.

Q: What about gold and silver ETFs?

A: Gold and silver ETFs do not have much gold, if they have any. Gold and silver ETFs lease their gold and silver from gold and silver banks. Gold and silver ETFs operate on the same fractional reserve system all paper assets, including money, operate on. For every ounce of gold or silver an ETF has leased, the ETF will sell 50 to 100 ounces of fake, paper gold and silver ETFs to unsuspecting investors.

When you sell your gold or silver ETF, the ETF will return money, that is going down in value, not gold or silver, which will be going up in value.

REMEMBER: The game the Big Banks and Wall Street plays is, "Heads I win. Tails you lose."

In 1972, I chose not to play that game.

Living in a Village Below an Avalanche

Nice, nice, very nice;
Nice, nice, very nice;
Nice, nice, very nice—
So many different people
In the same device.

Today, billions of people are living beneath the avalanche. They are trapped in a central banking system owned by the mega-rich. The central banks are not elected by the people and do not have to answer to the people. That is why gold and Bitcoin are a threat to central bankers.

Getting on your own gold and silver standard—before the last snowflake, before the avalanche—gives you a way off the mountain. If the avalanche knocks out the electrical system, government money and people's money are toast. ATMs will shut down, Wall Street will close, and people's money will disappear when the World Wide Web disappears.

Always remember, gold and silver were here when the Earth was formed, and gold and silver will be here when we are all gone.

That is why I agree with Rickards when he recommends we all keep 10 percent of our wealth in real money, real gold and real silver, outside the electronic, global banking system.

Q: What if you're wrong? What if nothing happens? What if there is no global catastrophe? What if the world economy keeps growing?

A: For the sake of the world, Jim and I *want* to be wrong. And, even if we are wrong, gold and silver will continue to increase in value. The value of the U.S. dollar will continue to decline.

Q: How can you be so sure?

A: I will let wiser men answer that question:

As Rickards writes in *Currency Wars*:

> "From its creation in 1913, the most important Fed mandate has been to maintain the purchasing power of the dollar; however, since 1913 the dollar has lost over 95 percent of its value. Put differently, it takes twenty dollars today to buy what one dollar would buy in 1913."

Voltaire (1694–1778), French Enlightenment writer, historian, and philosopher, is credited with saying:

> "Paper money eventually returns to its intrinsic value— zero."

George Washington (1732–1799) first president of the United States:

> "Paper money has had the effect in your State that it will ever have, to ruin commerce—oppress the honest, and open the door to every species of fraud and injustice."

Ron Paul, U.S. congressman and U.S. presidential candidate:

> "Because gold is honest money... it is disliked by dishonest men."

The Other Side of the Coin

Compare the above statements to those of a banker. On the other side of the coin is German banker Mayer Amschel Rothschild (1744–1812):

> "Give me control of a nation's money…and I care not who makes its laws."

There has been much debate, with many saying Rothschild did not make this statement. It has also been credited to the House of Rothchilds, as well as "the money lenders of the Old World." I often wonder how anyone would really know with absolute certainty. Is this just another example of more muddy water and fake news? We will never know.

What is real? Do the ultra-rich really control the money supply? Isn't it true the Rothschild banking dynasty own a controlling interest in most of the central banks of the world?

For chilling insights to those questions, it is time to listen to Nomi Prins.

The Story That's Not Being Told in America

We have been listening to wise men. It is time to hear from a wise woman.

In her book *Collusion*, Nomi Prins, like Jim Rickards, is a real teacher, an insider, having worked for Lehman Brothers, Bear Stearns London, and as a managing director at Goldman Sachs.

Like Rickards, Prins is an insider's insider. She has seen the innerworkings of the machine. In *Collusion* and as a guest on The Rich Dad Radio Show, Prins shared the real collusion story, a story not being told in America.

Her story is about Dark Money. I call it Fake Money. Here is real story in Prins' own words:

What is dark money?

Dark money is money electronically created or "conjured" by the Federal Reserve and other major central banks in the world that flows to big private banks and financial markets. Where it ultimately goes is untraceable. The Fed, together with the European Central Bank (ECB) and the Bank of Japan (BOJ), has created nearly $15 trillion worth of dark money. Adding in the People's Bank of China (PBOC) that figure is a staggering $23 trillion. That dark money goes to the biggest private banks and financial institutions first. From there, it spreads out in seemingly infinite directions affecting different financial assets in different ways.

Why is dark money bad?

Dark money represents a new kind of collusion between various governments, central banks and private banks. They work in tandem to siphon off more power and money for themselves using laws, power-brokering, and quid-pro-quos. Dark money is a version of fake money because it doesn't come from the real economy. It is an artificial stimulant to markets that comes from an external source. It can manipulate and distort markets, removing their ability to behave either as free or regulated markets.

Why are we in a new normal?

Central banks have become more powerful than governments by virtue of their ability to create massive amounts of money without any legal restrictions or limitations on the amount. The markets, banks, and speculators have become reliant on central banks to create money, not just in emergency situations, but as an ongoing subsidy for their activities.

Q: What does all of this mean?

A: It means that someone telling the truth when he or she said: "Give me control of a nation's money… and I care not who makes its laws."

A Fake Request for Money

In 2008, Hank Paulson, then secretary of the treasury, former CEO of Goldman Sachs, went before the U.S. government and American people to ask for $700 billion to bailout the "too big to fail" banks.

Q: Why was it a fake request?

A: That is the story Prins, like Paulson, an insider from Goldman Sachs, is telling in her book *Collusion*.

Simply put, "central banks" do not need to ask permission to print money. The Fed did not need Paulson, George W. Bush, Congress or the people of the United States for permission to print money.

Q: Is that the new normal? The Fed and the central banks of the world do what they want, without requiring permission?

A: I believe it is. Today, the ultra-rich do not care who makes the rules, what party is in power (Republican or Democrat, conservative or liberal) or if the country is capitalist, socialist, or communist.

Q: How did that happen?

A: The Emergency Economic Stabilization Act of 2008 created the TARP program. The Dodd–Frank Wall Street Reform and Consumer Protection Act, signed into law in 2010, reducing the amount authorized to $475 billion.

Q: So, the government said "No," to the $700 billion request?

A: Correct. The law makers reduced $700 billion to $475 billion.

Q: Then what happened?"

A: On October 11, 2012, the Congressional Budget Office (CBO) reduced it further to $431 billion.

Q: *Then* what happened?

A: Then Mayer Amschel Rothschild's words came true. When our leaders said "No," the central banks took over and, as Prins states, the new normal began.

Repeating Prins' words:

> "Central Banks have become more powerful than governments by virtue of their ability to create massive amounts of money without any legal restrictions or limitations on the amount."

On October 11, 2012, when the CBO cut TARP to $431 billion, Rothschild's words came true. As Prins states:

> "The Fed, together with the European Central Bank (ECB) and the Bank of Japan (BOJ), has created nearly $15 trillion worth of dark money. Adding in the People's Bank of China (PBOC) that figure is a staggering $23 trillion. That dark money goes to the biggest private banks and financial institutions first. From there, it spreads out in seemingly infinite directions affecting different financial assets in different ways."

Q: Does this mean my vote, who I vote for, the party I belong to, or who wins the election really does not matter?

A: I will let you answer that question for yourself. Many people want to believe their vote counts.

In her book *Collusion,* Prins gives you a glimpse inside the machine. At least you have seen the other side of the coin.

Now you can decide for yourself if your vote really counts.

Q: Does that mean financial markets are manipulated?

A: Yes, yes, yes. Once upon a time, professional investors could count on "price discovery." That meant the free market would determine the real price of an asset. Today, the central banks of the world control asset prices.

Q: Does that mean without "real price discovery," assets prices are fake?

A: Yes… manipulated dark money traded in dark pools, out of sight from you and me. Even the price of gold and silver are manipulated.

Q: If the price and gold are manipulated, why save real gold and real silver?

A: Same answer. Because gold and silver are God's money. Real gold and silver have no counter-party risk.

All fake assets have counter-party risk.

Counter-party risk means the value of the asset depends upon someone else, a counter-party. For example, the real value of the U.S. dollar depends upon the leaders of the U.S. government. The value of the stock depends upon the value of the company that issues the share of stock. If you lend your brother-in-law money, your money depends upon your brother-in-law.

Q: Who is the counter-party of gold and silver?

A: God.

When the central bank's house of cards comes crashing down, gold and silver will still be gold and silver… because gold and silver are God's money.

In the next chapter you will find out what you can do to prepare for avalanche and get out of the device.

YOUR QUESTIONS... ROBERT'S ANSWERS

Q: Do you believe that Jim Rickards and Nomi Prins are putting their lives in jeopardy by exposing these financial truths?

Amanda E. – USA

A: Yes. As you know, social media is often anti-social media. If someone wants to attack you, you will be attacked by a mob of angry righteous people. In the high court of social media, you are guilty... without any chance of being proven innocent.

This is not true for just Jim and Nomi. This is true for all of us.

Q: Do you think the U.S. government will ban the private ownership of gold again like they did in 1933?

José F. – Nicaragua

A: I doubt it, but you never know. In 2018 a few central banks began buying gold, the first time in 10 years. If the buying turning into a panic, and the U.S. dollar crashes, who knows what the U.S. government will do?

Q: How much longer (in years) do you think there will continue to be confidence in the U.S. dollar? If/when that's gone... what does the global economy look like?

Denes T. – Hungary

A: I do not know. What I do know is:
1. The U.S. government, economy, and people are floating on debt.
2. Entitlement programs are automatically funded.
3. Ten thousand U.S. Baby Boomers retire every day.
4. Baby Boomer pension funds are underfunded.
5. The United States fights terrorist wars we cannot win.
6. The United States continues to borrow money to pay bills.

7. AI, Artificial Intelligence, will destroy more jobs than China.

8. After 2008, the world stopped trusting the U.S. dollar.

If you trust our leaders to solve this problem, keep saving fake money.

Q: I don't see people ever catching on 100 percent to this deception—nevermind overthrowing the system. Convince us otherwise.

Akira Y. - Japan

A: Anger and frustration are growing, often spread by anti-social media. Watch for growing civil unrest, much like the unrest going on in Venezuela today. Mob rules will replace law and order.

Q: It's obvious the shadow bankers have full control over the rest of us. What type of final event would have to occur for them to lose control over it at last?

Renaldo J. - Philippines

A: The banking system has been ripping off savers for thousands of years. A thousand years ago, a saver gave a banker gold or silver to hold for safekeeping. The banker gave the saver a note, an I.O.U., for his gold or silver. The saver took that note and used it as money. The banker would lend the saver's gold or silver to a borrower. The banker did this over and over again.

Inflation is caused by too much money in the economy. Inflation decreases the purchasing power of money. The value of the saver's gold or silver declined in value as his own gold and silver expanded across the inflating economy.

Today this banking system is known as "fractional reserve banking." It is a system in which only a fraction of savers' money remains in the bank, as "reserves." Most of the savers' money is loaned out, over and over again, to more and more borrowers.

This is done to make more money for the bank in the name of expanding the economy.

The shadow banking system is an extension of fractional reserve banking. Individuals borrow money to loan money to people and organizations, outside the rules of the regulated banking system. The economy keeps expanding as more and more money is borrowed and loaned out. Everything is fine as long as the economy keeps expanding.

If one small company cannot repay its loan, the house of cards collapses, because fractional reserve and shadow banking have created far more real debt than there is real money.

China has a massive problem with shadow banking. If China's economy continues to slow, and loans cannot be repaid, a Chinese crash would make the 2008 subprime disaster look like raindrop on a puddle.

In 2008, banks dropped interest rates, some below zero and at the same time the banking system printed trillions in fake money.

Not only did savers lose the interest income on their savings, but their savings lost purchasing power to the trillions in fake money printed by the banking system.

The bankers who caused the disaster were bailed out and paid billions in bonuses, while savers became the biggest losers in world history.

The coming disaster will be much bigger than the 2008 crash, and yet schools continue to teach students to get out of debt and save money.

In 1971, the world changed but the education system didn't.

Chapter Eighteen

PREPARING FOR A BRIGHTER FUTURE

ACHIEVING SPIRITUAL HEALTH, WEALTH, AND HAPPINESS

Almost every morning, I follow the wisdom found in *The Miracle Morning,* written by Hal Elrod. Almost every morning, I practice a yoga routine for about 10 minutes, meditate for 30 minutes, read a spiritual book for 10 minutes, and journal, sharing my innermost thoughts on paper, to myself.

This early morning hour is the most important part of my day. This hour determines how I will handle the day and the quality of my future.

The Glass Ceiling

Corporate women often talk about the "glass ceiling." Men, and many times women, often perceive women to be not as competent as men… especially when it comes to the subject of money. Thank God that myth is dissolving.

My wife, Kim, has no glass ceiling. She is an entrepreneur who is at home with both men and women. And there are no limits to what she can earn or how far she can go.

Money and wealth do not discriminate. Money and wealth do not know the difference between men and women or discriminate based upon age, education, or race... but people do. Often, many people discriminate—even conspire—against themselves, as the Judas in them comes out saying, "I'll never be rich" or "I didn't go to college, so I'll never be successful"—all thoughts inspired by the Judas in them.

This is why meditation is important for me. Every morning, I need to turn *my* Judas off and move beyond silence until I find stillness.

Big Dogs—and Fake Big Dogs

Men, too, have a "glass ceiling." For men, it is the alpha-male syndrome. Much of history is about alpha-males who did great things in the world or great damage to the world, often massive crimes against humanity.

Alpha-males are often called "Big Dogs."

Many men are bullies, arrogant, and pompous, pretending to be Big Dogs. They are fake big dogs. Fake big dogs need "little dogs" to soothe their fragile, fake big dog egos.

Most financial disasters in homes, families, businesses, and the economy are caused by fake big dogs pretending to be Big Dogs— Big Dogs who pretend to know everything about money.

We all know fake big dogs of money.

Do you work for a fake big dog? Are you living with a little dog who thinks they are a Big Dog?

Fake Ceilings

Anyone with any ambition, man or woman, has had a glass ceiling or a fake big dog standing in his or her way.

In real life, most of us create our own fake glass ceilings and fake big dogs guarding the doors to our happiness.

Having fake glass ceilings, a fake big dog, or letting the Judas in us run our lives often manifests as limited success, shortage of money, being passed over for promotions, stuck in a dead-end job, dead-end relationships, troubled pasts, bad choices, limited happiness, addictions, depression, and more.

Fake glass ceilings are good, if you know you have one. Most idiots do not know they have a glass ceiling... until they crash into it. I have been that idiot many times.

The good news is that being the idiot has its benefits. All coins have two sides. On the other side of *idiot* is *genius*.

So, if you have ever been an idiot, the good news is that you are also a genius.

The Fairy Tale Is Over

Millions of people grow up believing in fairytales. You know a story is a fairytale when it ends with "...and they lived happily ever after."

The trouble with all fairytales is that all fairytales have glass ceilings. For example, Princess Diana, a beautiful young woman, marries a real prince and future king of England. Princess Di delivers two great young men: another future king of England and his heir-to-spare brother.

Diana Frances Spencer, born July 1, 1961, lived the dream of many young girls, the dream of being a fairy princess who marries a prince. A *real* prince.

Tragically Princess Di's real-life fairytale turned into a real-life royal nightmare. Her fairytale life began in a royal carriage on her wedding day... and ended in a twisted, mangled Mercedes stuck in a tunnel in Paris.

The lesson: even fairytales have glass ceilings.

Can Your Life Be a Fairytale?

Can ordinary people like you and me live in a fairytale? I say yes. But there is one condition.

We can live in a fairytale as long as we realize that on the other side of that coin is a nightmare.

Wake Up!

The good news is that the *nightmare* is the path to the *fairytale*. And the question is: Are you willing to *wake up*, and stay awake and alive through the nightmare?

Health, Wealth, and Happiness

What most all of us really want is a life of health, wealth, and happiness.

This chapter is about achieving the other side of the coin, a fairytale life we dream of… a life of spiritual health, spiritual wealth, and spiritual happiness.

Is it possible?

Spiritual Health

My cardiologist Dr. Radha Gopalan has been nudging me for years to meditate, reminding me that doctors and medicine are fake health… and that inner spirituality is real health.

Radha is a real teacher, mentor, personal friend, and author of *A Second Opinion*, a book about the power of combining both Eastern and Western medicine. It is a book with a message that is essential for anyone who values their health.

At our most recent three-day Rich Dad Advisor meeting last year Radha led a discussion on how illness can lead to health and spiritual enlightenment.

Dr. Gopalan is a cardiologist, as well as a doctor of acupuncture. He finally got it through my thick head that I was sacrificing my health and happiness for wealth.

Being a Type-A person, I loved what I was doing. Every day was fun. Every day was challenging. Every day was stressful—and I thrive on stress. The problem was, my ego was running me, not my spirit… and I loved that, too.

As Eckhart Tolle describes in his book *The Power of Now*:

> *Are you always trying to get somewhere other than where you are? Is most of your doing just a means to an end? Is fulfillment always just around the corner or confined to short-lived pleasures, such as sex, food, drink, drugs, or thrills and excitement? Are you always focused on becoming, achieving, and attaining, or alternatively chasing some new thrill of pleasure? Do you believe that if you acquire more things you will become more fulfilled, good enough, or psychologically complete? Are you waiting for some man or woman to give meaning to your life?*

Tolle might describe a person like me as running from my past because "the future holds the promise of salvation" even though that is an illusion.

Tolle adds:

> "Usually, the future is a replica of the past. Superficial changes are possible, but *real* transformation is rare and depends upon whether you can become present enough to dissolve the past, by accessing the power of the Now."

Until Radha nudged me to "wake up," meditate, read *spiritual* books (not just financial books), and practice yoga, as well as go to the gym, I was nothing but a little dog trying to become a bigger dog. What a waste.

I was unaware that I was destroying my future health, wealth, and happiness as I roared off to work every day.

As a little dog trying to be a Big Dog, I was working harder and harder, banging my head against my self-imposed glass ceiling, and turning my fairytale life, my marriage, and my business into a nightmare.

When I met Radha, I was already what most people would consider "successful." I had a wonderful wife, great life, money, some fame, happiness, and good health. The problem was I wanted *more*.

For Things to Change… First I Must Change

Today, I dedicate the first hour of my day to my spiritual health, wealth, and happiness.

Inspired by Radha, I began to look for new teachers, this time spiritual teachers. At a seminar, I met Hal Elrod, a young man who nearly died in a motorcycle accident and brought himself back to life. He gave me his book, *The Miracle Morning,* a book on the process he used to restore his life, his spiritual health, wealth, and happiness.

After reading Hal's book, I better understood what my doctor Radha had been nudging me to understand. By following the process in Hal's book, slowly but surely, my glass ceiling began to dissolve. The little dog in me stopped trying to be a bigger dog.

I had been running from my past… seeking salvation in my future. I could see that. And I wanted to change that. And I knew that change started with me.

Happily, I report, that miracles have been happening as I went through—rather than ran from—my nightmares.

Simply said, my nightmares were my path through my glass ceiling.

Another Spiritual Teacher

One of the books I studied during my miracle morning hours is *Awareness,* a book about waking up. I love *Awareness* because it is about my kind of spirituality.

Anthony de Mello is a real spiritual teacher. I have never met him. I only know him through his book *Awareness*. Anthony de Mello was a member of the Jesuits in Mumbai, India, and passed away suddenly in 1987.

If Anthony de Mello had not been a priest, I am certain he would have made a great Maine Corps drill instructor. His spiritual words of wisdom are direct, blunt, and definitely *not* politically correct.

I doubt de Mello would be allowed on college campuses today, because he might hurt teachers' and students' feelings.

His book *Awareness,* begins with this story:

> "A man found an eagle's egg and put it in a nest of a barnyard hen. The eaglet hatched with a brood of chicks and grew up with them.

> "All his life the eagle did what barnyard chicks did, thinking he was a barnyard chicken. He scratched the earth for worms and insects. He clucked and cackled. And he would thrash his wings and fly a few feet in the air.

> "Years passed, and the eagle grew very old. One day he saw a magnificent bird above him in the cloudless sky. It glided in graceful majesty among the powerful wind currents, with scarcely a beat of its strong golden wings.

> "The old eagle looked up in awe. 'Who's that?' he asked.

> "'That's the eagle, the king of birds,' said his neighbor. 'He belongs to the sky. We belong to the earth—we're chickens.' So, the eagle lived and died a chicken, for that's what he thought he was."

This story leads me to the question I want you to ask yourself: Are you an eagle… living with chickens? Or are you an eagle… trying to be a big chicken?

What Is Spirituality?

De Mello writes:

Spirituality means waking up. Most people, even though they don't know it, are asleep. They're born asleep, they live asleep, they marry in their sleep, they breed children in their sleep, they die in their sleep without ever waking up. ...

I want you to understand something right at the beginning, that religion is not—I repeat: not—necessarily connected with spirituality. Please keep religion out of this for the time being.

Time to Wake Up

Another story by De Mello:

A gentleman knocks on his son's door. 'Jaime,' he says, 'wake up!

Jaime answers, 'I don't want to get up, Papa.'

The father shouts, 'Get up, you have to go to school.'

Jaime says, 'I don't want to go to school.'

'Why not?' asks the father.

'Three reasons,' says Jamie. 'First, because it's so dull; second, the kids tease me; and third, I hate school.'

And the father says, 'Well, I am going to give you three reasons why you must go to school. First, because it is your duty; second, because you are 45 years old, and third, because you are the headmaster.'

Wake up, wake up! You've grown up. You're too big to be asleep. Wake up! Stop playing with your toys.

Most people tell you they want to get out of kindergarten, but don't believe them. Don't believe them! All they want is to mend their broken toys. 'Give me back my wife. Give me back my job. Give me back my money. Give me back my reputation, my success.' This is what they want; they want their toys replaced. That's all. Even the best psychologist will tell you that people don't really want to be cured. What they want is relief; a cure is painful.

Rich dad often said, "Everyone wants to go to heaven... but no one wants to die."

Rich dad also said, "Most people only want money. They don't really want to be rich. Working for money is easy. Anyone can work for money. Becoming rich is hard."

Rich dad often used the model of *Be–Do–Have.*

He would say, "There is a difference between being rich and having money. Most people focus on having money, rather than being rich."

Rich dad explained further, "Mother Teresa is rich because she does not need money to get her work done."

Eckhart Tolle, in his book *The New Earth*, says:

The ego tends to equate having with Being: I have, therefore I am. And the more I have, the more I am. The ego lives through comparison. How you are seen by others turns into how you see yourself. ... The ego's sense of self-worth is in most cases bound up with the worth you have in the eyes of others. You need others to give you a sense of self, and if you live in a culture that to a large extent equates self-worth with how much and what you have, if you cannot look through this collective delusion, you will be condemned to chasing after things for the rest of your life in the vain hope of finding your worth and completion of your sense of self there.

How do you let go of attachment to things? Don't even try. It's impossible. Attachment of things drops away by itself when you no longer seek to find yourself in them. In the meantime, just be aware of your attachment to things. ...

The ego identifies with having, but its satisfaction in having is a relatively shallow and short-lived one. Concealed within it is a deep sense of dissatisfaction of incompleteness, of 'not enough.'

'I don't have enough yet,' by which the ego really means, 'I am not enough yet.'

Repeating a rich dad lesson:

"*Being* rich is not the same as *having* a lot of money and things."

Q: What does being rich mean?

A: I do not know. The answer to that question is personal. Only you can answer that question for yourself. Here's what I do know: Billions of people *want* to have more money and *want* to have more things.

My glass ceiling was the little dog in me, running from being, running from *"I am not good enough yet."*

That is what I need relief from. Unfortunately, more money and more success were not a cure. More money and more success were only temporary relief.

Magic Pills

Back in the 1960s, there was a television and radio commercial that asked: "How do you spell 'relief'?" The answer was to spell out the name of the antacid the commercial was promoting. The announcer spells out, letter by letter, the product name: "R-O-L-A-I-D-S." Millions ran out and bought "relief."

Today, all over the world, we the people are pounded with "magic pill" promotions. Magic pills prey on humans' deep wanting, neediness, unhappiness, and feelings of "I am not good enough."

There are magic pills for losing weight, getting rich quick, finding the love of your life, quitting your job and never working again, and going back to school for an advanced degree.

My favorite magic pills are the weight-loss ads. Having struggled with being overweight all my life, I am a sucker for the ads showing before and after photos of a stunning man or woman, saying, "I took this magic pill and lost 55 pounds. I did it without dieting or exercise and look at me now!"

A few ads have been so convincing that I have taken out my credit card and ordered the magic pills. So far, none of the magic pills have worked. I continue to struggle with my weight.

As de Mello states, "What [people] want is relief; a cure is painful."

The pain would be sticking with the diet and exercise program that comes with every bottle of magic pills. That's the path to a cure.

Billion-Dollar Lottery

Relief from wanting money.

In 2018, the news was filled with stories of the lottery approaching $1 billion. As soon as that news got out, the lottery jackpot soared past $1 billion.

Why? Because millions of people were seeking financial relief, not a cure. Most people want the easy road to wealth… which is why most people never achieve great wealth or relief from real money worries.

The same thing happened when Bitcoin made the news. Suddenly millions of people were Bitcoin investors. I was one of them. I met a person who agreed to sell me five of the Bitcoins he owned, ones he bought early when no one knew about Bitcoin. We shook hands, but nothing happened. The seller and his attorney mysteriously disappeared, sparing me from my own foolishness.

It's not that Bitcoin is foolish. I was foolish. I was buying only because the prices were going up and I did not want to miss the boat. I was buying just five coins so I could get in the game to learn—a practice I recommend. I learn when I have "skin in the game." I did the same thing with gold and silver, stocks and bonds.

Eventually, I bought some lesser-known people's money, cybercurrency like Ethereum. I learn by buying a little, having some skin in the game, and then learning the game.

I suspect cybercurrency, people's money, will be government money's glass ceiling. I suspect the little dogs will bite the big dog's butts.

Why People Don't Wake Up

As de Mello writes, "Spirituality means waking up."

> *Waking up is unpleasant, you know. You are nice and comfortable in bed. It's irritating to be woken up. That's the reason the wise guru will not attempt to wake people up. I hope I'm going to be wise here and make no attempt to wake you up if you are asleep. It is really none of my business, even though I say to you at times, 'Wake up!' My business is to do my thing, to dance my dance. If you profit from it fine; if you don't too bad! As the Arabs say, 'The nature of rain is the same, but it makes thorns grow in the marshes and flowers in the gardens.'*

TRANSLATION: Magic pills do not work. Gurus do not work. A new wife will not work. A new Ferrari will not work.

When you look at Be–Do–Have, the deeper problem is the "wanting to have more."

Q: If relief—like a new Ferrari, a new wife, a bigger house, new shoes, clothes, or more money—does not work, how do you cure the *wanting?* How do I cure, "I am not good enough... yet?"

A: Remember, the thoughts, "I am not good enough… yet" are the Judas in you, the saboteur in you.

Judas is not the real you.

By being present with the pain, aware of the pain, you can begin the process. Rather than medicating the pain with alcohol, drugs, sex, food, and shopping.

Being present with the pain is a lesson in Radha's book *A Second Opinion*, Tolle's books *The Power of Now* and *The New Earth*, Hal Elrod's book *The Miracle Morning*, and Ryan Holiday's book *The Obstacle Is the Way*.

These books empower your spirit, which lives in your heart, to take control of Judas, who lives in your mind.

Q: So, my spirit is found on the other side of the coin?

A: Yes. It is. We all have strengths and weaknesses, courage and fear, loves and hates. Our genius is found by uniting, not by avoiding, ignoring, or medicating the other side of the coin.

As Radha would say, nudging me to wake up, each time I went in for a check-up, suffering from high blood pressure, and being overweight and pre-diabetic:

"Your spiritual health is found in your illness.

"Your spiritual wealth is found in your poverty.

"Your spiritual happiness is found in your sadness."

LESSON: Being present with your pain, your weakness, your darkness, and the Judas in you… is where your *real spirituality* is found.

Teaching Kids to Be Fragile

Education is in trouble. Education is the problem. Education educates the mind, not the spirit.

Earlier in this book, I wrote about Steven Brill's book *Tailspin*. *Tailspin* is about the damage higher education is causing in the world via very smart students corrupting the legal system and corrupting financial systems, producing fake financial assets that make the smart students rich by ripping off the rest of the world.

In the book *Big Potential*, author Shawn Achor, a Harvard graduate and lecturer, describes how the practices, methods, and processes of modern education keep students, even brilliant students, trapped in their small potential, not their big potential.

Another book, *The Coddling of the American Mind,* by Greg Lukianoff and Jonathan Haidt and published in 2018, paints an even more sinister picture of modern education.

Lukianoff is president of the Foundation for Individual Rights in Education. He is a graduate of American University and Stanford Law School. He specializes in free speech and First Amendment issues in higher education.

Haidt is a professor of ethical leadership at New York University's Stern School of Business. He obtained his PhD in social psychology from the University of Pennsylvania and taught at the University of Virginia for 16 years.

The Coddling of the American Mind is a book that addresses the underlying causes of today's hate, anger, intolerance, and discontent in global public discourse. For example: Why are people arguing rather than discussing? Why are terrorism and hate increasing? Why are there mass murders all across American and the world? Why do Republicans and Democrats attack each other rather than work together? And why are riots breaking out on campuses with students attacking speakers whose words "trigger" and "threaten" the students?

What Haidt and Lukianoff state in their book is: "What is new today is the premise that students are fragile."

They focus on the iGen (short for "internet generation"), those students born after 1995 as identified by social psychologist Jean Twenge, and the riots breaking out on campuses in 2014. The authors state:

> "Many university students are learning to think in distorted ways, and this increases their likelihood of becoming fragile, anxious, and easily hurt."

Before writing their book, the authors first submitted an article to *The Atlantic*, with the title "Arguing Towards Misery: How Campuses Teach Cognitive Distortions." That article evolved into the book *The Coddling of the American Mind*. They describe the process like this:

> *In that article, we argued that many teachers, parents, K-12 teachers, professors, and university administrators have been unknowingly teaching a generation of students to engage in habits commonly seen in people who suffer from anxiety and depression. ...*
>
> *Such thought patterns directly harmed students' mental health and interfered with their intellectual development—and sometimes the development of those around them. At some schools, a culture of defensive self-censorship seemed to be emerging, partly in response to students who were quick to "call out" or shame others for small things that they deemed insensitive—either to the student doing the calling out o to members of a group that a student was standing up for. We called this pattern* vindictive protectiveness *and argued that such behavior made it more difficult for all students to have open discussions in which they could practice the essential skills of critical thinking and civil disagreement.*

Q: What does all this mean?

A: Violence, hate, and disagreements will probably increase due to technology and mass higher education.

Today, teachers and students demand "safety." While physical safety is important, the concept of safety has spread to "safety" from ideas that may disturb the student. In other words, emotional safety. This means free speech is dead.

Making matters worse, if a student feels "threatened" by an idea, this new culture allows a person to retaliate, attack, even harm someone they have judged to have "triggered" uncomfortable emotions within the student.

This is why violence is increasing. Free speech is dead. Real education is dying.

The Coddling of the American Mind is an important book, especially if you have children in school or are an employer who works with the iGen (born after 1995). My friends who are in the military have noticed distinct differences between working with Millennials and those of the iGen.

Authors Haidt and Lukianoff state that it is the iGen that gives Millennials their flakey, combative reputation. The problem is that the attitudes of the iGen and today's teachers are infecting all generations, worldwide.

Q: How does one prepare for this brave new world?

A: *The Coddling of the American Mind* offers many solutions, one being insights from Nassim Taleb, author of *The Black Swan,* a 2007 bestseller and a financial bible for many professional investors.

Taleb is a statistician, stock trader, genius polymath, and professor of risk management at NYU. He states that too many investors look at risk in the wrong way. In complex systems and societies, it is impossible to see what will happen in the future, yet we persist in trying to calculate risk based on past experiences. Hence, that opens the door to unforeseen "black swan" events one is not prepared for.

Black swan (n): an unpredictable or unforeseen event,
typically one with extreme consequences.

This is why Jim Rickards believes that academic elites such as former Fed Chairman Ben Bernanke got it wrong. Rickards and Nomi Prins—real insiders, not fake academic elites—believe that we are making the future weaker, not stronger, by quantitative easing, QE, and printing more and more money.

Bernanke is a professor of the Great Depression. In 2008, he did what he believed the Fed should have done in 1929: print more money. Bernanke was driving into the future, but looking into the rearview mirror. As the old saying goes, "Generals prepare to fight the last war."

In 2008, Bernanke was fighting the War of 1929.

The Coddling of the American Mind and Nassim Taleb's 2012 book *Antifragile* take the position that our schools are inadvertently damaging students' futures by making them fragile, rather than preparing them for an unexpected black swan future.

Taleb asks us to distinguish between three types of people:

1. Some people are *fragile*, like fine china teacups. They break easy and *cannot heal themselves*, so you must handle with care.

2. Some people are *resilient* like plastic cups. They can withstand the great shocks of life. Parents usually give their kids plastic cups. The problem is, plastic cups do not benefit from falls and rough handling because plastic cups do not learn, grow, or get stronger.

3. Some people are *antifragile*. Antifragile people require stress, challenges, and hardship in order to learn, adapt, and grow.

VERY IMPORTANT: Antifragile systems grow weaker, more rigid, and less efficient when not challenged. For example, our muscles grow weaker and bones grow fragile, as do children's, because children and human beings have antifragile systems.

If a person spends a month in bed, his or her muscles atrophy because complex systems are weakened when deprived of stress.

When neurotically overprotective parents and school teachers protect students from real life, they are hurting the student and the future of our world.

On top of that, fragile people become violent people, defending their right to be protected from real life.

The Candle vs. the Campfire

The metaphor of a candle and a campfire is another example of this. If you blow too hard on a candle, the candle goes out. If you blow really hard on a campfire, the campfire grows stronger.

When our schools, teachers, and neurotic, overprotective parents protect their children from the real world, they raise "candles," children who will be unprepared for the black swans of the future and the world they will face as adults.

How to Prepare for the Future

Many people are resilient and strong. Again, the problem with strong, resilient people is they do not grow or learn, and fall behind as the world churns on into the future.

I will leave you with this thought… a quote, ancient words of wisdom that the authors of *The Coddling of the American Mind* use at the start of the book's first chapter, "The Untruth of Fragility."

> *When heaven is about to confer a great responsibility on any man, it will exercise his mind with suffering, subject his sinews*

*and bones to hard work, expose his body to hunger, put him
to poverty, place obstacles in the paths of his deeds, so as to
stimulate his mind, harden his nature, and improve wherever
he is incompetent.*

—Meng Tzu
Fourth century BCE

This is how humans turn into eagles.

Just as Radha nudged me to open my mind and learn:

"Your spiritual health is found in your illness.

"Your spiritual wealth is found in your poverty.

"Your spiritual happiness is found in your sadness."

Chickens are resilient. They survive but do not learn. They live
on the farmer's land and eat the farmer's food, and allow the farmer
to sell their eggs, enslave their chicks, and eat them when the farmer
is hungry.

Eagles are antifragile. They love the uncertainty of the winds,
the challenge of feeding their chicks, and the freedom of the sky.

These are my questions for you:

- Are you an eagle or a chicken?
- Are our schools teaching students to be eagles or
  chickens?
- What did school teach you to be?

Only you can answer those questions.

In the next chapter, you will learn how to soar like an eagle
while living in a world run by chickens.

YOUR QUESTIONS... ROBERT'S ANSWERS

Q: I've read Dr. Gopalan's book *Second Opinion* on Eastern and Western medicine philosophies—and the power each of us has to positively impact our health and wellness. How do we effectively spread this information to the great masses of ignorant people?

Monique B. - USA

A: We are all ignorant about something. No one knows everything. We all contribute to enlightenment when we share what we have learned in our lives. I commend Dr. Gopalan for sharing what he knows from both the worlds of both Eastern and Western medicine.

I commend you for reading his book. That is how we spread enlightenment

Q: Why do you think Dr. Gopalan's information and common sense philosophies aren't part of mainstream teaching on how to stay healthy?

Deepak J. - India

A: Dr. Gopalan says, "Today's health care is wealth care. Real healthcare is free." Both have their place in today's world. Personal healthcare costs would be less if people really followed Dr. Gopalan's advice and focused on health, not medicine, for healing.

Q: Can the "Judas" (as you call it) in all of us eventually be consistently controlled with enough practice?

Arturo S. - Mexico

A: No. Judas will never be controlled. The way to reduce Judas' power over you is to be aware and listen when Judas is doing the talking. The moment Judas knows you know he is doing the talking, Judas' power diminishes.

Chapter Nineteen

HOW TO SOAR WITH EAGLES... IN A WORLD RUN BY CHICKENS

TAKE CONTROL OF YOUR LIFE

Beware: This section may offend anyone who identifies with chickens.

As Greg Lukianoff and Jonathan Haidt warn in *The Coddling of the American Mind*, this section may be a "trigger" for those who are fragile like fine china. If you are one of those people, this final chapter is best avoided.

For those who are eagles, resilient or antifragile, this final chapter may be what you have been waiting for.

Conclusion: Lessons for Eagles

In 1972, I met a Vietnamese woman who was selling gold. She was a tiny woman whose teeth were red from chewing betel nuts, and she turned out to be one of my best teachers. I think of her often.

I remember that day vividly: flying behind enemy lines, looking down on burned-out wreckage of previous battles, landing on what I thought was firm ground, shutting the aircraft down, walking through the tiny village, smiling and waving to villagers who were selling fruit, vegetables, ducks, and chickens. The peasant farmers stared back, wondering what two U.S. Marines were doing strolling unarmed in "enemy territory," asking for directions to a goldmine.

On that day, I knew looking for gold behind enemy lines was stupid—very stupid. It was just an adventure. Today, I realize that looking for gold was one of the smartest things I have ever done.

The Vietnamese woman became my teacher when she refused to discount her gold. She wanted the *spot price*, the price of gold on that day on the international gold markets of the world.

At the time, I did not know what "spot price" meant. I was a college graduate. Yet, she knew more about real money, gold, and the real world of money than I did.

I thought about my rich dad and my poor dad. I wondered what else we supposedly educated Americans did not know about the real world of money. Why did I not know anything about gold? I wondered if we were being educated to be highly educated poor people.

The Vietnamese woman changed my future.

Today, my financial foundation is built on real gold and real silver, God's money… not manmade fake paper money and fake paper assets.

Stable Money, Stable World?

I think of that Vietnamese woman often. I wonder what our world would be like if our schools taught students what that Vietnamese woman knew about the real world of money. And, for me, it begs the question: If the world had stable money, would we have a more stable world? Would we have a world where the gap between rich, poor, and middle class was narrowing, rather than widening? A world that was bit more fair?

What Is Spirituality?

As Anthony de Mello writes in *Awareness:*

> "Spirituality means waking up. Most people, even though they don't know it, are asleep. They're born asleep, they live asleep, they marry in their sleep, they breed children in their sleep, they die in their sleep without ever waking up."

When the Vietnamese woman refused to sell her gold at a discount, she was saying to me, "Wake up, wake up, wake up."

Again, look at these charts and you will see the lessons she woke me up to see.

GOLD VS FAKE MONEY

MAJOR CURRENCIES AGAINST GOLD 1900 - 2018

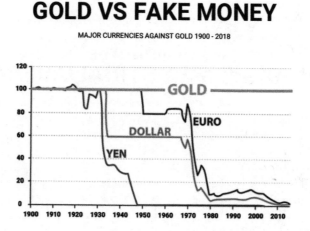

WHY SAVERS ARE LOSERS

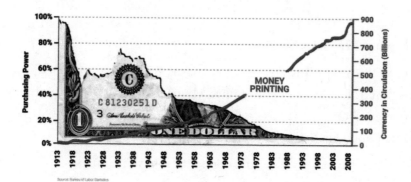

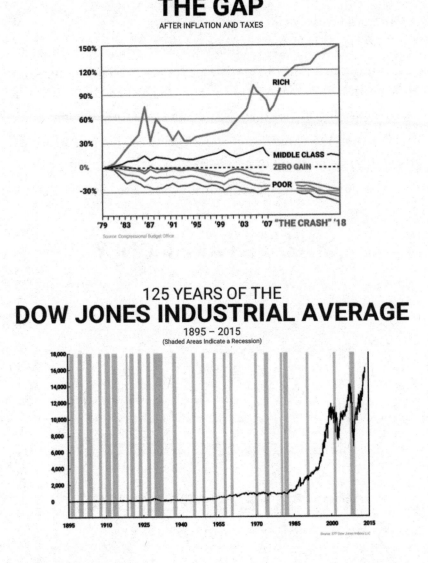

THE GAP
AFTER INFLATION AND TAXES

125 YEARS OF THE
DOW JONES INDUSTRIAL AVERAGE
1895 – 2015
(Shaded Areas Indicate a Recession)

Starting My Own Goldmine

In the 1990s, inspired by that Vietnamese woman, I began my search for my own gold mine. My partners and I eventually discovered one of the largest gold deposits in China. We took that mine public via the Toronto Stock Exchange.

Once we had a viable mining operation, the Chinese government took it from us.

As de Mello might say, I was waking up to the real world of money and power.

James Rickards in *The Road to Ruin*, writes:

> Paul Ryan, speaker of the House of Representatives, slipped a provision into a budget bill that increased China's voting rights at the IMF. This further validated China's membership in the exclusive club of countries that run the world money system.
>
> These triumphs for Chinese power went hand in glove with China's manic efforts to acquire gold since 2006, best understood as an initiation fee for this exclusive club. Publicly U.S. officials and those of the other major powers disparage gold. Yet, these powers hoard it as proof against the day confidence in paper money dies. The United States has more than eight thousand tons of gold, the Eurozone has more than ten thousand tons, and the IMF has almost three thousand tons. China's stealth acquisition of four thousand tons, with more on the way, gives China a seat at the table with other gold and [special drawing rights] powers.

LESSON: He who has the gold makes the rules.

This is one of the lessons the Vietnamese woman taught me. If not for her, I would not have begun my slow but steady accumulation of real gold and real silver… the real financial foundation for the wealth Kim and I have built.

If not for the Vietnamese gold vendor, I might have built my foundation on fake money, fake paper assets, and build an unstable real house of cards.

In December 2017, David Stockman, President Reagan's director of the Office of Management and Budget, sent out this warning:

"At the inception of an epochal pivot… there is literally a fiscal red ink eruption heading straight at the Fed's balance sheet shrinkage campaign that will rattle the rafters in the casino."

Is the End Near?

Consider this…

Barron's, November 15, 2018:

'We're Probably in a Global Credit Bubble' Says One of the Fathers of the Hedge Fund Industry

"We're probably in a global credit bubble, global debt bubble," Paul Tudor Jones II, the founder of hedge fund Tudor Investment Corp. and one of the industry's pioneers, said at the Greenwich Economic Forum in Connecticut today. The ratio of debt in the world relative to gross domestic product is at an all time high.

"I don't know whether we're supposed to run for the exits. But we are at a point in time that's really challenging to that paradigm of ever-growing debt relative to the carrying capacity.

"Since the United Nations Monetary and Financial Conference in Bretton Woods, New Hampshire, in 1944, debt levels have expanded because of an 'economic circle of trust,' he says, 'built upon central banks that began to coordinate with each other.' That persisted through the financial crisis. But those foundations are 'cracking.'"

Real Teachers

David Stockman and Paul Tudor Jones are real teachers. They are eagles who see the world from inside the global money machine.

The same is true for Nomi Prins and James Rickards. They sound similar warnings.

Like Dorothy in *The Wizard of Oz,* they have met the wizard… and they know the truth. The "wizard" is not a wizard at all.

The Vietnamese woman also saw the world from inside her tiny world of gold. That is why she was a real teacher. Take another look at the Higher Levels of Teacher illustration.

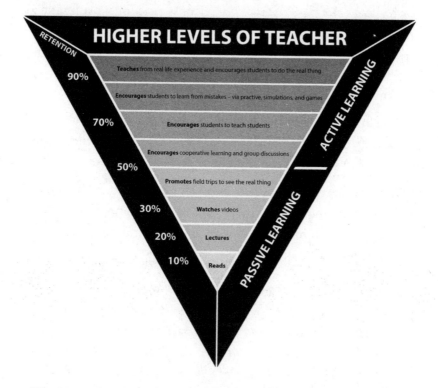

The Vietnamese woman saw the world from the top level. She was doing the real thing. She was selling gold for the owners of the gold mine.

James Rickards, in his book *The New Case for Gold,* verifies Steven Brill's statements that higher education began brainwashing the best and the brightest in 1970. Rickards states that, in the 1970s, the best schools began a campaign against gold, teaching students via John Maynard Keynes' line that, "The gold standard is a barbaric relic of the past."

Today, most financial experts are fake teachers. They condemn gold but know little about real gold and real money. They learned about gold in business school from fake teachers.

Most of today's financial experts are not eagles; they are parrots who mindlessly repeat the words their academic elite teachers taught them to say... *and dare not question.* This is true for most financial planners, stockbrokers, and pension fund managers, which is why many pensions are going broke. Most are parrots, not eagles.

Have You Been Brainwashed?

Most financial experts say "gold is a barbaric relic of the past" because they have been brainwashed. They repeat what they have been taught to say. That is why so few people own real gold.

Have you been brainwashed into not owning gold? Do you believe in saving money and investing for the long term in a diversified portfolio of stocks, bonds, mutual funds, and ETFs?

Anthony de Mello's words on brainwashing bear repeating:

> *There have been some interesting studies on brainwashing. It has been shown that you're brainwashed when you take on or "introject" an idea that isn't yours, that is someone else's. And the funny thing is that you'll be ready to die for this idea. Isn't that strange? The first test of whether you've been brainwashed and have introjected convictions and beliefs occurs the moment they're attacked. You feel stunned, you react emotionally. That's a pretty good sign—not infallible, but a pretty good sign—that we're dealing with brainwashing. You're ready to die for an idea that was never yours. Terrorists or saints (so called) take on an idea, swallow it whole, and are ready to die for it. It's not easy to listen, especially when you get emotional about an idea.*

I Woke Up

I woke up in Vietnam when I realized I was brainwashed. I woke up just before I murdered a little boy. I woke up realizing we were not fighting communism. We were fighting for oil.

I woke up when I realized I was brainwashed. I had forgotten that my professional education at the Academy was in oil and that I was an oil tanker officer. In our global economics class at Kings Point, the U.S. Merchant Marine Academy, we were taught that the United States did not want China to have access to Vietnam's oil. But I had forgotten all of that. I joined the Marine Corps and went to flight school to defend America against communism.

We were in Vietnam fighting for oil. We are still fighting for oil. Since 1914, all wars have been about oil.

Today, we are at war in Iraq, Iran, Syria, Yemen, and Afghanistan. That is why Russia is there.

The United States fights for Saudi Arabia against their mortal enemy Iran.

How do you think "terrorists" afford weapons? They sell oil.

Chickens become eagles when they wake up. I woke up in Vietnam.

How Eagles Learn to Fly

STEP 1: "Wake up."

When it comes to money, we have all been brainwashed. Brainwashed means taking on ideas that are not your own. Brain washed people are willing to die or fight for an idea. I was willing to die for America. I woke up when I realized I was killing for oil. We still are.

Brainwashed people become upset when I say things like:

Savers are losers.

Your house is not an asset.

The rich don't work for money.

The rich use debt as money.

The rich do not pay taxes… legally.

They become upset. A few become angry. They become emotional because they have been brainwashed. They become upset—"triggered"—by ideas that contradict their *fragile* beliefs.

Eagles know this. Chickens do not. Chickens will defend their right to pay taxes, save money, and invest for the long term in a well-diversified portfolio of stocks, bonds, mutual funds, and ETFs, even if they are losing money.

Again, as de Mello writes:

> "The first test of whether you've been brainwashed and have introjected convictions and beliefs occurs the moment they're attacked. You feel stunned, you react emotionally. … You're ready to die for an idea that was never yours."

You wake up when you will realize your savings, your house, and retirement savings are assets of the rich.

I am not saying do not buy a house, save money, or invest for the long term in the stock market. In fact, I recommend that people without real financial education hold on to their beliefs that they should buy a house, save money, get out of debt, and invest for the long term in the stock market. This mantra is best for the average person, someone who is not interested in investing time and money in their financial education.

All I am saying is, "Wake up." If you get emotional and want to defend those ideas, then you've been brainwashed.

The Side of the Eagles

If you become emotional or defensive, you cannot learn. You cannot see the other side of the coin, the side the eagles are on.

STEP 2: Eagles teach their kids about money. Chickens do not.

How do you think Jared Kushner knew about taxes, debt, and infinite returns and the reporter did not?

Did Jared learn about debt, taxes, real estate, and infinite returns at school, or from his father? Did Donald Trump learn about debt, taxes, real estate and infinite returns at school, or from his father?

Who taught me about debt, taxes, real estate and infinite returns? My poor dad?

Education is very important, but we must ask ourselves: what *kind* of education?

When I was nine years old, in a classroom with rich kids, I soon realized they were learning something I was not learning. Many were learning about money at home, from their fathers.

That is why my rich dad was teaching his son and me about money after school.

Rich dad often said, "Most family fortunes are gone in three generations. The first generation earns it, the second enjoys it, and the third generation loses it."

That is why he was teaching his son and me about real business and real estate. He did not want his fortune to be gone by the third generation.

Rich dad called it "dynasty wealth," wealth that is passed on from generation to generation. Rich dad also said, "Most poor and middle class parents only want their children to get good jobs."

James Rickards, in *The Road to Ruin,* tells a story of meeting a beautiful woman in Italy, whose family wealth was handed down for over 900 years. If you are familiar with Italy's history, you know that hanging on to dynasty wealth for 900 years has been nearly impossible.

When he asked her how their wealth was passed on for 900 years, she replied: "That is easy. We invest in things that last."

When he asked her what are investments that last, she replied: "Real estate, gold, and museum-quality artwork."

She did not mention cash, stocks, bonds, mutual funds, or ETFs.

This is another reason why Kim and I created the *CASHFLOW* game, write our books, and teach. We want *people to teach people,* and *parents to teach their kids* so that more family dynasties are created in which families grow and pass on their wealth for generations.

Eagles believe in passing on their wealth for generations. This is also known as capitalism.

Chickens believe in letting the government take their wealth and redistribute their wealth to other chickens. This is known as socialism and communism.

STEP 3: Eagles make mistakes and learn from their mistakes. Chickens do not.

Chickens never learn because they're often too chicken to make mistakes or pretend they did not make a mistake.

Nassim Taleb might describe a chicken as "resilient," durable, strong, tough, but unable to learn, change, and grow. Chickens do not learn and grow because school brainwashed them into believing that "people who make mistakes are stupid."

Schools teach students not to make mistakes rather than how to learn from their mistakes. Education seems to be teaching students to be fragile and attack anyone who disagrees with them or hurts their feelings. That is why there are more chickens than eagles.

STEP 4: Eagles cheat… they ask for help.

In school, asking for help is cheating.

Chickens are resilient, so they do not ask for help. They endure but do not learn, study, and grow. They fail to become eagles.

Eagles ask for help. Eagles have teams. They work as teams. They hire professional coaches. All sports professionals have coaches. Amateurs do not.

Money is a game. Schools teach students to play the game of money as individuals as Es and Ss.

How Es and Ss Play the Game of Money

Success Is Achieved Alone

In *Big Potential,* Shawn Achor describes the current methods of education as limiting students to their small potential. The best students tend to become high paid Ss, specialists such as doctors and lawyers. Asking for help is a sign of weakness.

Specialists in the S quadrant tend to pay the highest percentage in taxes. Chickens play the game of money as individuals.

How Bs and Is Play the Game of Money

The Game of Money Is a Team Sport

The New Zealand All Blacks, pictured above, are the greatest rugby team in the world and they represent one of the smallest countries in the world—New Zealand.

In *Big Potential,* Shawn Achor writes that learning to operate as a team increases an individual's big potential.

As any entrepreneur knows, the hardest part of a business is dealing with people, customers, employees, specialists, and government bureaucrats. That is why playing team sports develops important personal and people skills, which increase a person's big potential. Business and investing are team sports.

In school, taking a test as a team is called *cheating.*

Eagles play the game of money as a team from the B and I side of the CASHFLOW Quadrant. Chickens play the game of money from the E and S side.

The Game of Money Is a Game of Mindsets

Those in the E and S quadrants are rugged individuals. Their motto is: "If you want it done right, do it yourself."

Those in the B and I quadrants operate in teams. The minimum team for eagles is, first a bookkeeper, then an accountant, and an attorney.

An accurate bookkeeper is the least expensive member of a B-I team, yet what they contribute to the team is priceless. A B-I team cannot operate without accurate numbers.

Most S-quadrant entrepreneurs do their bookkeeping on their own, or their spouse keeps the books. Or they do not keep books. That is why most S-quadrant entrepreneurs hang out with the chickens.

When Kim and I were starting out, the first person we hired was Betty the Bookkeeper. We hired Betty when we had no money. Betty was another real teacher. If not for Betty, Kim and I would not be financially free today.

Chickens say, "I'll hire a bookkeeper when I have money." Which is why most chickens remain chickens.

Marriage and Money

Marriage is also a team sport.

Some marriages reflect a Tarzan-and-Jane relationship—where Tarzan manages the money on his own. Some marriages are business partnerships. Kim is the CEO of our marriage. Who is on your money team?

STEP 5: Eagles invest in what they love. Chickens do as they are told.

And what they're told is go to school, work hard, pay taxes, save money, and invest for the long term in the stock market. As de Mello would say, "They are asleep and brainwashed."

Most chickens believe in "Do what you love, and the money will follow." The problem is, studies show 70 percent of all chickens hate their job.

Eagles acquire assets they love. The financial statement below explains the difference.

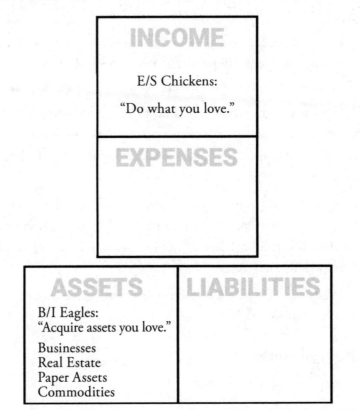

Business and real estate are the riskiest of all assets because they are the least liquid. If the investor makes a mistake, the asset drags him or her down. That is why businesses and real estate require the most financial education—and the best teams.

Paper assets and commodities such as gold and silver are liquid. If the investor makes a mistake, the investor can cut his or her losses quickly.

The Secret to My Success

If there's a secret to my success, it's love. I love being an entrepreneur. I love building businesses. I love real estate, using debt, and paying as little as possible in taxes. And I love gold, silver, and oil.

Eagles love their assets. Chickens do not.

STEP 6: Eagles invest for infinite returns. Eagles invest with OPM, other people's money. Chickens are the other people.

Infinite returns can be achieved with any of the four asset classes.

Paper assets are the easiest asset to achieve infinite returns, but not if you mindlessly turn your money over to a "financial expert."

Here's a simple—KISS—example:

> I buy 100 shares of stock for $1 each, costing me $100.
> The stock goes up in price to $10.

> I then sell 10 shares at $10. I now have my $100 back.
> The remaining 90 shares are my infinite return, money for nothing... my ROI, return on information, not money.

The Power of Leverage

Even higher ROIs can be achieved using stock options, puts, and calls. Again, do not try this without investing in stock option seminars.

Options in paper assets and *debt in business and real estate* are leverage. Remember and be cautious: the higher the leverage, the higher risks, the rewards, the gains, and losses.

If you are not willing to invest time and money in education and practice, practice, practice, it is smarter to be a little chicken.

Five Suggestions

The following are five suggestions on flying with the eagles. As you read the five suggestions, please be aware of what your "little voice"—that voice in your head—is saying as you read them.

"I can't afford to do that."

"That's silly."

"I don't care about money."

"I'll never be rich."

"I'm not smart enough to do that."

Remember that Judas lives in our minds. Judas stabs us and others in the back. In my experience, too many people listen to Judas.

Your spirit lives in your heart. Your spirit lives in silence, in stillness.

If you hear Judas talking to you, take a deep breath, take a look at life—a tree, a stream, a flower—and be silent, be still, and allow your spirit a chance to speak to you in silence.

More Secrets

The keys to realizing your full potential are love, education, and experience. If you love your asset class and you study, make mistakes, practice and learn, you will soon see ways of investing for infinite returns.

Kim and I love being entrepreneurs. We love real estate. We love gold and silver. I love oil more than Kim, because oil was my major at the Academy.

Stocks… vs. the Real Thing

If I invest $100,000 in paper assets—let's say stock in Standard Oil, a company I once worked for—I receive $0 in tax savings. If I invest $100,000 in a U.S. oil development project, I immediately receive a tax break of approximately 40 percent from state and federal taxes.

That means on $100,000 invested, I pay approximately $40,000 less in taxes.

Another way to look at this is that my tax savings offset my tax liability from income from my books of, say, $40,000. The tax break on my oil investment offsets the tax liability on other income that could result in paying nothing in taxes.

$ 40,000 in taxes owed from book income

LESS <u>< $ 40,000 ></u> in tax breaks from oil investment

$ 0

That is called $40,000 in "phantom income." Which is invisible income as a result of taxes not paid.

LESSON: Tax breaks for the Bs and Is are similar, yet slightly different in different parts of the world. The lesson is that having a smart tax accountant and tax attorney can be the smartest thing an eagle can do.

Chickens do not have bookkeepers, tax accountants, and tax attorneys.

It's important that I point out that everyone should check with both a tax accountant and tax attorney before making any investment for tax breaks.

LESSON: Most of the tax code is not about paying taxes, but about incentives for *how to pay less in taxes*. The U.S. government offers tax incentives to investors who partner with the government.

Civilization requires energy. Without energy, fossil fuels and renewables, civilization would collapse. The United States needs oil, lots of oil. If tax incentives were not offered, the price of gasoline would skyrocket and civilization would become chaos.

How Eagles Spend Money

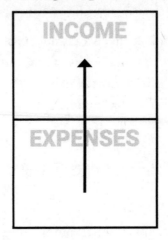

LESSON: Eagles spend money to increase income—on education (courses and seminars) and for professional advice from bookkeepers, accountants, and attorneys.

The best news of all? The government offers tax breaks to people who spend money to make money.

LESSON: Chickens who work hard and who work hard to keep expenses low so they can save money pay the highest taxes and receive the fewest tax breaks from the government.

How Chickens Spend Money

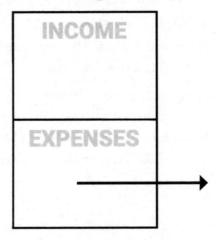

LESSON: Chickens spend money and the money never comes back.

Thank You

Thanks to Tom Wheelwright, author of *Tax-Free Wealth*, Rich Dad Advisor on taxes and accounting rules. Tom keeps tax education simple, yet accurate.

Why Chickens Lose

Chickens do as they are told and turn their money over to "financial experts," such as financial planners and fund managers to invest for them. The problem is that chickens learn nothing when the expert wins and learn nothing when the expert loses *their* money.

How Eagles Learn to Fly

In 1978, I made it to Xerox's President Club as number one in sales. I had achieved my goal. I had learned to overcome my shyness and fear of rejection, and learned to sell, although I was still shy and fearful of rejection. But I had learned the number one skill of an entrepreneur: the ability to sell.

In 1978, I announced to the Xerox Corporation that I was resigning to start my own business, and thanked them for four great years of real education.

In our spare time, a friend who also worked at Xerox and I had been building our start-up business—the first nylon and Velcro® surfer wallet company—across the street from the Xerox offices in downtown Honolulu.

Our first shipment of 100,000 nylon wallets had just landed in New York from Korea. It was time to start selling wallets. My friend and I were both excited and terrified. It was all or nothing.

As I was leaving, Elaine the receptionist smiled and said, "You're going to fail... and you will be back."

Over the years, Elaine had seen many young hotshot salesmen like me leave to start a business, only to fail and return to Xerox. One of my sales managers was one of those hotshots who failed and returned.

My friend, who is still one of my best friends today, and I succeeded. We were successful beyond our wildest dreams. Nylon wallets were an international hit. We were featured in sporting goods magazines, running magazines, surfing magazines, and even *Playboy*. Money poured in. We had achieved the American Dream. We were millionaires.

Then we crashed. We lost everything. It took me nearly eight years to pay my investors back, one of them my own father, poor dad.

It was a great, real education.

My reply to Elaine, on the day I left Xerox was, "I will fail... but I will never be back."

And I never did return. I kept succeeding and failing. I will always keep succeeding and failing, no matter how successful or rich I become.

That is what Nassim Taleb calls "antifragile." Just as our body needs challenges, stress, and adversity to stay strong, so does the human spirit. And our spirit lives in our hearts.

And that is how eagles learn to fly.

We are all eagles. We all have wings. We all have the God-given spirit to learn to fly.

The question is, do we have the courage?

More Words of Wisdom

I've heard it said that, "In the first place, God made idiots. That was for practice. Then he made school boards."

When it comes to money, are school boards made of wise men and women, or financially blind mice?

Rich dad often said:

"Any idiot can spend money. Spending money takes no special talent or education. It takes wise men and women to make money, hold on to their money, and most importantly, keep their money away from idiots."

I think of Mark Twain's words and ask myself, again, *is this why there is no financial education in schools?* I have my answer. What is your answer?

And from Albert Einstein…

"Education is what remains after one has forgotten what one has learned in school."

Since most people learn little to nothing about money, how much can anyone forget?

Einstein also said:

"Imagination is more important than knowledge."

Rich dad agreed. And he added:

"Imagination *is* more important than knowledge. But Einstein did not say, knowledge is *not* important. Knowledge is very important for knowledge empowers a person's imagination."

Rich dad also said:

"Everyone has million-dollar ideas. Without financial knowledge, ideas remain ideas, hopes remains hopes, and dreams remain dreams.

"Worst of all, without financial knowledge, many world-changing ideas, life-enhancing inventions, and products rather than weapons, products that could bring peace, remain trapped in that person's imagination."

"Without knowledge, information is worthless. Without knowledge, most people walk past millions of dollars every day.

"Knowledge has the power to turn imagination into reality, and ideas into money."

ROI—return on information—is only possible with knowledge. Without knowledge, information is meaningless. And information without financial education cannot be processed into wealth.

As R. Buckminster Fuller wrote,

> *I want you to think about this as individuals. An individual will say to me, 'What can I do? What can I do? I'm just a little tiny guy.'*
>
> *And, I say, what you can do—I'm repeating something I said to you earlier—that we are really in the final examination— I did get, last night, to you that we are a function in the universe. We're here for local universe information gathering, local problems solving in support of the integrity of an eternally regenerative universe.*
>
> *But integrity is the essence. In an invisible world there's no visible aesthetics. In an invisible world there's no visible aesthetics. In an invisible world the only aesthetic is integrity— in our great computer world we're going into.*

I thank my friend from Hawaii, Randolph Craft, for first of all for getting me to that event in 1981 in Kirkwood, California, near Lake Tahoe. Randolph was the person who nudged me to attend "The Future of Business" event with Dr. Fuller.

At the time, listening to Dr. Fuller was painfully boring for me. The conference sessions ran from early morning to late, very late, at night. I kept falling asleep. Again, it was Randolph who nudged me to stay focused on the five-day event rather than sleep through it as I did through most of my years in school.

Randolph helped me stay awake by being a crew member on the event's video-recording team. That is how I stayed awake and paid attention through one of the most important events I ever attended, a seminar that changed the direction of my life.

When Bucky Fuller talked about the Information Age being the Invisible Age, and that the Invisible Age was the Age of Integrity, I woke up.

At that time in my life, I was very unsuccessful. My business and my life were a mess. Fuller's words were my wake-up call— and his words made me take a look at my life and find out where I was out of integrity. And the list was a long one. After 1981, I was aware that I was out of integrity in many areas of my life and began "cleaning up my act."

At that first seminar, and during the two other summers I studied with Dr. Fuller, he would always say, "Integrity is the essence of everything successful."

What stayed with me were Fuller's words from his talk on Integrity:

> "I want you to think about this as individuals. An individual will say to me, 'What can I do? What can I do? I'm just a little tiny guy.'
>
> And, I say, what you can do—I'm repeating something I said to you earlier—that we are really in the final examination—I did get, last night, to you that we are a function in the universe. We're here for local universe information gathering, local problems solving in support of the integrity of an eternally regenerative universe."

Fuller passed away on July 1, 1983, about a month after my last time with him.

I was driving along the H-1 in Honolulu when I heard the news. And I pulled over and cried. I had assumed he would always be here to lead humanity out of this mess we were in... and now he was gone. His words kept ringing in my head, *"What can I do? What can I do? I'm just a little tiny guy."*

A few months later, I read Fuller's book *Grunch of Giants*.

As I read *Grunch of Giants,* the lessons from my childhood from my rich dad and my poor dad, crashing in Vietnam, the tiny Vietnamese woman refusing to discount her gold... then returning to Hawaii to find my poor dad unemployed because he stood up to one of the most corrupt state governments in the United States. I thought about different perspectives and points of view: my poor dad wanting me to get my master's degree and my rich dad recommending I learn about debt and taxes.

In 1983, I was still a little guy, but I knew what I was supposed to do. In 1983, I was in the rock and roll business. It was fun but not my life's purpose. So I gave my share of the business to my partners. I asked for nothing. I was done.

Fuller often said, "Free the scholar so he can return to his studies."

In 1983, I became a student for the first time in my life. For the first time in my life I was whole. I was complete. I was in integrity with my studies. I was no longer a fake student. I was now a real student. I became a student of *Grunch*.

In 1984 as I was preparing to leave Hawaii, I met the most beautiful woman in my life, we talked about our life's purpose, and we fell in love.

Although I had no job, no money, and no future, Kim and I held hands, took a leap of faith, and left Hawaii for California. We were homeless for a while, met horrible people and wonderful people, and had extreme highs and extreme lows. But we never looked back. Kim and I were in integrity with each other, with our life's mission, and our life's purpose. The harder life became, the more we became antifragile. Nothing was going to stop us.

Fuller's words—"Integrity is the essence of everything successful"—stayed with us then… and now. Today we realize that they carry additional meaning for the Invisible Age, today's world of invisible technology, invisible change, and invisible money.

Integrity (n.)
1: The quality of being honest and having strong moral principles; moral uprightness.
2: The state of being whole and undivided.

I will leave you with words of wisdom from Bucky Fuller, words that kept Kim and me going when we were without jobs and often without money.

"If success or failure of this planet and of human beings depended on how I am and what I do…

"How would I be?

"What would I do?"

YOUR QUESTIONS... ROBERT'S ANSWERS

Q: How worried should I be about physical counterfeit metals, especially gold and silver?

Shawn T. – Canada

A: You need to be aware that there are fakes and counterfeits and deal only with reputable gold and silver dealers.

Q: Is there ever a bad time to invest in gold?

Alexandra B – USA

A: Yes. When you are greedy.

Q: I've been skeptical to invest in gold and silver because of fear that the government will confiscate it. Do you see a scenario where this could happen in 2019?

Liu X. – China

A: Anything is possible. I doubt the U.S. government will confiscate our gold. On the other hand, you never know. That is why I always have a Plan B.

Q: What do you think Dr. Fuller would say to you today if he were still with us regarding your success and the creation of the *CASHFLOW* board game to teach others about money investing?

Iru L. – Argentina

A: I suspect he would happier that I read his book *Grunch of Giants*—and took action.